THE TRUTH ABOUT
GETTING IN

THE TRUTH ABOUT
GETTING IN

A Top College Advisor Tells You
Everything You Need to Know

KATHERINE COHEN, Ph.D.
Founder of IvyWise

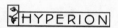

NEW YORK

ISBN: 0-7868-8747-8

Paperback ISBN: 0-7868-8849-0

Hyperion books are available for special promotions and premiums. For details, contact Hyperion Special Markets, 77 W. 66th Street, 11th floor, New York, New York 10023-6298, or call 212-456-0133.

FIRST EDITION

10 9 8 7 6 5 4 3 2 1

Designed by Michael Mendelsohn

For my students

CONTENTS

8. WRITING AN OUTSTANDING ESSAY

9. GETTING GLOWING LETTERS OF RECOMMENDATION

10. ACING THE INTERVIEW

ACKNOWLEDGMENTS

After I finished my Ph.D., I was certified in college admissions counseling at UCLA Extension. Much of the information in this book has come from my courses, books, and teachers at UCLA Extension. Moreover, those teachers, themselves admissions counselors, inspired and encouraged me to become an independent college admissions counselor and to start my company, IvyWise. They encouraged me to continue the learning process (as the requirements for college admissions change from year to year) by visiting campuses across the country and attending regional and national conferences like the Western Association of College Admissions Counseling (WACAC) and National Association of College Admissions Counseling (NACAC), where I have networked with various deans of admissions. I especially want to thank Linda Zimring, Esther Hugo, Julie Taylor, Youlanda Copeland-Morgan, Dr. Rae Lee Siporin, and the late Joe Allen. I respect them all for their work, enthusiasm, and sense of humor in what can be a frustrating field. They have truly enlightened me.

I could not have written this book without my students. Going over the college admissions process with each student, researching schools with them, solving their individual problems, answering their particular questions, helping them articulate and express themselves on paper—all of this has helped me identify the individual pieces in the intricate puzzle of college admissions. My students are the true inspiration for this book. If I can reach still others with this book, then I have achieved my goal in writing it.

I want to thank my friend and president of the West Coast Chapter of the Princeton Review, Lloyd Eric Cotsen. I started my career working for Eric recruiting students for the Princeton Review course after I finished the first Los Angeles SAT I course in 1984. Later, Eric trained me to teach the SAT I, and I have worked for him on and off over the last fifteen years. We have remained friends all this time and he has always supported me on my career path. He kindly offered to read the first draft of this book. His comments and criticism were invaluable and helped me finish.

I also want to thank my first assistant, Ben Jolliffe. Without him, this book would not exist. He amalgamated, organized, and synthesized all of its information. He put it together on my computer and formatted the entire manuscript. He was also my sounding board, as I would not add or cut anything without consulting him first. His opinions and input were always helpful and insightful. Furthermore, as my assistant, he made my life easier and enabled me to concentrate on getting the book done.

Huge thanks to my associate, Nina Bauer, director of IvyWise Kids Division, for helping me complete the 2001 update of *The Truth About Getting In*. I had looked at the book so many times, her fresh perspective was essential.

To Ed Schultheiss, website designer and all-around computer wizard, thank you for all your help in editing and reformatting.

I would like to thank Jeffrey Timon, who oversaw the final revisions of *The Truth About Getting In*. He was a true friend and a great detective throughout the process. Without him, this manuscript would never have been ready on time.

I would also like to thank my literary agent, Suzanne Gluck, at William Morris, and my editor, Mary Ellen O'Neill, at Hyperion. Suzanne was one of many agents who had read an article about me in *New York Magazine*. Overwhelmed with phone calls from agents, I began to interview them individually. It is not a coincidence that this process is similar to the college admissions process. I understood immediately how important it was for me to be working with the right agent—like the right college admissions counselor. Suzanne and I had both attended Brown University and had several friends in common. We immediately hit it off. Like a college counselor who matches students with the best college for them, Suzanne helped match me with the right publishing house. After just two days of interviews, I met with Hyperion's team. I felt like I had just stepped onto Brown University's campus for the first time. It was the gut feeling that this was where I belonged. Within twenty-four hours, the match was made and we began our work together. Mary Ellen has worked tirelessly with me through all of the book's phases. I thank her for putting up with my crazy schedule as the final edits of *The Truth* were due just as my students' early college applications were due. But with Suzanne's support and Mary Ellen's guidance, I was able to finish the book on time.

And last, but certainly not least, a huge thank you to my family, especially my grandmother Florence Lippman (matriarch of my family, my role model, and benefactress); my mother, Jane Barack (daily phone call supporter); my uncle Peter Barack (my attorney, adviser, and general paternal figure); my aunt Elise Barack (the most well-read person I know, sharer of knowledge and love of learning); my sister Emily Cohen (my comic relief); my brother Chris Cohen (always proud of me); and the Biddlepeople: my three cats, Icky, Daedalus, and Little Biddly. This book could not have been written without their humor, companionship, and emotional support.

INTRODUCTION

You've read the articles. You've heard the rumors in school. The flashy tell-all books recount the same thing—getting into college has become a high-stakes gamble. The coveted spots at the nation's most selective schools have become nearly impossible to obtain. Super-achieving high schoolers and their status-conscious parents will do almost anything to ensure a letter of admission from an Ivy League school, turning the once carefree years of high school into college admissions boot camp. Now more than ever, the nation's prestigious universities are able to hand pick their students—even admitting many early, before the legions of normal high school students get a chance to apply. I wish I could say it weren't, but the hype is true.

Why? Why this sudden pandemonium over postsecondary education in America? Why this sense that if you don't get into one of the nation's top colleges, your high school years will have been a waste? Why the pressure, the stress, the worry, and the cutthroat competition? First of all, it has to do with numbers. We are in the midst of a post baby boom, which is supposed to last until 2008. The U.S. Department of Education estimates that the number of high school graduates will rise to a record 3.1 million by the end of the decade, an increase of 12 percent over today.[1] The number of high school seniors taking the SAT I has been rapidly increasing over the years as well. In 2001, 1,368,850 students took the SAT I—a huge increase over the 1,260,278 students who took the test in 2000. But it also has to do with economic shifts in our country. The 1990s witnessed an unparalleled boom in the American economy. Despite the slight economic downturn at the beginning of the twenty-first century, most families still find themselves with more money for college fees and tuition than ever before. Accordingly, colleges' endowments have swelled and many schools are now able to offer financial aid to students who could not otherwise afford college.

Culturally speaking, this swelling generation of high school students born after 1982 is very unlike its more skeptical predecessors, Generation X.

---

[1] *U.S. News & World Report* 131, 10 (September 17, 2001): 90.

According to Neil Howe and William Strauss,[3] the "Millennials," as they call them, were born into a period of unparalleled economic and social stability, with parents whose ability to focus on providing their children with a busy, well-balanced life was unmatched by any previous parental generation. If you are reading this book now in preparation for college applications, then you are probably a Millennial. According to Howe and Strauss, you were most likely the product of a soccer mom and "sensitive" dad; your "Baby on Board" childhood during the Clinton boom years has given you an innate optimism; and the Columbine massacre was the awareness-raising event of your grade-school years. Now, of course, global terrorism and the World Trade Center and Pentagon attacks may be the defining moment of your young adulthood. Howe and Strauss believe this unique combination of historical events thrusts your generation into, to paraphrase FDR, "a rendezvous with destiny."

You are also the Internet generation, having officially replaced the "After-School Special" generation. You are more adept at using computer technology than your predecessors. With websites and e-mail, you have immediate access to more information than students did just five years ago. As a result, the number of online services devoted to college admissions is now staggering. You can research colleges and visit them online. At websites like Monster.com (which acquired collegelink.com), you can even fill out college application information, have it adjusted to fit the formats of hundreds of different college applications, and send it off—all with the touch of a button.

Although the applicant pool is growing, acquiring more resources, and becoming better informed, the number of spots at the nation's top colleges remains the same, creating a feeling of scarcity and fierce competition. And as competition grows, so does the pressure to perform. The college admissions process has unfortunately become one of the most stressful times in a young student's life, both physically and psychologically draining. And it's no walk in the park for parents, either. Frustrated at their inability to control the entire college admissions process, overwhelmed by the impending financial burden of a college tuition, and emotionally drained from the prospect of their children's departure from the family nest, parents today are just as stressed as their children when it comes to applying for college. I have met mothers and fathers who felt personally rejected when their child was denied admission to the college of their choice.

So what can you do?

---

[3] For more information, see Neil Howe and William Strauss, from *Millennials Rising: The Next Great Generation*. Vintage Books, A Division of Random House, Inc. New York, 2000.

To begin with, *relax*. Take a deep breath and remember that the most rewarding things in life are never a breeze. It might help to think of the college admissions process as a sport. Would you suddenly decide to run a marathon without training for months, even years, beforehand? Would you attempt to run a marathon if you were more gifted at the 100-yard dash? Surprisingly, when it comes to college admissions, many students do just that. They head blindly into the application process without the proper tools, strategies, or training. They base their college choices on the prestige and selectivity of a small number of schools without adequately researching what they want out of their postsecondary education. Finally, they make a series of mistakes on their admissions applications simply because they don't know how to separate the truths from the many college admissions myths.

My point is this: to get into the college of your choice, you must be performing at an optimal level when it comes to the college application. To do so, you need to begin training early on. You need a clear strategy, a bit of self-discipline, and a ton of good old-fashioned determination. But you also need someone who can separate the myths from the truths, someone who knows. That's where this book comes in. It is my mission to get you and your application into tip-top shape, to put you on the right track toward college admission, and to give you a leg up on the competition. That is why I have devoted the last fifteen years of my life to studying and working in all aspects of higher education.

That is also why I wrote this book: to provide you and your family with "the truth about getting in."

I am Katherine Cohen, independent college counselor, founder and president of IvyWise. Although no one person can guarantee admission to one of the nation's top schools, reading this book and following its exercises and tips will help you produce the best application possible. It will guide you through the complex issues facing today's college applicants, offering invaluable insights and trade secrets culled from my many years of experience on both sides of the college admissions process. I received my B.A. from Brown University, and an M.A., M.Phil., and Ph.D. from Yale University. I have taught SAT I courses and private tutorials. I have taught at Yale, where I also acted as a student advisor and read for the university's Undergraduate Office of Admissions. And I am currently an alumna interviewer for Brown University. In the course of my experience, I have evaluated and recommended hundreds of applications.

It is this background that has made my private practice so successful. With my personal experience at two Ivy League institutions, I am uniquely qualified to offer unparalleled advice on admissions to the top schools in the nation. But I don't stop there. Certainly, the Ivies aren't meant for everyone and not everyone is meant for the Ivies. With this in mind, I pride myself on finding "the right fit" for my students. For some, that means a small liberal arts college like Amherst or Wesleyan, for others it means a large state school like Berkeley or Michigan. No two colleges are alike and no two applicants have the same needs. More than referring to a particular destination then, the name *IvyWise* suggests a state of mind. If you are "wise" to what the most selective schools want, then you are wise to what any school in the country wants.

Of course, the college admissions process is not a science. Finding the right college and getting yourself in are highly subjective experiences. Working intimately with this book, you will gain a wealth of knowledge about the college admissions process, but, more important, you will also gain a wealth of knowledge about yourself. You will come to understand what you want from your education, what you want from the world, and where you wish to go in your life. The exercises and tips in the following pages encourage you to believe in yourself both academically and personally, to believe you deserve the best education possible, to believe you will ultimately go wherever your hard work and dedication take you.

Because that's the first truth about getting into college: when it comes to the application, colleges want to discover *you*—so get to know yourself first.

I remember when I was applying to college. I had very little guidance. In fact, I can barely remember the name of my high school college counselor. I attended a very selective all-girls school where my busy schedule of advanced placement (AP) classes and my unweighted 3.99 GPA only qualified me for eighth in a class of ninety. During a summer program at Andover, I visited Brown University and immediately fell in love. Unfortunately, my college counselor told me there was no way I would get in. Today, I understand that she was basing her decision on purely objective factors: there were two other young women above me in class rank who wanted to go to Brown and they would certainly be accepted before me. But the counselor never once looked at me as a unique human being with extracurricular interests that might make me a more interesting candidate. She didn't see, for instance, that my time spent with the American Field Service in Argentina, my photography portfolio, my extensive dance experience, or my employment might give me an edge over the slightly better-ranked students in my class. She didn't stop to consider my self-motivation, my commitment to community service, or my strong desire to attend Brown.

The day I got into Brown Early Action was one of the proudest days of my life. It was a testament to my commitment, as well as a strong expression of my independence. As rewarding as it was, however, I was acutely aware of the many students who lacked my self-motivation, students who fell through the cracks because they weren't pushed in the right direction or given the right tools. That is how IvyWise eventually came into being. This is why I am so eager to share my knowledge with you.

There are a lot of college resources out there. Believe me, I know. The intense competition that made college admissions such a high-stakes gamble in the 1990s has also made college admissions a big business. These days you can find all sorts of materials to help you get into the college of your choice: college admissions counselors both in and outside of school, test preparation courses and tutors, websites that offer online advice to help you write great essays, CD-ROMs that match you with the right colleges, not to mention the many books like this one. Personally, I don't believe that any one counselor, course, or book can get you into the college of your choice. Ultimately, only you can get yourself in. Even money can't "buy" admission. In 1998, for instance, a student whose father had donated $10 million to New York University was flat-out rejected. NYU kept the cash. I do believe, however, that you, the student, must be both educated and clear about what you have to offer a prospective college, what you want from your college education, which colleges best suit your needs, and how to get through the college admissions process without missing a step.

That is the goal of this book: to serve as an instigator, motivator, and coach. To challenge you to challenge yourself. It is a practical manual to college admissions, a source of insider knowledge and truths of the trade that will maximize your chances of getting into the selective school of your choice. It urges you to take your education into your own hands and be active in the college admissions process. Most important, it sifts through the dubious myths and questionable advice contained in other college admissions materials and gives you a clear picture of the truth about getting in.

So go ahead, make this book a part of your life. Scribble notes all over it. Photocopy its exercises and tips. Don't be afraid to get your hands dirty. And if the going gets tough, just picture yourself stepping under that ivy-covered archway onto the college campus of your dreams. That's it. That's what it's all about. A little hard work now, and you're already there.

THE TRUTH ABOUT
GETTING **IN**

1

THE ADMISSIONS APPLICATION

AN OVERVIEW

MYTHS AND TRUTHS

MYTH: You can increase your chances of admission by changing your profile to fit what you believe each individual admissions committee is looking for.

TRUTH: Committees change all the time, but each is looking to craft a well-rounded freshman class based on the current pool of applicants. Second-guessing will only deter you from being yourself. The truth of the matter is: if they don't want you to begin with, then you don't want them.

MYTH: Taking "serious" classes like AP biology looks better on your transcript than "unserious" courses like AP studio art.

TRUTH: If you are an artist, you should definitely take the AP studio art class. The longer you've been doing something, the better you are at it, and the more you follow through with it, the stronger your application becomes.

MYTH: You can start the application process in the twelfth grade.

TRUTH: The application process begins in the ninth grade. From that moment on, everything becomes a part of your academic or personal record.

MYTH: An A in a regular-paced course looks better than a B in an honors/AP course because your overall GPA is so important.

TRUTH: Colleges are looking for highly motivated students who challenge themselves with increasingly difficult courses, even if it adversely affects their overall GPA. Of course, it is always best to get the A in the honors/AP course.

MYTH: Your SAT I score is the most important thing in your application—if you've got a 1600, you're basically in.

TRUTH: Your transcript is the most important document in your application—and since so many students have excellent grades in demanding courses, the rest of your application takes on added importance. A high SAT score may keep you in the applicant pool, but alone, it is not your ticket in.

MYTH: Colleges look for well-rounded students with many interests.

TRUTH: Colleges look for well-rounded student bodies and seek individual applicants who display consistency and commitment in a handful of activities that are truly representative of their passions.

GENERAL REQUIREMENTS FOR THE APPLICATION

I cannot stress enough the importance of the college application to the college admissions process. It is, after all, the one document that admissions committees have by which to evaluate you. It sums up who you are as a student and as a person. It is your calling card. By way of introduction, then, I would like to present a brief overview of the college application in order for you, the student, to gain a better understanding of its component parts. The subsequent chapters will explain in more detail the individual elements of the application and guide you toward their completion.

Colleges may consider all or some of the following:

Academic Record

- Course work
- Grade point average (GPA)
- Standardized tests (SAT I or ACT, SAT IIs, APs)
- Class rank
- Grade trends

Personal Record

- Brag sheet
- Personal essay(s)
- Letters of recommendation (from teachers and high school counselor)
- Personal interview (with an alumnus and/or on campus)

Most schools will base the majority of their admissions decisions on your academic record. For the most competitive colleges, however, where multiple applicants with near-perfect records are vying for a limited number of spaces, your academic record is not enough. Selective schools will further evaluate you based on your personal characteristics as manifested in your letters of recommendation, essays, extracurricular activities, and interviews. Yet it is still not enough to have excellent grades and a stellar list of extracurricular interests indicative of a truly motivated and dedicated student. These things do not speak for themselves. Not anymore.

College applicants of today must learn how to differentiate themselves from the thousands of others with both the same academic records *and* the same activities. How do you do this? First of all, you must pay close attention to the way you talk about what you've accomplished and the language you use to express your personal characteristics. You must stress your personal and unique reactions to the events in your life, and penetrate beyond the where and the when to the *why* and the *how*.

In my many years on both sides of the college admissions process, I have encountered far too many applications that have ruined an excellent applicant's chances of getting into a top school. The following is a brief summary of common application mistakes.

- **Bad letters of recommendation.** A student with perfect grades and scores—4.0 GPA and a 1600 on his SAT I—as well as a number of extracurricular activities that attested to passion and commitment, did not get into the Ivy League school of his choice. Why? Because his teacher recommendations all left the distinct impression that he was arrogant, that he was taking his ability and his success for granted, and that he was not willing to lend a helping hand to his fellow classmates. In the minds of your teachers—as well as in those of admissions officers—there is nothing attractive about intelligence that doesn't benefit the world around it. It is not enough to be smart. Your character is what will make or break your college application. The secret is to cultivate teacher relationships early on in your high school career that will yield you the glowing recommendations your application needs in order to remain competitive. Another student left a bad impression by asking a friend to hand her recommendation forms to her chosen teachers, forgetting to supply a stamped and addressed envelope, and not leaving enough time for the teachers to fill in the forms before the application deadlines. Needless to say, her recommendations were far from glowing, despite her excellent academic record.

- **Bad essay topic.** Another common mistake involves the choice of an inappropriate essay topic. I remember one student who decided to write his essay about hunting. Not a bad idea, if he had approached the topic from a unique perspective, for example, stressing the time he got to spend with his father, his love of the great outdoors, or his passion for sport in general. Instead, he chose to spend his essay talking about how much he loved to kill animals. No one on the admissions committee had to be an animal lover or even a vegetarian to find the topic distasteful. Another student wrote her essay about being raped as a child by her uncle. Don't get me wrong; this student needed to tell her story—but to the police and a child psychiatrist, not to an anonymous admissions committee.

- **Gimmicks.** I have encountered numerous cases of unnecessary adornments to college applications that have done nothing but distract their readers. There are certain circumstances in which it is a good idea to include examples of your work, for instance, if you are a serious artist and want to include your portfolio. To draw butterflies and flowers all over your application because you think it makes it look pretty will only give an overall impression of immaturity. Another student who wrote her essay entirely in a circle only made her admissions readers dizzy.

- **A vague brag sheet.** Colleges want to know how you spend your time both inside and outside the classroom. They want details. That's why I have my students include a very detailed "brag sheet" with their applications. I remember one student who came to me because he had been wait-listed at Princeton. I agreed to take a look at his application. I was shocked to discover that on his brag sheet he had listed "athletics" as his number-one activity, followed by the equally vague "community service." This is not enough. How can an admissions committee form an opinion about you without any details? They want to know which sports, which positions, what level of competition, the duration of your participation, any awards you've won, and similar details. They want to know what community service organizations you belong to and what your precise responsibilities are. College admissions deans do not have ESP—so tell them. I am happy to say that with my advice, especially on how to prepare a greatly expanded brag sheet, this student got off the wait-list and into Princeton.

- **The common application and/or a "generic" essay.** Although using the common application will by no means disqualify you from contention at a selective school, it may give the impression of noninterest. The same goes for a "generic" essay you attempt to use for various applications with similar essay questions. Theodore O'Neill, Dean of Admissions at the University of Chicago, has said that he considers the whole college admissions process to be a "conversation" between the applicant and the college. If you turn in the common application, you're avoiding the conversation, reducing it to a simple "declaration," showing you didn't care enough to seek out the school's official application. The same goes for a "generic" essay: if you write an essay for one school, you should take the time to write a new essay for another school if the school asks a different question, thus maintaining your end of the conversation.

The best overall advice I can offer for your college application is to imagine that you are an admissions officer reading your own application. You have been sitting at your desk for twelve straight days, reading application after application and, quite frankly, you're getting bored. Your eyes are glazing over; the facts and figures on each application are blending into one another. The last thing you need is more work deciphering an application. What you want is a clear, concise, and straightforward voice that leaps off the page, giving you an honest and immediate sense of who the applicant is.

Keep in mind, however, that no two committees are alike. They are also bound to change from year to year, so don't try to tailor fit your application to what you've heard a particular committee is looking for. *Be yourself and express yourself clearly*—that's the secret to application success.

ACADEMIC RECORD: YOUR HIGH SCHOOL TRANSCRIPT

Your academic record in high school is the most important factor in your application. If you could walk away from this book with one college admissions truth, it would be this: there is nothing more important to a prospective college than your grades and your performance in the classroom. Do not forget that the main reason you are going to college is to get a higher education. The first question an admissions officer is bound to ask when he or she opens your application for the first time is: can you do the work?

Your specific course work, grades, grade trends, class rank, and standardized test scores are all aspects of the academic record that admissions officers will consider in appraising your application. This information is found on your high school transcript. Although transcripts vary slightly from school to school, the following information will be included on your transcript:

- All final academic marks earned by you at the end of each semester in grades nine through twelve.

- All course work attempted for which a mark was earned. It is important to note that if you receive a mark of D or Fail in a subject and that class is taken later and a higher mark is earned, the new grade is recorded on your transcript. However, the previous grade remains on your record and both grades are computed in your grade point average (GPA).

- Information identifying all schools that you attended while in high school and the dates of attendance.

- PSAT, SAT I, ACT, SAT II, Advanced Placement and other local and state testing information. (See Chapter 7.)

- Credits earned toward graduation.

- Classes taken at colleges, universities, accredited private schools, and programs in grades nine through twelve.

- Vital information: name, birthplace, birth date, Social Security number, parent or guardian name, address, and local telephone number.

- Incidents of dishonesty, truancy, or infringement of any state or federal laws may be recorded on your transcript and sent to prospective colleges.

Other information may be included on your transcript according to the local Board of Education's policies, including information concerning:

- work habits and cooperation

- significant honors and awards

- attendance records and disciplinary actions

All of this information is normally included in a transcript of about one to four pages. Through the high school registrar, parents may request a copy of this document periodically to verify its accuracy. Every high school and school district has a procedure by which parents can challenge and change incorrect information that appears on their child's transcript.

Course Work

Successful completion of specific course work in high school is one of the most important college requirements. The completion of basic requirements for graduation from your high school may or may not meet individual college entrance requirements. Therefore, when considering colleges, you should look not only at the minimum requirements, but also at the recommended course work. Also keep in mind that your courses reflect who you are as a person. Colleges will look to the electives you have chosen and begin to form an opinion about your personality. Therefore, whenever you have a choice, make it wisely and consistently. I had one student who wanted to take AP biology instead of AP studio art in his senior year because he was convinced it would "look better" on his college applications. I had recommended he take the AP studio art course, because he was an artist, had taken many art courses, and had even worked in museums and art galleries for a number of years. He did not listen to me and after three weeks in AP biology, he was failing the course and miserable. Although he was able to get out of the AP biology class with minimal damage to his transcript, he wasn't able to join the AP studio art class at such a late date. Colleges are looking for that extra sign of passion and commitment that an AP studio art course would have signified. This could have adversely affected his application, but I advised him to take an art class elective in school and another art class outside of school. He followed my advice and was admitted early decision to the University of Pennsylvania.

Look closely at Table 1.1 with your college counselor and your parents so you can decide on a program that will make you eligible for the universities of your choice. If your public high school does not offer the relevant classes, you may wish to explore those classes at a local community or state college. This shows motivation and determination and can make up for differences between public and private high school offerings. All in all, the best advice is to challenge yourself as much as possible whether you are applying from a private high school or a public one. Slacking off at a competitive private high school is not better than proving yourself to be highly motivated at a large public one. The truth is, no matter where you are applying from, colleges are looking for one thing: highly motivated individuals from a diversity of backgrounds who challenge themselves with an increasingly difficult course load. When taking any class outside of your local high school, you must remember to check with your counselor to ensure that those classes will be accepted for both graduation requirements and college admission. In the end, only you and your focused effort to achieve will get you into the college of your choice.

The College Planning table gives an overview of what classes an average, competitive, and very competitive college will expect prospective candidates to have taken in their final years of high school. Such schools recognize classes that are designated honors, college preparatory, international baccalaureate (IB), and advanced placement (AP). Each school will trace your courses in the same way they trace your grades and extracurricular activities. They will look for consistency and commitment. For example, if you have successfully completed Spanish 3 in tenth grade, you should continue on to Spanish 4 and 5, in eleventh grade and twelfth grade. Do not drop Spanish or suddenly take up a new language like French. However, you can add French 1 as an *additional* language, while continuing with Spanish 4 and 5. If you took honors English in the tenth grade, do not drop down to regular level English in the eleventh grade.

I always get the question: is it better to get a B in an honors/AP course or an A in a regularly paced course, even if it adversely affects your overall GPA? The answer that admissions officers always give, not without a wry smile, is that it is better to get an A in the honors/AP course. While this is certainly true, getting a B in an honors/AP course—as long as you are working your hardest—is better than getting an A in a regular-paced course, even if it adversely affects your overall GPA. It is better to challenge yourself than to take the easy route to an A. The truth is colleges like to see you push the envelope and

Table 1.1   COLLEGE PLANNING TABLE

Grade	Average College	Competitive College	Very Competitive College
8			Algebra (first year) Foreign language (first year)
9	Algebra (first year) English (one year)	Algebra (first year) English (one year) Foreign language (first year) World history/ geography (one year)	Geometry (one year) Foreign language (second year) English (one year) World history/ geography (one year)
10	Algebra (first year) or Geometry Foreign language (first year) Biology (one year) College elective (one year) English	Geometry (one year) Foreign language (second year) *Biology (one year)* College elective (one year) English (one year)	Algebra (second year) Foreign language (third year) *Biology (one year)* College elective (one year) English (one year)
11	Algebra (second year) or Geometry Foreign language (second year) U.S. History (one year) Chemistry (one year) College elective (one year) English (one year)	Algebra (second year) Foreign language (third year) *Chemistry (one year)* *U.S. History (one year)* College elective (one year) English (one year)	Trigonometry/math analysis (one year) *Foreign language (fourth year)* *Chemistry (one year)* *U.S. History (one year)* College elective (one year) English (one year)
12	Algebra (second year) Foreign language (third year) Government/Economics (one year) College elective (one year) English (one year)	Trigonometry/math analysis (one year) *Government/Economics (one year)* *Physics/science elective (one year)* College elective (one year) *English (one year)*	*Calculus (one year)* *Physics (one year)* *Government/Economics (one year)* College elective (one year) *English (one year)*

Advance placement courses are in italics.

challenge yourself. But, if you are getting a C or lower in the honors/AP course, you may have signed up for more than you can handle and should consider switching into the regular-level class.

GPA

Colleges pay special attention to the challenging courses you have successfully completed. They use a Grade Point Average (GPA) computed on a 4.0 scale with advanced honors, IB, and AP class grades usually weighted 1 point higher. For example, a B (3.0) in AP physics would be weighted as an A (4.0) and an A (4.0) in AP physics would be weighted as a 5.0.

The private schools, especially the Ivy League schools, will consider your GPA in relation to the competitiveness of your high school. For example, a B in a regular U.S. history course at a competitive private school might be given as much weight as an A at a public high school. However, AP courses should be about the same at any school, and are therefore weighted equally.

Standardized Tests (SAT I or ACT, SAT IIs, and APs)

The SAT I is a multiple-choice test that attempts to measure your verbal and mathematical abilities. It is a three-hour examination that can be taken more than once. Colleges usually take the highest scores of the math and verbal sections (which can be from two different test dates), although they always receive your entire College Board testing history. The scores for the verbal and math sections range from 200 to 800 each.

The ACT, or American College Test, is a single-format exam, testing for achievement in the areas of English, reading, mathematics, and natural sciences. There are four subscores—each on a scale of 1 to 36—plus a composite score. Most colleges will accept either the SAT I or the ACT. If you submit both scores, the college will use the one that reflects your higher achievement. (See Chapter 7.)

SAT IIs are one-hour exams in specific subject areas that measure your knowledge of particular fields and your ability to apply that knowledge. Check the requirements of the colleges that you are considering before deciding which tests to take. Some schools require certain tests, usually writing, math, and another test of your choice. Please note that not all tests are available on each testing date.

The College Board offers the Advanced Placement Program, giving high school students the opportunity to take college-level classes while in high school in thirty-three different curricular areas. In May of each year, the College Board offers exams for each of these classes. A student who is successful on these exams can earn 3, 4, or 5 units of college credit based on their score (on a 1 to 5 scale, 5 being the highest score). Please note that not all colleges give college credit based on a passing mark on the Advanced Placement exam. Also, any student can take an AP test, without being in an AP course. If you don't get into the AP course of your choice because of scheduling problems or lack of prerequisites, and you are able to study on your own, you should try to take the AP test to show you are challenging yourself and overcoming personal limitations.

Class Rank

Colleges look at your assigned class ranking relative to the others in the class. Class rank is important as a means of showing admissions officers the level of competition you have encountered and how well you have achieved relative to that competition. Not all high schools compute class rank, although most public high schools will. The Ivy League schools will determine a class rank for you based on GPA, type, and size of high school.[1]

Grade Trends

Selective universities will not only consider what grades you earn but will also look at your grade trends. They will want to see you achieve either:

- consistent A's in increasingly difficult courses (that is, with more and more honors and AP-level courses), showing consistent hard work and a high level of achievement, or

- an upward grade trend (low B's in ninth grade, B's and B+'s in tenth grade, A−'s and A's in eleventh grade, and A's in twelfth grade) showing a consistent rise in GPA as well as considerable effort and hard work, especially as the courses get more and more difficult.

  Conversely, you want to avoid

- getting B's in honors courses in ninth and tenth grade and then making it easier for yourself by taking regular-level courses in eleventh and twelfth grade and getting A's; this shows a lack of motivation and an unwillingness to take on challenges, counteracting the upward grade trend.

- a downward grade trend: getting A's in ninth and tenth grade and then dropping to B's and C's in eleventh and twelfth without taking more and

---

[1] It is better to receive a specific class rank rather than be assigned one by the College Admissions Board. If you rank in the top ten and are really ranked first, they might place you at fifth or tenth.

more challenging classes; this shows a lack of passion and commitment. Also, in the eyes of an admissions officer, it doesn't bode well for your potential achievement in college.

Another grade-trend scenario that sometimes shows up and must be investigated by an admissions committee is a temporary grade dip, for example if you have gotten A's consistently throughout high school and then fall semester of the junior year you suddenly dip to C-level work. This usually happens because of a personal problem, such as a debilitating sickness, a car accident, a death in the family, or any other traumatic experience that sufficiently distracts you and prevents you from attending class. If a grade dip is apparent on your transcript, it is up to your high school's college counselor to explain this dip in his or her letter of recommendation.

GRADE IMPROVEMENT STRATEGIES

I cannot stress enough the importance of your performance in the classroom. Luckily, there are many extra things you can do to improve your grades and to improve the relationships you have with your teachers. Many fine applicants have ruined their chances of getting into the college of their choice by being lazy and complacent. By contrast, many lower-achieving students have shown great heart by asking frequent questions and displaying a genuine love of learning. These students are usually rewarded with excellent letters of recommendation, making them stronger overall candidates.

To this day, I remember the teacher who first made me aware of the importance of self-motivation. His name was Dr. Deutsche. He was an eccentric AP physics teacher and we did not get along. And with a class of only four students, there was no hiding it. For the first time in my life, I began to zone out during class. The birds outside, my intricate desktop doodles, the laces on my shoes: anything was more interesting than listening to Dr. Deutsche drone on about physics. Then came our first test. I got a D. I had never even received a B before, let alone a D. Something had to be done. But what? I was on unfamiliar ground and I hated Dr. Deutsche because I thought he hated me. I'm sure you've been there. It's a tricky situation and is one reason so many students are underachievers. So I woke up one morning and had a little chat with myself. If I was ever going to salvage my grade, I told myself that I would have to swallow my pride and admit I needed help. Even worse, I would have to admit it to Dr. Deutsche. When I finally got up the courage to approach him and ask him if he would help me, convinced he would bark back some negative response, I was completely surprised by what happened next. He actually said yes. Moreover, he was genuinely impressed and flattered that I asked him. For the rest of the semester, I got to school one hour early—hard for a late riser such as myself—and Dr. Deutsche tutored me in physics. I found out that he was just as passionate about teaching as he was about physics. As we got know each other, our first impressions faded, and my grade jumped from a D to an A–. When I got a 4 on my AP physics exam, it meant so much more to me than any of the 5's I got on my other AP exams. The experience proved to me that with a little bit of honesty, a little bit of humility, and quite a bit of work, life can be a great learning experience.

Here are some time-honored strategies to help you achieve what you never thought you could.

1. Show up to class on time every day. Tardiness and absences can only bring negative attention to you; plus, you will miss valuable in-class discussions. And remember: no excuse, however creative, will endear you to your teacher, so don't set yourself up.

2. Be prepared and complete all homework assignments on time. Moreover, try to go above and beyond the call of duty. If you are reading something for English or history class, go to your local college library and search the MLA (Modern Language Association) database for articles and books written on the subject/book/author/period. Reading professional articles will help you with your writing because the papers you write for your high school assignments are essentially mini–critical papers. Also, you will be armed with more ideas and theories to bring up in class and to incorporate into your papers—after all, your teacher can only present a certain amount of information and certain points of view. This exercise will help you focus on your topic and get you more interested in what you are reading. Plus, your teacher will take note of how much extra work you are doing and this will reflect favorably on both your grade and any letters of recommendation he or she may write for you. Remember also that in college you will be looking up secondary sources to write your term papers, so it is a great habit to get into while you're still in high school. Just be sure to cite your sources when elaborating on them in class or in a paper. You don't want to commit plagiarism.

3. Be prepared to participate in class and have a few questions prepared in advance. Let your voice, opinions, and ideas be heard.

4. Be helpful and respectful of both your peers and your teachers. Do not go overboard, just be polite and courteous. Always address a peer or teacher

by name. It will get their attention and people like to hear their own name—it gives them a sense of authority.

5. Try to sit in the front row or as much in line with the teacher's vision as possible. This will force you to maintain eye contact with the teacher and the teacher will notice you. You will also be less likely to get distracted.

6. As you are listening to the teacher, take copious notes. Teachers usually test you on what they say in class. If they are bothering at all to say it, it must be important to them. Taking notes will also focus you on the discussion at hand, and will spark questions and comments you can contribute to the classroom discussion.

7. As you listen to your teacher and maintain eye contact, nod your head in acknowledgment of the points the teacher is making. I call this the "nod of approval." Teachers like to know that you're listening and comprehending what they are saying. Plus, nodding will get the teacher to notice you. It is like having a silent dialogue with him or her.

8. If you don't understand something that was presented in class, I suggest going to your teacher for outside help. Visit him or her during office hours. This is a good way for the teacher to get to know you better as a person. Let the teacher know what else you are involved in. Maybe this teacher will write you a letter of recommendation in the future, so it is a great idea to nurture this relationship. If you did poorly on a paper, for example, take it back to your teacher and offer to rewrite it, instead of filing it away in the back of your notebook—or in the trash. You can also offer to retake failed quizzes and exams. Offer to do it not for a better grade but for the sake of learning and understanding more fully what the teacher is looking for. You should show the teacher that you are eager to improve yourself academically. Ultimately, the teacher will improve your participation and effort grades, and may give some extra-credit points.

9. If going to the teacher is not enough, you may want to seek out that kid in your class who seems to understand everything. Invite him or her to lunch or dinner and try to study together. Do not copy from any other student, but have a peer explain something to you in his or her own words. Often this works well because you and your peers communicate in a similar way; that communication may be more effective than a teacher or adult's explanation.

PERSONAL RECORD

The second group of questions an admissions board will ask when they first open your application is: Who are you? Will you make a valuable contribution to your future campus community? What type of character traits do you possess? Are you going to show up on time for class, get along well with your roommate, and be nice to the service people in the dining halls? Are you responsible? Shy? Creative? A leader? A nonconformist? In many ways, these questions take on at least equal if not more importance than purely academic considerations. The admissions officers at the most selective schools say that 80 percent of their applicant pools are academically qualified to attend their institutions. How do they whittle that down to, say, the 20 percent they will accept? By looking at your personal record. The more competitive the school, the more this side of your application is stressed. These days, it is not enough to be a good student. You must also be a good person. The following is a brief overview of the application elements that comprise your personal record.

The Brag Sheet

The brag sheet is similar to a résumé or curriculum vitae. It should include a list of all extracurricular activities, honors/awards, community service, employment, summer experiences, and hobbies/interests, indicating when and how much time was spent on each activity. The brag sheet allows admissions officers to see how you have contributed to your high school or local community beyond regular attendance and participation, how you excel as a scholar, athlete, artist, leader, or in other outstanding ways. You should keep a record of such activities from the ninth grade onward or use the sample "brag" worksheets in Chapter 6 to make sure that you are not missing any opportunities to widen your range of activities. Remember, like courses and grades, colleges like to see consistency and commitment when it comes to your activities. It is better to be involved in three or four activities wholeheartedly, for several hours a week over four years, than nine or ten activities superficially, changing from year to year.

The Personal Essay

Since it is difficult for your personality and character to shine through your GPA, SAT, and class rank statistics, selective colleges and universities will most likely require you to write one or more essays on questions set by their boards of admissions. The essay, generally no longer than one or two typed pages, is a chance for you to express yourself directly to the committee, illustrating why you would be a perfect candidate for the school in question. It is the best opportunity, besides the interview, for your unique voice to be heard. In essence, the essay gives you the last word on your application. (See Chapter 8 for sample questions and answers.)

Letters of Recommendation

Admissions officers faced with thousands of applications also rely on letters of recommendation from teachers, counselors, and even coaches and employers, to assist them in making an accurate assessment of your character. You should make sure that each person writing a recommendation for you knows you well and has all the necessary information about you at his or her fingertips. Secure your letters well before the deadline. Many colleges and universities will give precise guidelines in the admissions literature as to what they expect in the letters of recommendation, and many provide specific forms to be filled out. (See Chapter 9 before you approach potential writers.)

Personal Interview

Many selective universities like to finish the admissions process with a personal interview so they can assess you in a face-to-face encounter. You should remember that the interview is, above all, a two-way street—take advantage of the opportunity to find out as much as you can about the college. The reputation and prestige of a particular university can sometimes make it difficult for you to decide whether it is actually for you. Will you thrive on that particular campus? Is the academic and social balance right for you? Your impression of the school will be just as important to you as yours is to it. (See Chapter 10 for more information on interviews.)

SUMMARY

The first question admissions officers will ask when they open your application is: can you do the work? If you have not taken a challenging course load, performed your best work in all of your classes, and achieved standardized test scores representative of the work you are capable of, the most selective colleges will have no reason to believe you are capable of doing college-level work. On the other hand, as colleges become more and more selective, the importance of your personal record increases. The nation's most selective colleges claim that 80 percent of their applicants are qualified academically. In order to stand out against the competition, you must spend considerable time putting together a great brag sheet of all your extracurricular activities, writing engaging and poignant personal essays, cultivating strong relationships with the teachers and counselor who will be writing your letters of recommendation, as well as preparing sufficiently for your personal interview.

INSIDER TIPS

Ten important things to remember about your college application:

✓ Choose the right classes. Choose a rigorous course of study with classes of increasing depth and difficulty, but also choose courses that reflect your interests, for example, doubling up in sciences or languages.

✓ Focus on your grades. Strive for consistent academic excellence or an upward grade trend; follow my grade improvement strategies (pp. 13–14).

✓ Prepare. Prepare well for all standardized tests and take them early so you can repeat them if need be.

✓ Distinguish yourself. Try to stand out from the competition with consistent extracurricular activities that show passion and commitment, not scattershot indecisiveness.

✓ Challenge yourself. Take as many honors/AP courses as you can realistically handle in a given semester.

✓ Sell yourself. Do not be afraid to brag—this is a highly competitive process and those who are too meek to get noticed will be passed over.

✓ Start early. Start compiling your brag sheet as early as ninth grade and remain aware of how each activity fits into the bigger application picture.

✓ Don't be shy. Colleges want to get to know you, so be self-probing and honest, especially in your essay.

✓ Get to know your teachers. Cultivate great relationships with the counselor and teachers who will be writing your letters of recommendation.

✓ Get out there. Take advantage of an on-campus interview; remember that you are interviewing them as much as they are interviewing you.

2

PLANNING
FOR
COLLEGE

MYTHS AND TRUTHS

MYTH: High school is essentially boot camp for the college admissions wars.

TRUTH: High school is a time of growth and separation during which adolescents and parents alike will learn a lot about themselves and the society in which they live. It is a time for internal and external exploration, not a test of whether you can jump through hoops. Of course, you will still have to go through the often-grueling college admissions process, but you can do so with tranquility and confidence if you keep your priorities straight and follow the many helpful exercises and tips contained in this book.

MYTH: It's okay to sit around all summer working on your tan.

TRUTH: Summer is a great time to be productive—to visit a foreign country, attend a sports camp, make up a class in summer school, start a business, get an internship, join a community service organization. Boards of admissions specifically look to see that you have remained productive during your time away from school. You may want to take a few weeks off, but use the rest of the time wisely.

MYTH: Early decision is for legacy or truly gifted students only, and doesn't really help normal applicants.

TRUTH: While the majority of early applicants tend to be in the upper echelons of the applicant pool, you have an advantage by applying early if you are ready.

MYTH: You can only apply to one school early decision or early action.

TRUTH: Unless your high school forbids it or a certain college puts limitations on its early decision/action policy, the consumer advocate point of view states that you are legally allowed to apply to as many schools early action as you like, and as many rolling admissions schools as you wish in addition to one school early decision. Like any well-balanced stock portfolio, this maximizes your chances of a high yield.

MYTH: Colleges are lenient toward dips in your senior year transcript—you're only human, after all.

TRUTH: Colleges play close attention to your senior year grades, even if you are applying early. Any dips in performance—academic or personal—may result in your chosen college rescinding their offer of admission.

MAKING THE MOST OF YOUR TIME

The demands made on you in the last three years of high school leave you little time for yourself and certainly not much time for planning ahead or preparing for college. You want to go shopping with your friends, watch your favorite TV shows, surf the web, listen to your MP3s, go to concerts and sporting events, even just plain chill out. I remember. I had the same struggles when I was your age. It's important to live; to explore your emotions and your love life; to travel and be free. I also know just how nerve-racking this period in your life can be—as your courses get harder and harder and your homework longer and longer, your parents seem stricter than ever. There just aren't enough hours in the day to keep up. I have witnessed the stress of teenagerdom hundreds of times from many different perspectives, not to mention my own experiences as a teenager.

The important thing to remember is that you are not alone. You have your family, your friends, your high school college counselor—as well as the tips and suggestions contained in this book. With help, you can tackle the many difficulties facing today's high school student; you can emerge on the other side a successful college applicant with many enrollment options. One word of advice, however: as you start to plan for your college application process, remember that the decision is ultimately yours. The truth is, all the outside advice in the world should not change your mind once it is made up. This means it is important for you to voice your opinion, to explore your options, and to set about making your dreams come true.

I've devised the following calendars with your busy schedule in mind. They give you detailed and practical advice about where you should be focusing your efforts each month of each year. I hate to say it, but your first priority is always studying hard and keeping up your grades. With competition ever more intense, your best shot at getting into a selective school is to distinguish yourself academically. Your relationships with teachers and college counselors also need to be nurtured and encouraged whenever possible. This begins early in high school, so pay attention. If you keep a close eye on these monthly activities, you'll find yourself becoming a star college applicant while still leaving enough time to enjoy your busy, exciting life.

SOPHOMORE MONTHLY COLLEGE-PLANNING CALENDAR

SEPTEMBER

Update your brag sheet with your summer experiences or jobs.

Register for the PSAT.

Discuss with your teachers and counselors how many courses beyond the minimum required it is feasible for you to take.

Nurture relationships with your teachers.

OCTOBER

Take the PSAT.

Colleges take sophomore grades into consideration, so be sure to study hard.

Begin researching possible colleges.

Get involved with your extracurricular activities; be a leader in and outside of school.

NOVEMBER

Focus on academics and consider doing extra-credit work for one or more classes.

Find some volunteer work in your neighborhood.

Begin reviewing your personal preferences, strengths, and weaknesses. (See Chapter 6.)

DECEMBER

Talk to your older friends about their applications and about which colleges they have visited.

Be sure to keep up background reading (novels, newspapers, etc.) for your SAT next year. The more you read, the higher your verbal scores are likely to be.

JANUARY

Use your school's library to research possible colleges for admission; use handbooks, videos, computer programs, and all available materials.

Using your PSAT scores, begin narrowing down the range of colleges that you intend to apply to.

FEBRUARY

Consider a college summer program. Do research.

Continue with volunteer work, club activities, or a part-time job.

Schedule a meeting with your college counselor and your family to discuss college options and summer programs.

MARCH

Register for AP exams.

Begin visits to nearby colleges.

Research interesting and challenging summer courses, jobs, or activities.

APRIL

Sign up for SAT IIs; if you are in algebra II, take the math I in May and June. If you take biology in the ninth grade, take the biology SAT II in May and June of the ninth grade.

Use spring break to visit colleges far from home.

Apply for college viewbooks.

Attend the National College Fair.

MAY

Prepare for SAT IIs.

Plan challenging academic courses with your college counselor for the following year.

Repeat any classes where you scored lower than a C. Consider summer school.

Make a tentative list of colleges you want to visit or investigate further.

JUNE

Take SAT IIs. Remember that many selective universities require writing, math, and a third subject.

Plan visits to colleges over the summer; keep a log of college visits.

Consider doing something very productive with your time over the summer: for example, a study abroad program in a country whose language you are studying, or an academic program at a university campus. Make sure you do something for a long period of time, at least ten full weeks. No two-week-long teen tours!

Research scholarship and financial aid eligibility.

JUNIOR MONTHLY
COLLEGE-PLANNING CALENDAR

SEPTEMBER

Register for the PSAT.

Be sure that you are taking a strong academic program.

Purchase or borrow college reference books.

Plan the next two years' extracurricular and community service activities.

Confirm your Social Security number.

Confirm your high school's CEEB code number.

Nurture relationships with your teachers and counselor.

Sign up for October, November, December, and January SAT IIs: writing, Math I, and another of your choice. Make sure you are prepared for any SAT II you take. You may want to consider taking the SAT I for the first time in January if you can start preparing early.

OCTOBER

Take the PSAT.

Colleges take junior grades into consideration, so be sure to study hard.

Find some volunteer work in your neighborhood.

Begin reviewing your personal preferences, strengths, and weaknesses. (See Chapter 6.)

Take October SAT IIs.

NOVEMBER

Work on your brag sheet. Keep it up to date throughout the year.

Begin researching possible colleges.

Take November SAT IIs.

DECEMBER

Talk to your senior friends about their applications and about which colleges they have visited.

Discuss PSAT results with your counselor to determine how to improve.

Be sure to keep up background reading (newspapers, novels, etc.) for your SAT—the more you read, the higher your scores are likely to be.

Take December SAT IIs.

JANUARY

Use your school's library to research possible colleges for admission; use handbooks, videos, computer programs, and all available materials.

Using your PSAT scores, begin narrowing down the range of colleges that you intend applying to.

Begin intensive SAT I preparation. Sign up for March SAT I.

Take January SAT IIs. If you have time prepare for the SAT I over winter break, I suggest taking the SAT I in January for the first time, and March for the second time. This will leave May and June open for SAT IIs in the year-long subject courses you are taking junior year. You could then have two opportunities at the end of the school year to take three subjects.

FEBRUARY

This is the last semester that counts in your GPA/class rank; go for it.

Plan spring testing schedule with your counselor.

Consider a college summer program.

MARCH

Take the SAT I.

Register for AP exams.

Sign up for May SAT I if you need to take the test for the second time. If you are not taking the SAT I again, or plan to take it again in October of your senior year, then sign up for May and June SAT IIs in your year-long subject courses. Sign up for the ACT.

Begin visits to nearby colleges.

Research interesting and challenging summer courses, jobs, or activities.

Schedule a meeting with your college counselor and your family to discuss college options.

APRIL

Use spring break to visit prospective colleges.

Take ACT test.

Apply for college viewbooks.

Attend the National College Fair.

Keep reading.

MAY

Take SAT I or SAT IIs.
Take AP exams.
Plan challenging senior academic courses with your college counselor.
Register for ACT.

JUNE

Take SAT IIs (those that correspond to junior year courses, e.g., foreign language, U.S. history, science).
Plan visits to colleges over the summer.
Take ACT test.
Study hard for finals.
Register with NCAA Clearinghouse if applicable.

SENIOR MONTHLY
COLLEGE-PLANNING CALENDAR

SEPTEMBER

Update brag sheet with your summer activities and new or continued club or team activities.
Begin approaching teachers for recommendation letters.
Find out if any of your possible choices for colleges make fall presentations on your campus or nearby.
Obtain any college applications that you have not yet received.
Start narrowing down your choice of colleges; be sure to include a combination of safety, target, and reach schools.
Begin a file for each prospective college; use College Tracker.
Begin work on your personal essay(s).
Register for a retake of SAT I or ACT or SAT IIs if necessary in October and/or November.

OCTOBER

Take the SAT I or ACT and confirm registration for SAT IIs: remember, many selective colleges require writing, math, and a third SAT II of your choice.
Confirm all college application deadlines.
Follow up on letters of recommendation and transcripts to be sent with your application: remember self-addressed, stamped envelopes.
Double-check all recommendation letters. Thank teachers.

Follow up on any application requests not yet received with the relevant college.

Complete college essays and have them checked for style and grammar.

Determine your college costs and personal financial resources.

Research scholarship and financial aid eligibility in your college office and on the Internet.

NOVEMBER

Take SAT IIs.

Early action and early decision deadlines should be mailed by November 1 or 15.

Send in rolling admissions applications—the sooner the better.

Keep working on January- and February-deadline applications.

If you apply to a community college, be aware of priority registration dates, usually November–April.

Research scholarships offered by companies, parents' employers, civic and/ or church groups.

DECEMBER

You should complete SAT I, II, and ACT testing by this month. Walk-in registration is possible if you did not sign up on time.

Talk to your senior friends about their applications and about which colleges they have visited.

If accepted early decision, withdraw applications to all other colleges by mail.

If deferred early decision, write to the college, stating it is still your first choice and you will attend if accepted in the spring.

Begin filling in the Free Application for Federal Student Aid (FAFSA) and/or the PROFILE financial aid form (if applicable) for January mailing; the earlier you file, the better chance of a larger grant.

JANUARY

Complete and send financial aid applications, ensuring you have completed FAFSA and PROFILE if required.

If a seventh-semester transcript is required, ask your counseling office to send it.

Private college applicants need to supply a mid-year report.

Continue to research scholarship information.

Maintain your second semester grades and beware of senioritis/laziness. The year is not over academically and colleges can rescind their acceptances if your grades drastically plummet.

FEBRUARY

Check that colleges have received all materials: application, letters of recommendation, test scores, and financial aid forms.

Carefully read all information from colleges, including acceptance procedures, scholarships, financial aid, housing, registration, and orientation.

Encourage parents to complete tax returns early so they can supply a 1040 Income Tax form for determining financial need eligibility.

Continue checking with your college office for scholarship information.

MARCH

Report any admissions problems to your college counselor.

If colleges require additional information, send it immediately.

If accepted by a college, notify your counselor.

Register for AP exams.

APRIL

All colleges should respond by early April.

Meet with counselors and parents to discuss which college you should attend.

Consider financial aid packages carefully as offers arrive.

Try to visit all colleges that have offered you a place, if you have not done so.

Listen to advice of parents and counselors, but insist on your choice if it feels right for you: do not be overly influenced by college name prestige.

Follow acceptance instructions carefully.

Students on wait lists should write letters expressing interest and send any additional information.

MAY

Balance preparation for AP exams with final exams, term papers, and other course work.

Use AP preparation guides and/or study groups to help you in the exams.

Make final college selection if not already made; send deposit by May 1.

Follow up on financial aid package if you've heard nothing by mid-May.

Fill out housing forms.

Inform colleges you will not be attending that you have declined their offers.

JUNE

Graduation.

Order final transcript form from counseling office to be sent to the college of your choice.

Confirm that the college has all your relevant information.

Make sure you respond for state and Pell Grants or any other financial aid offered to you. Failure to do so will result in the aid offer being withdrawn.

WHEN SHOULD I APPLY?

Standard Admission (or Regular Decision)

Regular decision means that applications and supporting documents must be submitted by a set date in your senior year. The dates vary from November 30 through March 15, but most selective schools' regular decision applications are due January 1, 15, or February 1. The college then takes action on all the applications and notifies all students of its decisions at the same time. Notification dates are in the spring of the senior year, usually around April 1. If accepted, you must notify the college by May 1 of your intent to accept or decline their offer of admission.

Early Decision (ED)

This program is for students who select a particular college as a definite first choice. When applying early decision, you are signing a binding agreement that if accepted, you will withdraw the remainder of your applications and attend that school. This means that this school should be your number-one choice, because if you get in, you are committed to attending. You are essentially telling the college that it is your first choice; and you are rewarded by a significant increase in admit rate during this period. For example, in 2001 Yale accepted 26 percent of its early decision applicants, while it accepts only 13 percent of its regular decision applicants. The application, as well as all supporting documents, must be submitted early in November, usually between November 1 and 15 of your senior year for ED 1 schools and a few weeks or months later for ED 2 schools. Some universities give the applicants two early decision dates, usually one sometime in November and another that coincides with the regular decision deadline. The ED 2 period is for students who know the college is their number-one choice and who would commit to the school if admitted, but are not ready to apply by November. Junior-year grades are therefore extremely important for the ED applicant, although first quarter senior year grades may be submitted as well. It is best to check with your individual schools about transcript policies for early applicants. If you are a sopho-more reading this book and are thinking of applying early decision, it's already time to lay the groundwork for a productive and successful junior year.

After applying early, the college will take action and notify you, usually in December, whether you have been accepted, deferred, or rejected.[1] If you are deferred, your application will be held and you will be considered on the same schedule as the rest of the regular admissions applicants. If accepted early deci-sion, you are obligated to attend that institution and must withdraw all other applications. You may apply to only one school early decision, although you may simultaneously apply early action (see below) to other schools as well as to schools with rolling admissions policies, depending on the specific guidelines set by your high school's college counseling office and the university in question. For example, if you apply to Princeton early decision, you cannot apply to any other schools early decision or early action, so you'd better make sure you have a good chance of getting into Princeton early if you apply there early. Otherwise, you might be missing other opportunities for admission at early action schools that you like.

Early Action (EA)

This program is similar to early decision, but you are not required to attend the target school if accepted and may continue to apply to other schools. This program was not created to identify a number-one choice school. It is for stu-dents who really like the university and who have their acts together (stan-dardized tests completed, grade trend stabilized, essays done) early enough in the year to submit their applications early and find out early if they get in. The college can deny admission as well as accept or defer in December. Some selective schools that offer EA are: Cal Tech, the University of Chicago, Har-vard, Georgetown, MIT, and Notre Dame. Brown no longer offers an EA plan, having opted for a binding ED program instead. You can apply to more than one school EA, even if you are applying to one school early decision.

Early Admission

This option is for truly gifted students only. If you have exhausted your high school's graduation requirements and have finished all your testing early, you may apply to college at the beginning of your junior year or earlier. In your applica-tion—and in your letters of recommendation especially—you must demonstrate a level of social and emotional maturity commensurate with college-age students. I

---

[1] This varies from school to school. Some will not reject early, only defer. Others will accept, reject, and defer.

knew a ninth grader who was in senior-level classes and had no problem, either academically or emotionally, dealing with his peers. He was an excellent early admission candidate. If you apply early admission, you must go through the same standard admissions procedure, simply a year or more earlier. Again, these situations are very rare and should be handled on a case-by-case basis.

Rolling Admissions

The many state universities and private schools that use rolling admissions act on an application as soon as its file is complete. The college notifies the applicant of its decision within weeks of receiving the completed application. The deadline for this type of admission is usually not until May 1 and these colleges usually continue to accept students until they reach their capacity enrollment; therefore, it is best to send in your application as early as possible—in September or October of your senior year.

Open Admissions

Some colleges offer admission to all students who apply. Community colleges are an example of this type of admission.

THE TRUTH ABOUT APPLYING EARLY

In recent years, early decision and early action programs have been at the center of an ongoing debate about college admissions policies. Some studies and articles have shown that early applicants may increase their chances for admission anywhere from 20 percent to over 70 percent, depending on the college. Columbia University, for example, has a selectivity rate of 14 percent for regular admission. That number jumps to 40 percent when it comes to early applicants. In the study "Early Decision: The View from Different Perspectives" by Christopher Avery and his colleagues at Harvard's Kennedy School of Government, Avery finds that "applying Early Decision has the same effect as an increase of 100 points in the SAT score. Applying Early Action has a similar but slightly smaller effect." There is some controversy, however, over the effects of these now-popular programs. In an article in *The Atlantic Monthly* devoted to college admissions,[2] James Fallows has attacked the early decision program, arguing that although there are many incentives for a student to apply early, there are even more incentives for colleges to encourage early applicants:

[2] James Fallows, "The Early Decision Racket," *The Atlantic Monthly* 288, 2 (September 2001).

1. Colleges want enthusiastic students who identify them as their number-one choice—it boosts campus morale and gives schools a much better indication of a student's likelihood of accepting their admission offer.

2. Early decision facilitates the college's enrollment planning, so that the college does not overshoot or undershoot its incoming class.

3. Early decision improves the college's selectivity and yield, raising the college's *U.S. News and World Report* ranking.

4. Early decision knocks out the competition for applicants who might otherwise be applying to other selective schools.

5. Early decision reduces the financial aid burdens of the college, because the college can lock a student into a certain package before the student has a chance to compare it to packages offered by other schools.

It is the third point that especially aggravates Fallows. He believes that in the rush for prestige, colleges will stop at nothing to increase their reputation in the eyes of the public. Various national ranking systems help determine that reputation and colleges will do anything to increase the two major indicators that determine their national ranking: selectivity (the percentage of applicants admitted—they want this to be low) and yield (the percentage of students who accept their offers of admission—they want this to be high). Not only does this foster a competitive environment among colleges—as a loss in rank can easily translate into a loss of alumni donations—but, according to Fallows, ED programs are also by nature elitist. They tend to favor legacy candidates, wealthy candidates who can afford not to wait for offers of financial aid from other institutions, and students whose high schools are already well-staffed and connected enough to encourage students to apply early in the first place. In addition, besides favoring well-heeled students with established connections to the corridors of power, binding ED programs encourage competition among students, further alienating them from the underlying goal of their adolescent years: education, both academic and emotional. Finally, ED programs contribute to the myth that only a small number of highly selective colleges in America are capable of providing an excellent undergraduate education. Fallows cites studies that have shown that enrollment at one of the nation's top colleges does not necessarily translate into future economic success. At the very least, enrollment at any of the nation's other fine institutions, public or private, does nothing to hinder a determined student's ability to make it in this world.

On the other hand, a recent study by the College Board comparing the qualifications of early applicants to those of the entire freshman class at all schools that offer early plans (about four hundred) reverses many of the findings fueling both the Harvard study and Fallows's attack. According to this study, although the vast majority of schools with ED 1, ED 2, and EA programs are private (90, 100, and 90 percent, respectively), and a full 80 percent of them are on the East Coast, they are not necessarily elitist. Minority applicants, the study shows, are only slightly underrepresented in the early applicant pools; the class rank, GPA, and test scores of the early applicants are only marginally better than those of the freshman class as a whole; the percentage of students with financial need is similar to the percentage of students in the regular pools; and financial aid awards are not significantly lower for early applicants, undermining the theory that schools use ED and EA programs to lock students in at lower award levels. Of course, the College Board study only compares award offers *within* individual schools, so the suspicion that a student applying ED to a particular school is cheating herself of possibly higher aid offers from other schools is still valid.

In addition, Charles Deacon, Dean of Admissions at Georgetown University, has argued that the all-important yield statistics no longer mean anything since the numbers have been so manipulated by colleges based on subjective, nonpublicized factors. According to Deacon, early admissions programs were created to award academic excellence, not to increase alumni giving through higher rankings. He is also fundamentally opposed to binding early decision programs because of the unnecessary competition they create among college applicants. Accordingly, Georgetown does not allow students applying EA there to apply ED somewhere else. Also, Georgetown does not accept legacies or student-athletes early unless they have the same high level of academic achievement as their other EA accepted students—that is, unless they have an average SAT I score of 1430 as compared to the average of 1320 for regular decision admits in 2000. Dean Deacon also debunks the idea that early admissions either helps or hinders applicants in gaining admission to college at Georgetown. At Georgetown, the EA admit rate stands at 22 or 23 percent while the overall admit rate is just slightly lower at 21 percent. With 27 percent of their overall pool applying early, their yield has actually dropped from its 1999 level of 66 percent to the 2001 level of 44 percent. In other words, early action, as practiced by Georgetown, neither helps the student nor the institution—it is simply there to reward those students who have displayed a higher level of academic achievement throughout high school.

In line with this thinking, Georgetown also refuses to deny students who apply EA, opting instead to defer them to the regular admissions pool. Dean Deacon and his colleagues believe this to be less psychologically damaging for students, especially as they are about to rush their other applications to the rest of their chosen schools right before the holidays. Some college counselors disagree with this practice, arguing that it keeps false hopes alive and discourages students from taking their other applications seriously. Either way, it is up to you to decide what a deferral from a school really means—if it comes from a school such as Georgetown, it obviously is less encouraging than being deferred from a school that also maintains an outright early rejection policy.

Elsewhere, colleges and universities and high schools have taken matters into their own hands. Trying to discourage the current early application frenzy, some have attempted to limit the number of early applications their applicants are allowed to submit. Harvard, for example, used to include a caveat in its early action application allowing students to apply to as many schools early action as they wish, but forbidding them to apply early decision *anywhere*. That policy was recently changed in 2002. Now, if you apply to Harvard early action, you can apply somewhere else, like Yale, early decision. If you are admitted to both institutions, you must honor the early decision and attend, in this case, Yale. Georgetown states that it does not appreciate a student applying to any other school either early action or early decision; although the school cannot prevent you from doing so, if they found out that you applied somewhere else early, it would negatively affect your admissions decision. On the other hand, schools like Princeton and Brown, which have early decision programs, strictly forbid students from applying anywhere else early decision or early action. While these policies restricting applicants technically go against the National Association of College Admissions Counseling's (NACAC) definitions of ED and EA and the consumer advocate's position, private schools *can* enforce their own application procedures. Therefore, you must follow the guidelines of the individual universities.

In addition, some high schools limit the number of early applications their students are allowed to submit—one for either early decision or early action. They do so because they want to be able to tell each college that their early applicant is dead set on attending the school if accepted, thereby maintaining their mutually beneficial relationship with the deans of admissions at the selective schools in question. Dalton, a private high school in New York City, limits its students to applying to only one school EA or ED. I disagree with their policy, because other students around the world who can apply to many schools EA and one school ED will have an advantage over Dalton applicants. Dalton is trying to make EA schools into ED schools. EA was *not* created to identify a university as the student's number-one choice (otherwise, it would *be* an ED school). If this is this case with your high school, I urge you to petition your principal or school board to get this changed because it limits your choices and puts you and your fellow classmates at a disadvantage in relation to other students who apply under no such restrictions. According to NACAC, as a consumer you have a right to apply to one school ED, as many schools EA, and as many schools rolling admission as you wish. Until this dilemma is resolved, however, you must follow your individual high school's policy. Otherwise, they will not support your applications.

Fallows cites Edward Hu, of Harvard-Westlake school in Los Angeles, as one who is seeking a solution to this dilemma. Hu has suggested that all students apply to college only after they have graduated from high school, everyone essentially taking a year off to find themselves, go on interesting adventures, and apply to well-researched colleges, all at the same time. The late Joe Allen, former Dean of Admissions at the University of Southern California, proposed a far less radical approach. If most admissions officers and most high school college counselors agree that early decision applications have gotten out of control, then why not put a moratorium on the entire idea? If some of the top schools dismantled their ED or EA programs, surely others would follow. Once the effects have been diagnosed, schools could return to binding ED programs if they wished—but with full knowledge of their true effects.

Early decision is clearly not an option for students seeking the best financial aid package possible. Early decision also forces many students to make a decision they are not ready to make; they apply early somewhere because they know their chances of getting in are greatly increased. Colleges, on the other hand, are leery of students using their ED plans as strategies to get in, instead of as an indicator of the college as their first choice. Competition is so fierce and strategy so important in this process that some students are using early decision to apply to their *second* choice school, just to ensure an admission *somewhere*. I think the whole situation has gotten out of hand. Colleges are afraid to get rid of their ED plans because if they manipulate their numbers and take a larger percentage of their incoming class early, they can increase their yield and decrease their regular decision admit rate in the spring, thereby increasing their selectivity and raising their ranking in *U.S. News & World Report*. A higher ranking means more potential future applicants and more alumni donations. For colleges, ED is about rank, prestige, and, ultimately, money. Every year that I have attended NACAC, it seems that more and more people are bemoaning the iniquities of early decision. My question is why has not one selective college with an EA or ED plan stepped forward to abolish it completely? Why have we been discussing the same issues surrounding early action and early decision for at least the last five years? Personally, I am starting to feel like Bill Murray's character in the film *Groundhog Day*; I am bored with this conversation. And talk is cheap. Colleges want students to take action and make perhaps the most important decision of their young lives early, yet I don't see many colleges taking any action to address the problems surrounding early decision (except perhaps UNC Chapel Hill, which replaced their ED plan with an EA plan in 2001—a change I applaud). I consider it hypocritical for highly selective colleges to say that they are looking for leaders, pioneers, even. Yet these same colleges are too afraid to be the leader in this initiative. In 2001 the president of Yale said that Yale would be happy to abolish its early decision program, but only if a slew of other highly selective colleges joined Yale in the endeavor. Why can't they be the pioneer, set an example, and do it alone? Students are looking for leaders, too, in their college choices. If colleges are afraid of not getting their good press in *U.S. News & World Report*, I think they should fear not. The first highly selective college to abolish its early program will get more press in more publications than they know what to do with. And, as they say, the only bad press is no press at all.

For now, as long as there are early decision and early action plans available at the schools of your choice, it remains in your best interest to apply early—if you are ready—because this will increase your chances for admission. "Ready" means: you have decided under no uncertain terms that this school is your number-one choice (ED); you have visited and researched the school extensively; your essays are polished by October of your senior year; your grades through your junior year are indicative of your outstanding academic performance; and you have completed all necessary testing and are content with your scores.

A Note on Deferral

In the event you are deferred under either an early decision or an early action program, the last thing you want to do is wait around in the wings, hoping you have what it takes to survive the next round of applications. On the contrary, if you are deferred, there are a number of strategies you can employ to increase your chances of being accepted in the spring. First of all, I recommend you write a letter to the admissions office at the school in question, informing them in writing that if you are admitted in the spring, you will definitely attend their school (you can obviously only write *one* letter like this). Remember, schools are looking for a commitment in order to increase their yield; that is why early admissions programs are so attractive to them in the first place. Second, you need to keep in constant contact with your school. Write or e-mail them with any relevant updates to your application. You may even want to retake some standardized tests and submit new scores. Relay any new experiences you've had and any new positions or honors you've obtained, using the network of contacts you developed during the application process. This will plant your name and profile squarely in the minds of the admissions officers and make your application stand out from the influx of applications about to flood their desks. This is also another reason why it's so important to keep up your grades during your senior year, even if you are applying early to your top choice—they may have deferred you precisely in order to see those grades.

BEWARE OF SENIORITIS

Once your application is in and you're waiting to hear back from your schools, beware of that dreaded disease called "senioritis," an unofficial yet highly contagious case of "slacking off" that plagues many high school seniors. The college you choose will eventually receive your final semester grades and if they are significantly lower than the rest of your transcript, it could jeopardize your offer of admission. All college acceptance letters clearly state that your offer is contingent on your maintaining the same level of academic and personal excellence that made you such a strong applicant in the first place. So whatever you do, don't slack off, either academically or personally. Don't give them any reason to change their minds.

Believe me, I know the allure of a "senior slide." I know how much pressure there is to let loose and have fun. A good friend of mine was admitted to Harvard from an elite boarding school. He had gotten into some trouble earlier in high school but had recovered from the slip-up. Unfortunately, he got involved in an incident his senior spring involving alcohol. Although the circumstances left it unclear as to who was to blame, he lied to get himself out of a tricky situation. When his high school's dean discovered the lie, my friend was required to withdraw from high school—for *dishonesty*, not drinking. When Harvard got wind of this, they were understandably upset. Had the official disciplinary report simply read "drinking," they may have forgiven him (though it's doubtful). But dishonesty is a far more serious charge. It was no longer a question of his judgment, it was a question of his character. Harvard rescinded its offer of admission, although my friend finally wound up at an excellent alternative, the University of California, Berkeley. As a college freshman, he was unexpectedly summoned to the dean's office at Berkeley, even after a stellar academic performance his first semester. It turns out they wanted his final transcripts from high school. When he reexplained the circumstances under which he was kicked out of high school, the dean nearly kicked him out too. Finally, after providing sufficient proof that he was emotionally capable of thriving in an adult, college environment, he was allowed to stay. Do you really want the moment you've been waiting for your entire life to be haunted by the fear that you'll be called into the dean's office and made to answer for your horrible senior spring semester?

Or worse yet, do you want to forget about that moment altogether? I also heard about a student from a prestigious preparatory school who applied early decision to Duke. He was accepted, although they were concerned about a B– he was getting in calculus. They even warned him, telling him and his high school college counselor it was important that he do something about it. But he didn't listen. In fact, he became cavalier after getting in and let his grade slide even further to a D. Later that spring, Duke rescinded its offer of admission. Needless to say, the student was devastated. His parents were none too happy either. Since he had not applied anywhere else, the student ended up taking the year off to work. He retook calculus, got an A, reapplied to Duke, and got in. This may sound harsh, but Duke knew what it was doing. Anyone who would pull a stunt like that is clearly not mature enough to go to college. A very humbling year later, the student finally took his first step onto the Duke campus, a bit older and a whole lot wiser. Again, all I can do is ask you to envision that same first step onto the campus of your dreams. It is a moment of ultimate freedom. You are finally an adult in the eyes of the world. You have your entire future at your feet. Don't mess that up.

SUMMARY

To make the most of your time in high school is the single most important recommendation I can offer for a successful college application experience. If you have planned your time well, you can greatly increase your chances of gaining admission to the selective college of your choice. There are, of course, many pressures to distract you. Once you have turned in all your application materials, beware of the dreaded "senioritis." Colleges will be receiving your final transcripts and any irregularities in either academic or personal performance could force a college to rescind its offer of admission. Just remember this time-honored truth: a little hard work now will pay big dividends later as you take that first step onto the college campus of your dreams. As you apply to college, you will want to consider the following types of admission: standard admission (or regular decision), early decision (ED), early action (EA), early admission, rolling admission, and open admission. Each school varies in the types of admission it offers. Review the appropriate sections in this chapter for more details.

INSIDER TIPS

✓ Use your time wisely. Get started on the application process as early as possible so that you can enjoy your teenage years.

✓ Plan well. As in all things, a little balance and moderation in your academic planning go a long way toward securing your future college happiness. Check and double-check that you are satisfying all requirements.

✓ Apply early. As long as there is some early plan available at your first-choice college, you should apply early *if you are ready*.

✓ Beware the dreaded "senioritis." Colleges will rescind their offers of admission if you do not maintain your demonstrated level of achievement throughout your senior year.

3

COLLEGE RESOURCES

MYTHS AND TRUTHS

MYTH: As a college-bound student, you have to rely primarily on your parents' and your own knowledge and research as you wade the difficult waters of college admissions.

TRUTH: There are a number of excellent resources available to you, including your high school college counselor and independent college counselors, as well as guides, books, and Internet sites devoted to the complex issues facing today's students.

MYTH: Most source materials are impartial representations of the relative strengths and weaknesses of the colleges and universities covered.

TRUTH: All source materials are flawed or opinionated in some way. You should not trust any one single reference to guide you through the college admissions process. Instead, you should familiarize yourself with as many as possible, then supplement their assessments with your own firsthand experience visiting and researching the institutions that interest you.

GETTING STARTED

In this chapter I would like to introduce you to the various resources available to you in your quest for the perfect college fit. These lists are by no means exhaustive, but if you follow my suggestions, they should provide you with a solid foundation on which to base the majority of your application decisions. Only through exposure to as many colleges as possible will you be able to assess their relative strengths and weaknesses and decide which ones are right for you. In Chapter 4, I will guide you through a number of exercises that will help you pinpoint exactly what you are looking for in a college or university. For now, please spend some time looking through the following resources and familiarizing yourself with their offerings. Again, nothing beats a little hard work now, especially when it comes to making one of the biggest decisions of your life.

USING YOUR HIGH SCHOOL COLLEGE COUNSELOR

The myth in this case is that a normal American high school doesn't have the resources to help you prepare for your college applications. The truth is, you will find one of the most useful sources of college admissions information right in the middle of your high school: your high school college counselor. While he or she may have large numbers of students to aid and assist through the college admissions process depending on the size of your graduating class, your college counselor should have access to the current year's university admissions literature as well as individual advice based on his or her contacts and experience. Counselors are expertly trained and highly experienced guides to the labyrinth of college admission. As you will have seen from the planning calendars in the previous chapter, you should try to cultivate a relationship with your high school college counselor as early as possible in your high school career so he or she can best help you in the months to come, eventually writing a great letter in support of your application.

There are also a number of independent counseling options available to students and parents who feel they might need extra help facing the challenge of applying to college. Although there has been some disagreement between school-based and independent college counselors in the past, ultimately both are working with the best interests of their students in mind. I prefer that my students inform their college counselors that they have retained my services; when working together, I always try to cooperate with them, hoping to make their sometimes overburdened jobs a little easier.

What Your High School College Counselor Should Be Doing[1]

Although a high school college counselor's responsibilities vary from school to school, he or she should:

1. Guide and counsel you and your parents through the formulation of your postsecondary school plans.

2. Organize and maintain a College Counseling Center containing college catalogues, brochures, handbooks, videotapes, and other reference materials for all types of postsecondary school options.

3. Attend pertinent district, regional, and national meetings regarding college admissions, financial aid, and testing.

4. Coordinate and implement ongoing dissemination of information to you, your parents, faculty, community members, and staff at local elementary schools pertaining to the college admissions process.

---

[1] Attachment A, Memorandum No. 47, Los Angeles Unified School District, Office of the Associate Superintendent, Schools Operations.

5. Motivate and encourage you to prepare for college admissions by taking the appropriate tests and course work as well as provide you with specific information and time lines regarding entrance requirements.

6. Provide necessary information and materials for you regarding PSAT, SAT I and IIs, American College Testing (ACT), Test of English as a Foreign Language (TOEFL), Advanced Placement tests (APs), and other college entrance or placement tests.

7. Interpret test results for you, your parents, and your school's staff.

8. Provide current information regarding college costs, financial aid opportunities (local, state, federal, organizational, and institutional), and fee-waiver eligibility.

9. Maintain your files regarding postsecondary school plans for the purpose of counseling you and your parents.

10. Offer you and your parents workshops to provide information and assistance in accurately completing up-to-date forms; provide follow-up interpretation.

11. Write a letter of recommendation for you for all admissions and scholarship applications.

12. Provide assistance to faculty and staff in writing letters of recommendation and completing secondary school reports.

13. Coordinate opportunities to meet with college representatives on campus and at local college fairs. Organize and implement field trips to college campuses.

14. Design and prepare the school profile.

15. Organize a system for dissemination of transcripts for college admissions and/or scholarship purposes. Facilitate processing of applications for admissions and/or financial aid.

16. Coordinate and administer school and community scholarship programs, including identifying candidates and planning the selection process.

17. Plan and organize senior awards ceremony.

18. Train and supervise personnel assisting in your high school's College Counseling Center.

19. Provide information regarding off-site college courses for concurrent enrollment along with summer program options.

Your High School College Counselor's Required Skills

Your high school college counselor should be able to:

1. Work well with you, your parents, faculty, and postsecondary school educational representatives, as well as school community groups.

2. Represent the school in a positive way.

3. Accurately assess your maturity level; emphasize the processes of goal setting and decision-making.

4. Help you assess interests and abilities and make course choices that will lead to appropriate careers.

5. Understand test construction and interpret educational test data.

6. Know district graduation requirements and parallel entrance requirements for postsecondary institutions.

7. Plan, organize, and implement meetings involving a variety of topics.

8. Have effective oral and written communication skills.

9. Maintain current knowledge of frequently changing laws, application requirements, and procedures.

10. Motivate you and provide academic incentives for your success.

11. Understand the relationship between high school and college programs.

Your high school college counselor must also be able to show that he or she is a certified employee of the local school district with an active teaching credential, as well as a credential that authorizes counseling services.

THE INSIDE SCOOP ON PRIVATE COUNSELORS

As the number of professional college admissions services increases, so does the number of independent counselors who have neither the proper credentials nor experience to guide you adequately through the college admissions process. As with any outside services you seek, be very careful when hiring an independent college counselor. If, after consultation with your parents and your high school college counselor, you are interested in retaining the services of an independent college counselor, I would strongly suggest asking them the following questions first. You should also talk to some of their current or recent clients before deciding to hire them.

1. What is their experience in the field of college counseling? Have they worked in a high school setting? Have they sat on an admissions committee? If so, where and for how long? How long has their private practice been running?

2. Are they certified to be college counselors in their state or through one of the national organizations? Do they belong to the National Association for College Admission Counseling (NACAC) or to the Independent Educational Consultants Association (IECA)?

3. What is their academic training? Do they have any degrees in counseling? Have they taken any certification courses? Are they certified to handle developmental problems in adolescents?

4. What are their fees? What services do those fees include? Are reduced rates available for lower-income families?

5. How many colleges have they visited? How recently? Do they go on college tours every year? Are they familiar with your high school's academic program?

6. Do they have long-standing relationships with deans of admissions at the nation's selective colleges?

7. Do they attend national and regional conferences set up by NACAC or IECA?

8. What is their reputation in the community where they live?

9. What is their legal/business status?

For more information on both high school and independent college counselors, contact: NACAC: (800-822-6285) or *www.nacac.com*; IECA: (703) 591-4850) or *www.educationalconsulting.org*.

HELPFUL RESOURCES

In addition to the assistance available from your high school college counselor and from independent college counselors around the country, there is much reference information readily available from many different sources. *But*—and this is essential to your future well-being in college—please keep in mind that each of these books and guides tries to create the myth of its own importance. Often, the goal is to sell you on buying their book, not necessarily on presenting the most accurate, up-to-date, and helpful advice about college admissions. In other words, use the following books and websites as *guides*—each is opinionated, flawed, and incomplete in its own way. The trick is to familiarize yourself with the information they contain *only as a starting point* for the much more valuable and rigorous research you will be doing in Chapter 4 as you narrow down your college list and delve into examining your personal aspirations. The truth of your college needs and desires is in you, not out there in some book.

Guidebooks

Most guidebooks contain the following information: enrollment, admissions, selectivity, curriculum, costs, financial aid, faculty, majors/programs offered, campus life, student body makeup, and profiles of the freshman class. These materials are available or can be ordered from most bookstores. I happen to prefer the *Fiske Guide* for its combination of compressive facts and figures and personal anecdotes and descriptions of each campus. They may take a bit longer to read than a quick reference guide, but each entry leaves you with an indelible impression of the academic and social life at the college in question. Please refer to the list below for a selection of currently available titles.

General Guides	
Barrons	*Profiles of American Colleges*
Cass and Birnbaum	*Comparative Guide to American Colleges*
College Board	*The College Handbook*
———	*The Index of Majors*
———	*10 Real SATs*
Custard, Edward	*Student Advantage Guide to the Best 310 Colleges*
———	*The Complete Book of Colleges*
Fiske, Edward	*The Best Buys in College Education*
———	*The Fiske Guide to Colleges*
Lovejoy	*College Guide*
Peterson's	*Annual Guide to Four-Year Colleges*
———	*Competitive Colleges*
———	*Paying Less for College*
———	*Sports Scholarships and College Athletics Programs*
Townsend, Kiliaen	*The College Comparison Guide*
Yale Daily News	*The Insider's Guide to College*

Books

Bailey, Robert	*How and Where to Get Scholarships and Financial Aid*
Bear, John	*Finding Money for College*
B'nai B'rith	*Hillel Guide to Jewish Life on Campus*
Bromwell, Perry and Howard Gensler	*The Student Athlete's Handbook*
Cassidy, Daniel	*The Scholarship*
Chany, Kalman	*Paying for College Without Going for Broke*
Coburn, Karen	*Letting Go: A Parents' Guide to Today's College Experience*
Davis, Kristin	*Financing College*
Fiske, Edward	*How to Get into the Right College*
Gourman, Jack	*The Gourman Report, A Rating of Undergraduate Programs*
Greene, Howard	*Scaling the Ivy Wall in the 90's*
———	*The Select: Realities of Life and Learning in America's Elite Colleges*
——— and Matthew Greene	*Making It into a Top College*
Hartman, Ken	*Internet Guide for College-Bound Students*
Hayden, Thomas	*Handbook for College Admissions*
Hernández, Michele	*A Is for Admission*
Kaplan, Benjamin	*How to Go to College Almost for Free*
Leana, Frank	*Getting into College, a Guide for Students and Parents*
Levin, Shirley	*Summer on Campus*
Light, Richard	*Making the Most of College*
Margolin, Judith	*Financing a College Education, The Essential Guide for the '90s*
McKee, Cynthia, and Phillip McKee	*Cash for College, The Ultimate Guide to College Scholarships*
Mitchell, Joyce Slayton	*Winning the Heart of the College Admissions Dean*
Moll, Richard	*Playing the Private College Admission Game*
———	*The Public Ivys*
Paul, Bill	*Getting In: Inside the College Admissions Process*
Peterson's	*College 101*
Pope, Lauren	*Colleges That Change Lives*
Rugg, Frederick	*Rugg's Recommendations on the Colleges*
Shields, Charles	*The College Guide for Parents*

Books	
Spencer, Janet and Sandra Maleson	*Visiting College Campuses*
Steinberg, Jacques	*The Gatekeepers*
Sullivan, Robert	*Ivy League Programs at State School Prices*
Turner, O'Neal	*The Complete Idiot's Guide to Getting into College*

The Internet

The Internet has fast become the most sophisticated and comprehensive research tool for obtaining college and university information. Since you are just beginning your research, you can start by looking at the education sections of well-known search engines such as Yahoo!, Google, or Excite. While they do not offer very detailed or specific information on each university, they have useful listings that can help you narrow down your search, as well as links to individual institutions where you can take virtual tours. I happen to think that individual college websites offer some of the best insights into what each school has to offer, both academically and socially—but remember that such websites are essentially promotional tools for the colleges and therefore are not completely impartial. The following is a list of useful websites for the college-bound student.

College Admissions Process and Planning
College Express: *http://www.collegexpress.com*
This is a well-organized, student-oriented site that offers a full range of college admissions information. It is a free site that is broken down into categories such as College Search (find your college, request information, view maps and directions), Admissions (read tips on getting in, consult their admissions dean, and apply online), Financial Aid (estimate costs and locate scholarships), Student Center (ask questions and explore campuses), Sports Source (athletic information on colleges), and Parents' Corner (how parents can help). It is most useful for its financial aid and college homepage links as well as detailed information on generic admissions procedures.

College Net: *http://www.collegenet.com*
This is a searchable database of colleges, scholarship opportunities, and academic resources. With web-based admissions applications, you can apply to more than five hundred colleges online. You can also search and apply for scholarships and financial aid. For $9, you can sign up for college recruiting

and make your profile available to all participating colleges. The site also offers information on college resources and a virtual bookstore, with discounted books, software, and CDs on sale through the site's affiliate, Barnes & Noble.

College Choice Website: *http://www.gseis.ucla.edu/mm/cc/home.html*

This is a nonprofit information service for college-bound students with brief recommendations on: preparing for college, selecting a school, the college application, paying for college, your first year away, time lines, links to other informative sites that cover testing (the Princeton Review, Kaplan, SAT I, AP tests), minority students, scholarships and grants, articles and essays about college, and college life.

Cynthia Good's Home Page: *http://www.users.massed.net/~cgood/*

This site has a plethora of useful links but you have to sort through it all to find exactly what you're looking for. The topics include: the college application process (college choice), essay evaluation (for a fee), college selection (college link), financial aid, testing, careers, and study skills.

National Technology Institute:
http://www.collingswood.k12.nj.us/high/guidance/TI/guidlinks.htm

This National Technology Institute guidance website offers links to information on preparing for college, financial aid, scholarships, college rankings, online applications, distance learning, testing, career planning, and international colleges.

Students' Link to Government: *http://www.students.gov*

This is a U.S. Department of Education site that is your gateway to the U.S. government. It is an excellent collection of links that range from precollege planning and repayment of loans to how to register to vote and community service opportunities. This website also offers information on internships, fellowships, programs affiliated with diversity, and military service.

My College Guide: *http://www.mycollegeguide.com*

"One-stop College Information on the Web," including *The College Guide Magazine,* a college search engine, and financial aid information. You can download the common application here or ask the guru any question relevant to college admissions. The most recent and frequently asked questions by students are posted, with answers from the guru.

NIEP: *http://www.niep.com*

National Institute for Educational Planning's site offers a program where students and counselors can pay for various services, including planning college tours and college and graduate school admissions counseling.

Peterson's Education: *http://www.petersons.com*

Peterson's college database is available on their homepage, as is other educational and career information. You can search for colleges through College Quest as well as tap into distance learning options. There is a section for international students with information on requirements and testing. You can search for accredited colleges by specialized programs such as nursing, culinary school, visual and performing arts, and schools that have distance learning options. This site also offers information on career guidance, summer jobs, community service opportunities, and summer programs. You can also purchase Peterson's books at a discount rate.

New York Mentor: *http://www.nymentor.edu*

New York mentor is an online resource for you and your family to plan for New York's colleges and universities. It has direct links to the schools' websites and contains all you need to know about a particular school. You can e-mail the site's support for specific questions or reference their FAQs. It contains useful information for international students. This site also offers Apply Now!, which allows you to view applications and apply directly online. In order to view applications online, you need Adobe Acrobat Reader.

NACAC: *http://www.nacac.com*

The National Association of College Admission Counseling homepage includes a regularly updated list of National College Fair dates as well as the *www.OnlineCollegFair.com* link to virtual college fairs. NACAC is an association of secondary school counselors, college and university admissions officers, and counselors and related individuals who work with students making the transition from high school to postsecondary education. One can find the Statement of Principles of Good Practice, the code of ethical conduct for all individuals and institutions involved in admissions. As a student you can ensure that your counselor is fulfilling his or her obligations to you. You can also go to *www.nacac.com/p&s/steps.html*, which has specific information for parents and students regarding financial aid, tips on writing a college essay, test-taking strategies, general admissions, and college visits. In addition, NACAC maintains a constantly updated list of useful web resources.

College Views and Tours
College View: *http://www.collegeview.com*

This website contains a "lite" version of the proprietary college information, software, virtual college tours, a searchable database and scholarship, and financial aid data. The site offers electronic applications free of charge through NetApply and AppZap, which are printable and can be sent online. However, there are not many selective schools on the list and no Ivies. The site does have a test prep center, as they are affiliated with Kaplan Test Prep; you can enroll for test prep courses through Kaptest.com on this site. Other links: Career Center, Campus Bookstore, Guidance Office, and Game Room.

Campus Tours: *http://www.campustours.com*

This is a great source for virtual college tours, webcams, campus maps, college videos, and movies and pictures. Their college finder allows you to sort through over 3,200 colleges and universities to find the one that is right for you by having you answer questions in a survey in order to narrow down your search. Online applications are also available.

Collegiate Choice: *http://www.collegiatechoice.com*

As they are not authorized by the colleges themselves, these video tours provide a raw, inside look at all aspects of campus life, including those unflattering sides of the schools so difficult to come by in "official" tours. You may purchase their video tours.

College Visits: *http://www.college-visits.com*

If you are having trouble planning your college visits, try accessing this site, run by Robert Rummerfield, for upcoming group tours to specific geographic areas that cover a number of colleges in only a few days and include information sessions. These trips are well-planned and affordable. I take a college trip with Bob every year. Call (843) 853-8149 or (800) 944-2798 for more information.

College Link Pages
American Universities:
http://www.clas.ufl.edu/CLAS/american-universities.html
Direct links to the homepages of approximately 1,102 American universities.

Community Colleges:
http://www.mcli.dist.maricopa.edu/cc/search.html
Links to 450 community colleges in the United States, Canada, and other foreign countries.

Global Computing: *http://www.globalcomputing.com/university.html*
Direct links to 620 American universities.

International Universities:
http://www.mit.edu:8001/people/cdemello/univ-full.html
More than three thousand links to universities all over the world.

Applying Online
The Princeton Review: *http://www.princetonreview.com*
The Princeton Review recently bought Embark, a service that makes it easy to
apply to college online. You can sign up for free and apply to undergraduate and
graduate schools online. The site helps you find the schools you are best
matched for. You can do virtual campus tours and plan college visits. There is
also a special section for international students and transfer students with related
links on visa applications, academic and testing requirements, and application
deadlines. This site offers comprehensive advice on the entire college admissions process, including financing your college education, the pros and cons of
early action/early decision, tips on how to write a good college essay, and interview preparation.

Monster.com: *http://www.monster.com*
This popular career site has recently made the foray into college admissions
services, vowing to help students evaluate their educational needs as they
relate to their potential careers. In addition to admissions matching services
that screen for up to forty-five points of data, Monster.com has recently
acquired the financial aid website FastWeb, a free scholarship search database
that saves your profile and e-mails new sources of private merit aid to your
mailbox. They also recently acquired the online college application service
College Link. This service greatly simplifies the application process by allowing you to input your application information once and then automatically
reformat the data to fit application forms for more than one thousand member
colleges, thus giving the impression you have taken the time to fill out each
individual college's application separately. There is no charge for the service.
They also have College Search Tools, Student Diaries, access to over $1 billion

in scholarships, and are developing software to allow you to immediately upload your application onto a college's internal application database.

Testing
College Board Online: *http://www.collegeboard.com*

The College Board's homepage identifies itself as the "starting point for students, parents, counselors, admission, and high school and college faculty members." You can link directly to more than five hundred college websites, e-mail their admissions offices, and apply online. The site also provides testing information, financial aid forms, essay writing tips, and sample SAT questions. You can prepare and register for the SAT I and SAT IIs online.

Educational Testing Service: *http://www.ets.org*

This site provides valuable information on guidelines for standardized test-taking, rules and regulations for test-taking, information for students with learning disabilities, standards for quality and fairness, information on testing locations, registration, and computer-based testing.

The Princeton Review: *http://www.princetonreview.com*

This site helps you search for schools, manage the application process, and find the finances to pay for it all. It contains guidance as well as articles on college admissions, school rankings, visits, and online test preparation. Recent updates to the site include: a chat room, a parents' guide section, and an informative list of FAQs. The Princeton Review also publishes more than 150 reference and tutoring titles. Please note that the Princeton Review is not affiliated with Princeton University, although founder John Katzman attended Princeton as an undergraduate.

Fair Test: *http://www.fairtest.org*

The National Center for Fair and Open Testing (FairTest) is an advocacy organization working to end the abuses and flaws of standardized testing and ensure that the evaluations of students are fair and educationally sound. It also lists 281 schools that have eliminated or reduced the SAT and ACT requirements for admission.

Athletics
NCAA: *http://www.ncaa.org*

The National College Athletics Association's information site includes rules and eligibility for NCAA, comprehensive scholarship information, information on recruiting, the clearinghouse, records and statistics of college-level sports, and links to schools by conference, division, and NCAA region.

Study and Work Abroad
Study Abroad: *http://www.GoAbroad.com*
This site allows you to search for many different programs abroad by subject or location, as well as for jobs, internships, adventures, teaching positions, and language schools. Travel guides can also be found on this site and *www. StudyAbroad.com.*

Financial Aid and Scholarships
Financial Aid: *http://www.finaid.org*
Top-quality homepage of links to many financial aid–related sites. The EFC (Estimated Family Contribution) estimator is one of the highlights of this site.

Financial Aid Library: *http://www.nt.scbbs.com/finaid*
A variety of useful links serve as a financial aid "desk reference set."

Loan Repayment Estimator: *http://www.student-loans.com/Repay.html*
Estimates monthly payments for various college loan programs/amounts.

Nellie Mae: *http://www.nelliemae.org*
Sallie Mae: *http://www.salliemae.org*
Information on Nellie Mae and Sallie Mae college loans.

SUMMARY

Research is perhaps the most important aspect of the college admissions process. The more you know about your options, the more likely you are to find the right fit. Your high school college counselor is an invaluable resource for this information. Independent college counselors are also available if you need more personalized attention and guidance through the college application process. Increasingly, the web has become a major source of college admissions information along with the many guidebooks, brochures, and ranking reports currently available. All in all, you will want to expose yourself to as many different sources of information as possible in order to gain an objective and broad understanding of the choices facing you.

When beginning your research, please bear the following tips in mind.

INSIDER TIPS

✓ Research first. Your high school counselor is extremely busy. Do as much research as you can on your own. Know what you want from your counselor well in advance of any deadlines.

✓ Seek guidance. Once you know what you want, do not hesitate to ask. Know what your high school college counselor is and isn't qualified to do before you visit. If you want to retain the services of an independent college counselor, research their credentials and make sure they have a good track record with previous clients.

✓ Do your own work. As you research schools, do not be fooled by name recognition alone; look closely at what each school has to offer and think carefully about what you are looking for in a college.

✓ Form your own opinion. Throughout the process, try to remember there is no such thing as objectivity—all sources are flawed and opinionated in some way.

✓ Speak up. Don't ever be afraid to voice your opinion when it comes to making one of the most important decisions in your life. You will be confronted with many differing perspectives—if you keep a level head about it, the right fit will come to you.

4

CHOOSING YOUR COLLEGES

MYTHS AND TRUTHS

MYTH: Only a top name college will provide you with the educational and social opportunities necessary to succeed in today's society.

TRUTH: Very few top executives and national leaders went to "elite" colleges. There are literally hundreds of colleges and universities that offer excellent opportunities to all types of students—the trick is to know what you're looking for so you don't fall prey to the allure of a prestigious name.

MYTH: College is a time for ultimate freedom. You should seek out a school with as little structure as possible.

TRUTH: Every single college applicant has different needs. And every single college experience is different. For some, structure may be necessary, for others freedom may provide the best basis for self-realization. The truth is: you have to know who you are before you apply anywhere.

MYTH: It's okay to apply to a list of colleges supplied by a counselor or parent, or simply to follow the *U.S. News & World Report* rankings.

TRUTH: If you don't know why you're applying to a certain school, then don't apply. You are the one who has to live with your decision and you will not be happy if you're not at the school that's right for you.

MYTH: College is an academic experience—you should therefore choose a college based on your proposed major alone.

TRUTH: College is an academic but also a social experience. The average college student changes majors at least twice in the course of his or her college career. You should make sure the colleges you research boast a number of strong departments in multiple areas in which you are interested.

CHOOSING YOUR COLLEGES

Now that you have spent some time gaining an overview of the myriad college options available to you, it's time to start considering in more detail which colleges offer what you truly want out of your postsecondary school experience. The myth is that you must apply to and be accepted by one of the top name colleges in the country in order to receive an excellent education. But as Caitlin

Flanagan has argued in *The Atlantic Monthly*, this is far from the truth.[1] An "elite" college frenzy is currently gripping America, one whose worst consequence is not a mailbox filled with rejection letters, but the literally hundreds of excellent educational opportunities passed up at the rest of the nation's excellent educational institutions. If you do the proper amount of research—delving deeply into both your prospective schools and yourself—you will soon see that many colleges fit your criteria. As you will also see, there are hundreds of factors to consider when faced with choosing where you would like to continue your studies. Not only is there a bewildering choice of courses and places to take them, there is also a wide range of social, financial, and environmental questions you need to ask yourself before choosing the right college. I suggest you make use of the following questionnaires to create a profile of the college that would best fit your needs and interests. You will then be able to take a second, more informed look at the available information from specific colleges on your way to finalizing the list of colleges to which you will apply.

The following series of questions was inspired by Linda Zimring's extensive work in the field.

Physical Factors

Which areas of the country will you consider?

West: _____ Pacific Northwest: _____ Southwest: _____

Rocky Mountains: _____ Midwest: _____ New England: _____

Northeast: _____ South: _____ Midatlantic: _____

Which of the following would suit you the best?

Urban: _____ Suburban: _____

Small town: _____ Rural: _____

On what was your decision based:

Climate: _____ Culture: _____

Other: _____

How often do you plan to return home? _____

Do you prefer to be close to home or far away? _____

---

[1] Caitlin Flanagan, "Confessions of a Prep School College Counselor," *The Atlantic Monthly* 288, 2 (September 2001).

Would you prefer to:

commute from home? _____

live on campus? _____

live in a rented accommodation? _____

Do you require guaranteed housing for all four years? _____

Will you be taking a car to school? _____

Would you consider a college that does not allow freshmen to have cars?

_____

If you plan to be on campus, what type of dorm would you prefer?

single sex: _____ coed by floor: _____ totally coed: _____

theme dorm: _____ co-op: _____ other: _____

Campus Size and Social Issues

Sense of community you seek: cozy? anonymous? in-between?

Average class size you seek: _____

Given your priorities, what campus size(s) are you currently interested in?

20,000+: _____ 15,000–19,999: _____

10,000–14,999: _____ 7,500–9,999: _____

4,000–7,499: _____ 2,000–3,999: _____

Under 2,000: _____ Don't know: _____

Are campus cultural issues such as religion, socioeconomic level, or race

important considerations in choosing your school?

_____

Are cultural amenities such as museums, theaters, movies, malls, or pro-

sports events important to you?

_____

Do you want your school to have a strong Greek life with many sororities and fraternities?

_____

What degree of school spirit (football, cheerleading, campuswide traditions, sense of history, etc.) do you want your school to have?

_____

What degree of political activism—issues such as workers' rights, affirmative action, gay and lesbian issues, protests and marches for/against various political figures—do you want your school to have?

_____

Would you prefer a liberal or a more conservative atmosphere on campus?

_____

What types of activities should be available as the "fun" part of campus life? Dances, concerts, sporting events, mixers, arts festivals, excursions, movie nights, etc.

_____

Does the degree of drug/alcohol use on campus concern you? If yes, in what respect?

_____

Academic and Extracurricular Factors

What kind of college would you like to attend? Liberal arts, business, engineering, trade, or technical?

_____

Would you prefer a general or specialized curriculum? Do you plan to declare a major immediately?

_____

Would you prefer a set curriculum or a flexible curriculum that you can design yourself?

_____

How much academic structure is important for you? Some smaller, liberal arts colleges have abandoned grades altogether while others offer self-paced, self-designed courses and even self-administered exams. By contrast, large state schools tend to enforce strict core and distribution requirements while offering more standardized examinations. Remember, the less structure there is, the more self-discipline you must have.

_____

_____

What academic level is most suitable for you? How hard do you want to work?

_____

_____

Would you prefer a trimester, semester, or quarterly calendar? Semesters have the benefit of longer summers, but trimesters and quarters give you an opportunity to take a wider array of courses.

_____

_____

How important is the level of intellectual stimulation in classes and among your peers?

_____

How important are the following factors:

academic guidance: _____ career counseling: _____

ease of course enrollment: _____

breadth of course offerings: _____

faculty accessibility: _____ prestige of college: _____

Are there subjects that you particularly want to avoid at college? If so, which ones?

_____

Conversely, what are the academic areas in which you have an interest and that a prospective college must offer?

_____

_____

Extracurricular Activities/Community Service/Athletics: What do you plan to get involved with?

_____

_____

Speciality Interests: Music/Art/Drama, etc._____

_____

_____

Financial Factors

Can you attend college without financial assistance? _____

Are you able to consider private schools, which can be extremely costly compared to public institutions?

_____

Is the availability of on- or off-campus jobs important to you? _____

_____

Is the cost of living of the surrounding community a factor to consider?

_____

REQUESTING INFORMATION FROM COLLEGES

Once you have filled out the above questionnaire, take another look at the college resources in Chapter 3 and approach your high school college counselor with a short list of schools you would like to research in more depth. He or she will be able to help you clarify your priorities. Then, in order to inform yourself further, write to these colleges individually, requesting copies of their literature, and refer to their websites for other relevant information. (You should check whether the colleges require payment for hard copies of materials before writing.) Please refer to the following sample letter as a model.

Your Name
Address
City, State, Zip

Date

Director of Admissions
Name of College
Address
City, State, Zip

Dear Admissions Officer,

I am a (sophomore/junior/senior) at _____ High School and am considering applying to your school. I would appreciate your sending me the following (and I am enclosing a check to cover the cost of your catalog*):

Course catalog
College view book
Application for admission
Financial aid forms
Special program brochures
Information pertaining to your _____ department
List of extracurricular activities/clubs/organizations
List of community service organizations

Thank you in advance for your prompt reply.

Sincerely,
Your signature
(Print or type your name)

*If applicable.

THE SECRET TO A BALANCED PORTFOLIO

Once you have studied the relevant information from your initial selection of possible colleges, I strongly advise you to break down your choices into "safety" (60–90 percent chance of gaining admission), "target" (30–60 percent chance of gaining admission), and "reach" schools (less than 30 percent chance of gaining admission). By doing so, you will give yourself the best chance of getting into as wide a variety of schools as possible. To get a better sense of your chances at each school, you can compare your own academic record with statistics of the previous year's admitted freshman classes. You can get this information on the colleges' websites or in books like the *Fiske Guide*. You can also get statistics on admit rates of students from your high school's previous graduating classes. Finally, have a frank discussion with your high school college counselor, your parents, or anyone else you feel has an objective view of your abilities in order to help balance your profile with the right colleges. List your relevant statistics below and use that information to compile lists of your safety, target, and reach schools.

Your Statistics

Cumulative GPA _____

SAT I Verbal _____ Math _____ ACT _____

Rank in Class _____

Safety Schools

Use the following table to help you assess two to three colleges you consider "safety" schools where your profile is significantly stronger than the typical freshman and you would have roughly a 60–90 percent chance of getting in.[2]

College	% Accepted Applied/ Accepted/ Enrolled	SAT I Scores Mid 50% of those accepted	Freshman Academic Profile in HS class	Admissions Deadline (ED/EA Regular)	Tuition Board Fees
Example:					
Tulane	78% 8388/ 6542/ 1635	600–690 V 590–680 M ACT N/A	52% in top 10% 97% in top 50%	EA11/1 1/15	$23,500 $6,908 $1,890

[2] Statistics in the following tables are taken from *The Fiske Guide to Colleges 2001*.

1.

2.

3.

Target Schools

Choose four to five "target" schools where your profile is similar to that of the typical freshman and you would have roughly a 30–60 percent chance of gaining admission. It is most likely that the college you attend will come from this group.

College	% Accepted Applied/ Accepted/ Enrolled	SAT I Scores Mid 50% of those accepted	Freshman Academic Profile in HS class	Admissions Deadline (ED/EA Regular)	Tuition Board Fees
Example: George Washington University	49% 14,326/ 7019/ 2105	560–660 V 570–660 M ACT 24–29	47% in top 10% 99% in top 50%	ED 11/1 ED 12/1 12/1,1/15	$22,340 $8,210 $1,035

1.

2.

3.

4.

5.

Reach Schools

Finally, you should choose two to three "reach" schools. These will probably be quite selective (less than 30 percent acceptance rate). Often one of these schools is your top choice. To increase your chances of admission, apply to your top choice early decision or early action, *if you are ready*.

College	% Accepted Applied/ Accepted/ Enrolled	SAT I Scores Mid 50% of those accepted	Freshman Academic Profile in HS class	Admissions Deadline (ED/EA Regular)	Tuition Board Fees
Example:					
Princeton	11% 14,875/ 1,636/ 1,129	680–770 V 680–770 M ACT 30–35	92% in top 10% 100% in top 25%	11/1 1/2	$25,430 $7,206 $2,684
1.					
2.					
3.					

BEYOND THE IVIES: FINDING THE PERFECT FIT

While my advice has focused largely on selective, top-tier schools, including those of the Ivy League, you may want to look beyond these colleges (see the Appendix, Forty Elite U.S. Colleges and Universities) at the increasingly wide range of specialist schools that offer great educational opportunities. The following websites will give more detailed information on college life, academic and social opportunities, and other defining characteristics. You may be sick and tired of hearing it, but the next four years are going to be crucial to your future and a little research now will pay huge dividends later on. The truth is: you must go forth and seek if you want to end up in the right place.

Alternative Admissions Policies: *http://www.fairtest.org*

Some colleges have admissions policies that look beyond the narrow portrait given by traditional GPA and test score statistics. For a complete list of 281 schools that have eliminated or reduced SAT I and ACT requirements for admission into bachelor degree programs, visit the FairTest website or contact them by phone at (617) 864-4810.

One of the websites listed below may also be of interest.

Historically Black Colleges: *http://www.blackhighereducation.com/hbcu.html*

Women's Colleges: *http://www.dir.yahoo.com/Education/Higher_Education/Colleges_and_Universities/United_States/Women_s_Colleges/*

Jesuit Colleges: *http://www.ajcunet.edu*

Jewish Interest: *http://www.hillel.org/*

Trade and Vocational Schools: *http://www.overview.com/colleges/*

SUMMARY

There are thousands of factors to consider when choosing which colleges to put on your final college application list. Once you have given careful consideration to all of your academic, social, geographic, and financial options, you should be in a position to narrow your choices down to seven to ten schools. Of these schools, two or three should be "safety" schools where you have a 60–90 percent chance of getting in; four or five should be "target" schools where you have a 30–60 percent chance of getting in; and two or three should be "reach" schools where you have less than a 30 percent chance of being admitted. When coming up with this list, do not be swayed by name recognition alone. Think long and hard about what it is you want from your institution of higher learning. Look off the beaten track and think outside the Ivy League box. There are literally hundreds of excellent schools you may never have heard of, which offer great opportunities for your academic and social future.

INSIDER TIPS

✓ Get the inside scoop. Ask friends or family who have attended one of the schools on your list for insights and tips.

✓ Keep an open mind. Do not limit yourself to one type of school. Try not to go on name recognition alone.

✓ Balance your portfolio. Choose a broad array of schools. Make sure to include some "safety" schools that you would still love to attend.

✓ Network. Contact professors in your field of interest and let them know you are thinking of applying. They might give you good advice.

✓ Do the work. Nothing beats good research. Start with a large list and narrow it down according to your specific interests.

✓ Contact. Get in touch with schools personally. They will register the interest and open a file on you right away.

5
PREPARING
TO
APPLY

MYTHS AND TRUTHS

MYTH: To apply to college, I just need to fill out a few forms, right?

TRUTH: Wrong. You should treat each college application like you would a job application. Research the school's offerings, research your needs, then develop a precise vision of how the two would come together at each school you're interested in. Literally imagine you're there before you even apply.

MYTH: Letting your parents take over the application process will greatly increase your overall chances.

TRUTH: Allowing anyone else to write or overly influence your application will only make it more complicated and less authentic. Remember: colleges want to get to know you, not who your parents think you should be.

MYTH: The college visit is pretty much optional.

TRUTH: In order to know if a particular college is a right fit, you should visit it. Nothing beats your firsthand impressions of a school as you visit its campus, talk with its professors and students, check out its dorms and dining halls, and walk around its surrounding community. If you and your family cannot afford your own college tour, there are a number of other, more affordable options available to you.

MYTH: I'll remember everything about a school if it really moves me.

TRUTH: Take as many notes as possible as you research and visit your schools. Don't let the details get hazy—you must be specific in your essays and interviews in order to make each school feel wanted for its unique offerings.

MYTH: Colleges hate nothing more than a persistent student—contact them only when absolutely necessary.

TRUTH: The more you keep in contact with the schools you are applying to, the better your chances of receiving a favorable reading of your application. Colleges like knowing you are interested in them; you can best express this interest through e-mail, phone, and written correspondence. The office of admissions at each of your target schools will open a file on you the first time you make contact—the more your interest shows in that file, the better.

PREPARING TO APPLY

Now that you have spent some time getting to know the schools that interest you and coming up with a list of colleges, it is time to zero in on each one in preparation for your actual applications. In order to better understand what you are looking for and what each college has to offer, you will have to do some in-depth research. Don't shy away from this. Nothing can take the place of hard work when it comes to strategizing your approach to your college applications.

Here's the hard truth: in today's increasingly competitive college admissions environment, you essentially have to think of your college search as a job search. If you were applying for a job at the company of your dreams, what would you do? Surely you wouldn't go in cold, with no knowledge of what the company has to offer or what you might be able to offer the company. You would do research. You would look into the history of the company and the kinds of products and services it offers. You would examine the structure of the company to know how the job you're applying for fits into the big picture. You would contact your potential coworkers in order to gain a better understanding of your future work environment. And you would develop a precise vision of what you could contribute to the company community if hired. Finally, you would use the results of this research in your cover letter and in your interview, in order to give the company every reason to hire you.

The same goes for the college application. You must get to know the schools to which you are applying, research their histories, communities, current course offerings, professors, and student bodies. By getting to know each school well, you will form a clear picture of how you might enhance its community. If you have this picture clearly in mind, you will write better applications and impress your interviewers. You will also have a much better idea of why and where certain schools belong on your final list. If you are having trouble imagining you're there during your research, then you may have to weed out some of the colleges on your list. Try to keep an open mind if this happens. You may have fallen in love with a school from its website, its brochure, or from word-of-mouth praise, but when you visit it or imagine yourself going through a typical day there, something negative is revealed. It may be a school to cross off your list, but don't get discouraged. The selection process can be grueling. Look long and hard at all the information available to you and try to form an honest, well-researched opinion about each school. Try to filter out the inevitable influences from the outside world—friends, college ranking magazines, even parents—and form your own opinion. Remember: the decision is ultimately yours.

IMAGINING YOU'RE THERE

I have used this exercise quite successfully in my private counseling practice. I find it inspires my students to pinpoint what they are looking for in a prospective college. Essentially, they get to go to college before actually attending. The exercise also gets them involved in the college application process early on in their high school careers, encouraging a detailed and methodical approach to college admissions. Ideally, you should begin doing this type of in-depth research during your sophomore year and continue all the way through the end of your junior year, so you are not making up a last minute college list during your senior year. This way, bit by bit, you will become your own expert on the many college choices available to you. Think about what I call the three Cs—classroom, campus, and community—which exist in concentric circles. Picture the environment in the three Cs and articulate how you would contribute to each of them in a productive and valuable way.

1. Begin by choosing one of the schools from your list. Access and review any and all available materials. That means: read the college's brochure; tour its website; analyze its course catalog; research its core and distribution requirements, its major programs, and its admit rate. Finally, realistically determine your chances of getting in.

2. Your next step is to envision your first year at the college in question. Literally pretend you are there, living in your dorm with your new roommate, eating in the dining commons, sleeping in a strange new bed. Picture yourself going through this first year, drawing on all the knowledge you have gathered about the school during your research.

3. Choose your courses. What subjects are you interested in? What core requirements do you need to satisfy in your first year? Which professors are you interested in? Sign up for the courses, being sure to take on a typical first semester course load. Imagine yourself sitting in lecture, venturing a question in seminar, buying your books at the bookstore, lugging that first load of assignments home to your dorm room.

4. Now look more in-depth at the academic environment. How accessible are professors, according to the resources you have checked? What is the overall student to teacher ratio? What articles or books have professors published recently? Call the department that interests you and ask them for a list of the latest papers published by members of their faculty. Go and find some of their works in your local library. If you can't find them there, check the Modern Language Association's (MLA) database in your local

college library for a list of currently available titles. You might also log on to your local state university's library network and find a professor's work that way. If all else fails, you can usually find works by professors at the campus bookstore during your campus tours. Once you have found something a professor has written that is of particular interest to you, *read it*.

5.   Now you are ready to move outside the classroom. College, after all, is more than just book learning. It is a series of life lessons that equip you to be an active member of society at large. Research extracurricular activities available at the school in question. What do you think you will be doing in your free time? Imagine joining various clubs and organizations, continuing what you have been pursuing in high school (colleges want to see consistency and commitment). Get the names of current club and organization members and contact them, asking them direct questions about their membership requirements, funding, work opportunities, etc. Some examples of clubs to write to are: a singing group, an acting troupe, a political organization, a jazz band, a vegan co-op, an honor society, a debate team, an intramural sports team, an ethnic or theme house, etc. If you write for your school newspaper, request copies of all campus publications. Which one would you want to write for? A daily? A humor magazine? A political journal?

6.   Now move further outside the classroom. Research community service opportunities available at the school. Remember: colleges want students who are valuable and productive members of their campus communities and the larger communities surrounding the campus. Which activities might you pursue? Can you continue the type of volunteer work you are doing now? Write to the school and ask them direct questions. Will you realistically have time to devote to community service or will other interests interfere?

7.   Now comes what is perhaps the most important step: *visit the school*. You cannot learn everything from a website, brochure, or catalog, and nothing beats actual, firsthand experience with the campus and its atmosphere. An extensive college tour of Northeast colleges reminded me about such interesting things as the monkey carrels at Williams (which are like bunk bed desks; you can climb up to the upper desk), the new Bicentennial Building at Middlebury, and the completely red room at Amherst where the course Murder is taught. Knowledge of specific details such as these is only possible with a campus visit.

8.   The final secret to this exercise is to produce a pros and cons sheet for each college you have researched. Try to keep it to one page for easy ref-

erence. You may be surprised by what you find—some schools you never thought of as top choices might turn out to be better suited to your needs than your first, more obvious choices.

What does this exercise accomplish? First, it makes you an expert on a number of colleges. You are now ready to apply to them with a full understanding of their relative strengths and weaknesses. Second, the knowledge you have gained in the process will come in handy if you are ever asked to answer the typical "Why this school?" question on an application. Third, this is excellent preparation for an interview. If you have pictured yourself at the school and researched every last detail of your first year there, then you will be able to artic-ulate that vision to an interviewer. In turn, the interviewer will be able to pic-ture you there too. You will also be able to formulate intelligent questions by incorporating a number of salient facts and details about the school that only a well-researched person would know. For example, you might ask an inter-viewer: "I know that Judith Rodin, president of the University of Pennsylvania and the first female president of an Ivy League institution, teaches a freshman seminar called Body Obsession. Could you tell me how hard it is to get into?"

Finally, and most importantly, this exercise makes you appear like a legacy applicant. One reason why legacy applicants are so attractive in the eyes of col-lege admissions committees is because children of alumni are always better informed about the school than other applicants. They grew up hearing their par-ents talk about the school, going to reunions with them, hosting alumni dinners. Schools know this. They know the legacy candidate is making an educated deci-sion when he or she chooses to apply. And they also know the legacy student is more likely to attend if accepted. The truth is: colleges want students who know them well and want them. Showing you have done the research can sway a com-mittee to your side, giving you a leg up on the competition. The officers know you're serious; they know you care; they know you have the resolve and deter-mination it takes to be an excellent member of their college community.

COLLEGE VISITS

The next step in preparing to write your college applications is to arrange a number of campus visits to the colleges you have selected. Again, the truth is clear: words, websites, and any amount of careful research cannot replace your actual firsthand impressions of a school. You can plan a college tour with your parents, go alone, or travel with an organized tour. You should plan your visits during your junior year—any time you have time off: religious holidays, Columbus Day, Thanksgiving, winter break, Presidents' Day weekend in February, spring break, or any weekend. You can also plan your visits during the summer between junior and senior years, although this is less ideal because regular classes are not usually in session.

The tours can be done with relative ease. Simply call the admissions office at each school well in advance of your visit to set up a tour and information session. If you plan correctly, it is possible to visit a few colleges in a single day, although I recommend spending a good, solid day getting to know each one. There are also a number of excellent private tour services that provide cost-effective ways of visiting a group of colleges in a specific geographic area. Such services can be beneficial as they will often expose you to colleges you might never have considered. College Visits (see p. 50) is an excellent provider of such a service.

If you keep the following suggestions in mind during your visit, you should have a good idea of whether or not the school is right for you. Again, take your time, ask a lot of questions, and listen carefully to everything you are told.

1. Try to visit while school is in session. You will get a much better feel for the size of the campus, its student diversity, and its atmosphere. Even more informative is the campus tour arranged through the admissions office usually conducted by students. If you know any students from your high school currently studying at the college you are visiting, ask to meet with them, for they will be in a much better position to give you advice and answer your questions. Make sure to wear comfortable clothes and shoes on your tour, as you will be walking a lot. Also, bring a camera or videocamera and make sure to get the good, the bad, and the ugly, as well as some candids of students. These pictures will help you remember what you saw on your tour. Ask yourself: Do I feel comfortable in this campus environment? Can I picture myself attending this school?

2. In addition to the tour, you should call the admissions office at least a month in advance to arrange an information session. There are usually two sessions given on a single day (one in the morning, one in the afternoon), normally by an admissions officer or the Dean of Admissions. Make sure to bring a notebook or a tape recorder. Write down as much information as possible and ask questions specifically related to your interests. When you are asked, "Why this school?" in an essay or an interview, these notes will help you immensely.

3. Get the business card of the person who gives your information session and open a line of communication; tell him or her how much you enjoyed the session; then keep in touch periodically.

4. Bear in mind your responses to the questionnaire in Chapter 4 regarding physical, academic, and financial factors. While touring campus and listening to the information session, ask yourself, "Does the school meet all or only some of my needs?"

5. Visit the college's admissions office. Introduce yourself to one of the admissions officers or someone who reads applications—preferably the area reader for your application. Get that person's phone number and e-mail address. You can obtain a great deal of information concerning the college directly from the admissions office. Fill out a card with your information (name, address, high school, your interests, what information you are seeking) so the reader can start a file on you and have a record of your visit. This file can be a plus when you apply, because the college will have evidence of your early interest. Try to keep in touch by writing, e-mailing, or calling every month with questions or updates on the progress of your application.

6. Ask about and investigate the school's student support services, including tutorials, student advising, career counseling, and health services.

7. Evaluate the school's activities and athletic programs, including major sports, intramural sports, clubs, and organizations. Even if it isn't part of the organized tour, try to visit the school gym, theater, playing fields, and student centers, or any area of interest to you. Other good sources of campus-life information include: the school newspaper, college radio station, local community newspaper, department newsletters, as well as the many notice boards that dot every college campus.

8. If school is in session, try to audit a class. Ask the admissions office at each particular college for permission. Make sure to pick up a course catalog from the admissions office as well. Ask yourself, "Do I like the courses they offer? Does this school meet my educational needs? Does it offer the courses and major in which I am interested?" Beware of subtle differences. For instance, a lot of students want to study business but many small liberal arts colleges only offer economics, which is not the same.

9. Talk to a professor in your area of interest, a coach in your chosen sport, and other students. Ask a student why he or she chose this college. Ask about likes and dislikes. Talk with students about weekend activities as well.

10. Make sure to visit a representative freshman dorm during your tour. Check out things like the bathroom situation, closet space, windows, and Internet connections. You can even arrange with the admissions office to stay overnight with a freshman and attend class with him or her.

11. The day of your visit, try to have lunch in one of the school's cafeterias. Do they have a good selection of food, such as ethnic, healthy, or vegetarian options? Do they contract out to a caterer or hire their own chefs?

12. Think about the weather. For example, visits to Eastern schools are often scheduled in the spring or summer when temperatures rarely drop below 60 degrees. Can you live in snow, sleet, hail, and temperatures that may drop below zero for four or five months out of the year? Can you survive the constant rain and fog of the Pacific Northwest? The humidity of the South? The landlocked flatness of the Great Plains?

13. Once the tour is over, walk or drive around the community surrounding the campus. Adjusting to life away from your immediate family can be challenging at first, so you may want to consider if there are any relatives or family friends close to the school you are considering. If you are touring the school with your parents, I urge you to break away from them for a while at some point and walk around town and through campus alone, soaking in the atmosphere, trying to picture the independent life you will soon have.

14. Do, however, consult with your parents on your impressions of the campus. They will most likely be helping finance your college education and they might make useful suggestions and offer different perspectives on cities, locations, and schools. The more they feel like they are being included in the process, the more likely they are to listen to your opinion when it comes time to choose.

If an actual college visit is prohibitively expensive for you and your family, fear not. First, you can try calling a college and explaining your circumstances. It is not unheard of for colleges to offer to pay for your visit, provided such funding is available. Second, in addition to actual tours, you can order walking-tour videos of hundreds of different campuses from Collegiate Choice (*www.collegiatechoice.com*). These "objective" videos are made from real campus tours, and include the good, the bad, and the ugly. This is a far better option than ordering a video directly from the school in question. In-house college videos are bound to show you the campus on its best day, editing out any construction, dilapidation, protests, foul weather, or other unappealing aspects. If you do order a video directly from a school, keep in mind that such videos are largely promotional in nature.

Also, do not forget that college representatives will be visiting your high school to give information sessions. Be sure to attend these sessions—they are excellent networking opportunities. Also be sure to get the representative's card and e-mail address and open a line of communication. The earlier a college knows you are interested, the better. And the more you are in contact, the more your interest will pay off.

You may find it helpful to use the following form to remind you what questions to ask when visiting a school and to keep a record of your findings. Make a worksheet for each school you are considering. Use your answers to compare your impressions of each college visit.

COLLEGE VISIT WORKSHEET

Name of College

Address and website

Admissions office phone number and e-mail

Contact person

Expense

Tuition

Room and board

Application fee

Total

Location

Distance from home

Setting (urban/suburban/rural)

Natural Offerings (mountains,

bike trails, ocean, lakes,

hiking, skiing, sailing,

surfing, etc.)

Cultural Offerings (movie theaters,

restaurants, shops, museums,

nightlife, etc.)

Size

Enrollment

Campus area

Admission Requirements

Tests required

Average scores

GPA

Recommendations

Interviews

Essays

High school courses

Admit rates of previous year,

    both regular admission and

    early decision/action

Special requirements

Student Body

Male/female ratio

Student/teacher ratio

% minority

% international

Housing

Availability

Quality (size of rooms, windows,

    location of bathrooms, closet

    space, etc.)

Residence hall requirement?

Types and sizes (high-rise,

    brownstone, co-op, special

    interest/theme houses;

    singles, doubles, triples,

    quads, suites?)

Food plans/options (number of

    dining halls, quality of food,

    types of food, operating

    hours, etc.)

Cars on campus?

Campus parking

Financial Aid

Required forms (FAFSA,

    PROFILE, etc.)

Available scholarships

Work-study opportunities

% receiving aid

Need-blind admissions?

Community work opportunities

Special Programs

Study abroad programs

Summer internships

Transfer semesters

Orientation

Learning disabled support

Handicapped facilities

ROTC

Student athlete support

Mentoring/tutoring

Social Environment

Student center

Weekends

Nightlife

Greek life

Campus drug/alcohol policy

Athletics

School spirit/traditions

Clubs/organizations/activities

Religious affiliations

Community service opportunities

Academics

Core curriculum

Distribution requirements

Electives

Calendar (semesters, trimesters,

    quarters)

Time line (declaration of major;

    max./min. of units to

    graduate; time off, etc.)

Majors

Minors

Quality of education (rank of

    school programs; awards;

    renowned professors; size of

    classes; etc.)

Faculty accessibility

    (student/teacher ratio; role of

    graduate student instructors;

    office hours, etc.)

Personal Opinions

Love/like/hate?

Apply?

Safety/target/reach?

Notes

SUMMARY

Once you've adequately researched a number of colleges and narrowed down your list of potential candidates to two or three safeties, four or five targets, and two or three reaches, it is time to zero in on the schools you have chosen and gain an in-depth understanding of their offerings. The first step in this direction involves what I call "imagining you're there." For each school on your list, you should picture yourself during your first year in the classroom, on campus, and in the surrounding community (i.e., waking up in your dorm room, eating at the dining commons, going to your classes, participating in your activities, and doing some sort of community service). In order to do so, you must research the course offerings of the school in question, look up professors' works, and contact campus clubs and organizations to ask them about their programs. Not only will this make you an expert on a number of colleges, it will also come in very handy if you ever have to answer the "Why this school?" question on an application or in an interview. Most important, however, this preparation makes you appear like a legacy applicant. After you have completed this exercise, you are ready to start visiting the schools on your list. Keep a detailed account of everything you see and hear on your college tour and in your information session.

Bear some of the following insider tips in mind and you will come away with a clear opinion as to the relative strengths and weaknesses of each institution.

INSIDER TIPS

✓ Make yourself known. During your campus tour, visit the admissions office, introduce yourself to an admissions officer, and fill out a card. They will record your early interest in the school. Once you have made contact, keep in touch approximately once a month.

✓ Get in there. If school is in session, audit a class. There is no better way to sample the academic fare.

✓ Ask questions. During your visit, try to talk to a professor in your area of interest, a coach in your chosen sport, or other students. Ask them anything and everything you want to know about the school.

✓ Check out the digs. Make sure to visit a freshman dorm during your tour. Check out things like the bathroom situation, closet space, windows, Internet connections. You'll be living there for four years.

✓ Break away. If you are on a tour with your parents, break away for a while. Walk around. Take pictures. Soak it all in. Soon you could be living here and you want to make sure it's right for you.

6

SELLING
YOURSELF

MYTHS AND TRUTHS

MYTH:　Selling yourself means putting a positive spin on everything.

TRUTH:　Weaknesses are great learning experiences and failures can make great essay topics, so be sure to consider any and all meaningful experiences you have had in your life.

MYTH:　You have to be a leader in everything you do in order to appear desirable in the eyes of an admissions committee.

TRUTH:　If schools admitted only leaders, who would be left to follow? Colleges are looking for all types of students, and just because we tend to lionize leaders in our culture does not mean that everyone is supposed to display that one, very particular character trait.

MYTH:　Doing the minimum amount of community service required by your high school is good enough for most colleges.

TRUTH:　You should be doing far more than the minimum number of community service hours—but you should also be doing something you love, and doing it over a long period of time.

MYTH:　Get involved in everything—colleges are looking for a brag sheet chock full of activities.

TRUTH:　Overall, it is better to be involved in three or four activities wholeheartedly, than nine or ten superficially, because colleges look for consistency and commitment when it comes to your activities.

MYTH:　If there's one thing colleges hate, it's bragging.

TRUTH:　Don't be shy. Brag—that's why they call it a brag sheet. Be proud of who you are and all that you have achieved. Colleges are never going to learn about you unless you tell them.

SELLING YOURSELF

Congratulations! You are now ready to begin the official application process. I know it seemed like a long, hard road at times. But with all the research and preparation you've already done, the actual applications will come easy. You already know what each and every school has to offer—now it's simply time to explore the other half of the college admissions equation: you.

The truth is, colleges are not admitting facts and figures. They want living, breathing human beings with likes and dislikes, passions and aversions.

Accordingly, they want to know what makes you tick. So before you begin to tackle your applications, you will want to ask yourself: Who am I? What do I love to do? How do my friends and family describe me when I'm not around? What have been my proudest moments? My most disappointing failures? My most intense learning experiences? How will I get all these admirable characteristics and experiences across to the colleges of my choice?

These are the questions you should be asking yourself as you begin to address the personal elements of the college application. Through the brag sheet, the personal essay, your letters of recommendation, and the interview, you have a chance to come alive in the mind of the admissions reader, to stand out as a unique individual with drive and determination whose love of learning and commitment to your community make you a star applicant. In other words, it's time to start exploring yourself, to start assessing your own strengths and weaknesses, goals and aspirations, so that you can give a compelling and accurate view of who you are on your college applications.

To facilitate this, I have developed a number of exercises that will give you a leg up on the competition by helping you come closer to a vision of who you are both as a person and as a candidate for college. As you navigate this section, be honest with yourself. No school is looking for one particular type of student, so don't try to mold yourself into something you're not. Examine yourself thoroughly and let your actions and aspirations speak for themselves. If you can communicate both the global and the personal significance of what you have done, then your top colleges will come running.

Don't be daunted. This can be a trying, soul-searching experience. Take your time. Think about everything you've ever done that has brought you either pleasure or pain. Don't be afraid of a little self-analysis. And don't compare yourself to other students—everyone has their own unique qualities that make them attractive in the eyes of an admissions committee. Everything else aside, getting to know yourself and what you want from life is the secret to writing an outstanding application and getting into the college of your choice.

WHO ARE YOU?

Assessing your strengths and weaknesses and differentiating yourself from the competition is a crucial part of selling yourself to a school. Careful forethought and preparation are half the battle. Honesty in self-assessment is the other. Don't be afraid of the negative. As we all know, moments of failure are often more rewarding as learning experiences than moments of success. The Personal Strengths Questionnaire will help you pinpoint your strengths and skills as well as prepare you to write your brag sheet and sell yourself to the college of your choice. Once you have filled in the questionnaire, you should discuss your answers with your high school college counselor, your parents, and your friends, as they will often mention things you have overlooked or not considered. You may find that the process of answering these questions will suggest potential essay subjects as well.

Completing this general self-assessment questionnaire will assist you in deciding what you can offer a college. It will be of use in preparing you for a range of standard interview and essay questions. I thank Linda Zimring for her inspiration with this questionnaire.

PERSONAL STRENGTHS QUESTIONNAIRE

Overall strengths and preferences: Of all the things you do in your life, both in and out of school, which three do you feel you do the best?

1. _____

2. _____

3. _____

List three experiences that have had the greatest impact on your life. Briefly describe them.

1. _____

_____

_____

2. _____

_____

_____

3. _____

_____

_____

Of all the things you do in your life, both in and out of school, which three do you enjoy the most? (Please include relevant work experience.)

1. _____

2. _____

3. _____

Which of your academic strengths have been most helpful to you?

1. _____

2. _____

3. _____

Describe one academic weakness and how you overcame it.

_____

_____

_____

List three social strengths that have helped you get along with other people and develop good relationships. Include one area where you feel you could improve.

1. _____

2. _____

3. _____

4. _____

List the strengths that have been most helpful to you while playing sports. Include one area you feel is your weakness and how you might remedy it.

1. _____

2. _____

3. _____

4. _____

How would your best friend, boy/girlfriend, sibling, or parent describe you?

1. _____

2. _____

3. _____

4. _____

List five adjectives that best describe the strengths and weaknesses in your character.

_____

In what specific ways do you hope to contribute to your college's activities and campus life?

_____

_____

_____

_____

Describe your typical day.

_____

_____

_____

Describe your typical weekend.

_____

_____

_____

Describe a challenge, obstacle, failure, or problem and how you solved or overcame it.

_____

_____

_____

In your opinion, what are the most important things in life?

_____

_____

_____

What do you feel this form has not given you an opportunity to express?

Please be sure to include anything that comes to mind, as your unique

qualities will help to distinguish you from all other candidates.

_____

_____

_____

_____

THE BRAG SHEET

Everything you do, especially outside the classroom, tells the admissions committee what kind of person you are. From the quality and duration of your participation in certain activities, your reader will gain a more in-depth understanding of your personality and character. Now that you have spent some time exploring who you are, it is time to organize the supporting evidence into what is commonly known as the brag sheet. It is essentially a résumé of all that you have done outside the classroom from the beginning of the ninth grade on. You will attach your brag sheet as a separate document to your college applications, but be sure to read the instructions carefully on each application first. You will usually be asked to fill out an "activities" grid, which sometimes does not provide enough space for detailed descriptions. After filling in the grid, you may add at the bottom: "Please see attached brag sheet." Do not worry if the admissions officer is getting some of the information twice. Most likely, he or she will go directly to the attachment and read about you in full.

The brag sheet should not exceed three pages, and each page should have your name, the name of your high school, and your Social Security number in the top right- or left-hand corner.

The brag sheet format I have my students follow contains six major sections:

1. Extracurricular activities

2. Honors and awards

3. Community service

4. Summer experiences

5. Employment and internships

6. Hobbies and interests

Use the following charts to keep track of everything you have done outside the classroom since the ninth grade. You will use the information you provide to create your brag sheet. If you keep detailed records of everything you do outside the classroom, you will have no problem producing a great brag sheet that will effectively sell you to your top college choices. As you will see, Brown University requires a slightly different format. Either way, it is always a good idea to read each application carefully for specific instructions pertaining to attached materials.

Extracurricular Activities

Use the following worksheets to keep a record of what you have been doing outside the classroom to ensure that you do not miss any opportunities to highlight activities that will raise your admissions profile.

The truth about college admissions today is that selective universities are not looking for well-rounded students, but for well-rounded student bodies. In other words, you should not get involved with ten school clubs just to appear to be a Renaissance student. Besides, a one-hour per week activity is usually considered insignificant. Instead, get involved in a few activities that truly interest you, activities you will want to spend at least two hours a week on. Also, do not jump around from club to club year after year just to have a long list of clubs for your brag sheet. If you have been playing soccer since ninth grade, do not drop it in twelfth or suddenly take up a new sport. You do not want to appear noncommittal or fickle when it comes to your activities.

Overall, it is better to be involved in three or four activities wholeheartedly than with nine or ten superficially, because colleges look for consistency and commitment.

Please list your activities in order of their importance to you.

Activity (Student government, newspaper, music, art, drama etc.)	School years	Hours-per-week/weeks-per-year	Positions/honors (captain, editor, etc.)

Organizations and clubs	School years	Hours-per-week/weeks-per-year	Positions/honors

Teams/athletics	School years	Hours-per-week/weeks-per-year	Positions/honors

Awards and Honors

You should keep track of all awards and honors you have won, collecting the individual documents in a file. If you have been written up in the school or community newspaper, keep copies of those articles as well. Awards and honors can include: school, regional, or national prizes in any subject; most improved player awards; sports competitions; national sports rankings; All-Star teams or Dean's List nominations; National Merit Scholar, Finalist, or Semi-Finalist; Westinghouse/Intel finalist, among others.

Unfortunately, it is often difficult for students in the humanities to find national prize competitions for expository and creative writing on par with the competitions available to math and science students. For those of you in the humanities, Princeton University holds both poetry and one-act play writing competitions for eleventh graders, as well as the Humanities Symposium for high school seniors. The symposium, organized yearly around a specific theme, draws sixty-five seniors from around the country (chosen by their high school college counselors) for a series of lectures, films, seminars with Princeton professors, and sessions with Princeton undergraduates. It is an excellent accomplishment to include on your brag sheet if you are a student of languages, literature, philosophy, religion, history, or the creative or performing arts, and it offers an invaluable sampling of college-level academic life in the humanities. Contact your high school college counselor or the Princeton University Office of Admissions for more information.

In addition, the *Concord Review*, edited by Will Fitzhugh, provides a forum for history students to submit their work for both competition and evaluation. Now in its forty-seventh issue, with more than five hundred high school history papers and College Board AP history essays to its name, the *Concord Review* is an excellent opportunity for history students from around the country to submit their four- to six-thousand-word essays for publication. Each work chosen for publication is automatically submitted to the Ralph Waldo Emerson Prize competition, which awards four prizes of $3,000 each year. Subscribers around the world are given a chance to read the published essays and use them as examples of exceptional writing in their high school history classes. In addition, many students choose to include their published essays along with their college applications. There is a marginal fee for each submission.

The *Concord Review* website also hosts the National Writing Board, a group of high school history teachers who evaluate essays against an independent academic expository writing standard. Twice a year, in November and June, the board rates submissions and sends students a report, which they can choose to include in their applications to their colleges. There is also a fee for this service. Whether or not you are chosen for publication or receive a favorable report from the board, accessing the *Concord Review* website provides a great learning experience for high school history students, as it contains fifty-one downloadable examples of the best high school writing in the country, which you can use as inspiration for your own work. But do not be tempted to submit work that is not your own or to copy portions of the published essays. The *Concord Review* requires you to sign a letter verifying authorship of your essay, signed by your teacher, your principal, and a notary public. Infringement of this letter will result in disciplinary action from your high school. Also keep in mind that, thanks to the Internet, high school teachers have access to websites such as *www.plagiarism.com* and *www.turnitin.com*, which search essay databases for essays they feel may have been plagiarized. For more information on the *Concord Review*, visit them at *www.tcr.org* or call (800) 331-5007.

Finally, there are also the Scholastic Art and Writing Awards administered by the Alliance for Young Artists and Writers, a nonprofit organization dedicated to recognizing excellence among secondary school educators and students. Since 1923, the Scholastic Awards have been a great venue for young artists and writers in grades seven through twelve to receive recognition and awards for their creative achievements. Each year more than 250,000 students submit their art and writing samples for over $1 million in awards in sixteen art and eight writing categories ranging from architecture, ceramics, computer graphics, drama, drawing, humor, jewelry, and journalism to painting, poetry, photography, sculpture, short story, and video/film. A full fifty thousand of these submissions receive regional awards and 1,100 are selected for national awards by panels of professional artists and writers, many of them top names in their field. The award-winning works of art are honored at an awards ceremony and exhibition at the Corcoran Gallery of Art in Washington, D.C., while the writing award-winners are invited to attend a reading/reception, also in Washington, D.C. For more information on these excellent opportunities to bolster the awards section of your brag sheet, encounter the work of your fellow young artists, and travel to our nation's capital, call (212) 343-6892 or visit *www.scholastic.com/artandwritingawards/index.htm.*

On the following chart, list your honors and awards beginning with the most recent.

Academic and athletic honors and awards	School years	Honors/title

Community Service

If your school does not require community service, I suggest you start getting involved in your community by contributing to activities such as working with the homeless or a local environmental organization. If there are areas of special concern that are not being addressed in your community, consider starting your own organization or teaming up with local groups to achieve what you would like to see done.

Although you will not need proof or documentation of your efforts in this area, it is not unheard of for admissions officers to check up on your activities, just as an employer might check up on an employee's résumé. It is essential, therefore, that you not exaggerate or lie about what you have done.

List your community service activities beginning with the most recent.

Organizations and volunteer work	School years	Hours-per-week/weeks-per-year	Positions/responsibilities

Summer Experiences

You may not like hearing it, but the truth is, your summers are just as important as your school years to an admissions committee, so hopefully you are not spending them lounging on the beach working on your tan. In order to remain competitive in the college admissions process, you should be productive with your summers. Get involved in a summer travel program, attend summer school at a college that interests you, participate in an Outward Bound program, attend a summer camp or sports camp, do independent research, or start a community service project in your months away from school. If you cannot find something to do for the summer, go to your high school college counselor—he or she should have many brochures on appropriate summer programs.

List four summers starting with the summer before twelfth grade and ending with the summer before ninth grade. If you work for money during the summer, you should list that under "Employment/ internships" or combine the two sections into "Summer experiences and employment."

Summer Experiences	Summer (year)	Hours-per-week/number of weeks	Description/ responsibilities

Employment and Internships

One of the best things you can do as a student is work. It is not necessarily important to make a lot of money—it's the experience that counts. Holding down a job, learning a business or skill, striking out on your own in some entrepreneurial pursuit—all of these are experiences that display commitment, maturity, and responsibility. Jobs can be anything from research assistant, lab assistant, camp counselor, newspaper or pizza deliveryperson to waitperson, baby-sitter, dog walker, law firm or hospital intern. You can even start your own business by being a website designer or party DJ. Working outside of school shows a type of work ethic different from study habits that admissions boards like to see, especially if you can hold down a job for an extended period of time. It will speak well of you as a young adult capable of college living, and you will not appear lazy or spoiled. It can also give you an edge over candidates who may display more academic, rather than real-world knowledge.

List your employment experience beginning with the most recent. If you have earnings, you should note how much you earned and what you did with that money (savings, car insurance, new computer, college tuition).

Employment/ internship	School years or summer	Hours-per- week/weeks- per-year or weeks-per-summer	Positions/ responsibilities

Hobbies and Interests

It can also be helpful to list hobbies and interests that are not organized activities per se. For example, if you spend many hours a week reading novels, the admissions officer will only learn this about you if you mention it. In fact, reading is probably one of the best hobbies you can have, as it helps you become a better writer and prepares you for the often grueling reading lists in college-level courses. Another typical interest is computers. If you spend two to three hours a day surfing the net, researching, reading, chatting, or programming, write it down in this section.

A word of warning, however: you should exercise restraint when it comes to the amount of detail and breadth you provide. Do not include something you do for only a few hours a year like bird-watching with your grandfather. If you play with your dog every day, that may not be the most salient detail to include. However, if you develop your passion for dogs into a private dog-walking service that earns you extra spending money over the summer, this is something that shows initiative, commitment, and entrepreneurial spirit, and you will definitely want to include it in your brag sheet.

Think of everything you do in your free time from yoga to yodeling and list these in order of their importance to you.

Hobbies and interests	School years	Hours-per-week/weeks-per-year	Description

SAMPLE BRAG SHEETS

Have a close look at the following sample brag sheets, which you can use as guidelines to create your own.* I have included two from the first student, Ronald Siegal. One is a general brag sheet, which he sent to most schools. The second he reformatted specifically for Brown University. Brown University asks for your activities in a particular way that is unlike any other college, so I have included it here.

Notice the way in which all three contain a wealth of detail. When I was attending an information session at Yale University this year, the admissions officer gave specific advice to potential applicants: "Don't be shy! Brag! Give us as much information as possible, because you are up against thousands of other applicants and if you really want us to get to know who you are, then tell tell tell!"

You should list extracurricular activities and hobbies in order of their importance to you. You should list everything else in reverse chronological order, beginning with the most recent. You should also indicate how much time (hours per week and weeks per year) you spend on each activity. Remember, a school year is usually forty weeks long, a summer is usually twelve weeks long, and a sports season is usually fifteen weeks long. If the activity calls for a description or a location, put it underneath the activity. Finally, do not forget to list your positions, titles, or responsibilities for each activity.

---

* Please note that all students' and high schools' names as well as Social Security numbers have been changed to protect the anonymity of my clients.

Ronald Siegal
123-45-6789
Swanee High School

Extracurricular Activities	School Years	Hrs.-Per-Wk./ Wks.-Per-Yr.	Positions/Honors
National Art Honor Society— responsible for beautifying the high school mainly by painting murals	10, 11, 12[1]	6/40	President, Art Historian/ Parliamentarian (12), Treasurer (11), Secretary (10)
Newman Art School (Cleveland, Ohio)	9, 10, 11, 12	4/40	Student-Studio Art, Elements of Drawing and Painting
Spanish Club	9, 10, 11, 12	4/40	Activities Coordinator/VP (11), Secretary (10), Member (9)
The Swan School Newspaper	9, 10, 11, 12	7/35	Editor (11, 12), Business Manager (11,12), Reporter (9,10)
Peer Counseling	10, 11, 12[2]	3/40	Chosen to Counsel (11, 12) Member (10, 11, 12)
Patrons of Music and the Arts	11, 12	3/20	Student Liaison (11, 12)
National High School Honor Society	11, 12[3]	3/40	Member
Cleveland Teen Center	10, 11, 12	3/40	Assistant to Executive Treasurer (11, 12), Hiring Interviewer (10)
Group Skills	10, 11[4]	3/40	Treasurer
Class Government	9, 10, 11, 12	2/20	Cabinet Member
Student Activities Committee	9, 10, 11, 12	2/35	Club/Society Rep. (10, 11, 12), Voting Member (9, 10, 11, 12)

Honors and Awards Presented By:	School Years	Honors/Description
State of Ohio, Office of the Attorney General	11	Triple "C" Award in Recognition of Outstanding Character, Courage, and Commitment to the Swanee High School and Cleveland Communities

[1] Unavailable to ninth graders.
[2] Also unavailable to ninth graders.
[3] Unavailable to ninth and tenth graders.
[4] Only available to tenth and eleventh graders.

Ronald Siegal
123-45-6789
Swanee High School

Swanee High School	10, 11, 12	Major Volunteer Service Award— Shapiro Learning Center
Swanee High School	11, 12	Major Volunteer Service Award— *March of Dimes Foundation*
Swanee High School Student Government	11	Special Recognition for the Art Honors Society and the beautifi- cation of Swanee High School
Patrons of Music and the Arts	11	Only student art chosen to be displayed in MADE (a World Music, Dance and Community Art Show[5])
Talisman	11, 12[6]	National High School Honor Society
Summer Discovery at Michigan	11	John Davidson Leadership Award— only given to four students out of 200 at Summer Discovery
Swanee High School Art	9	Art chosen for display in *The Free Space Gallery*, a student art show
Cleveland Community Window Painting Contest	9, 10	Best overall for my age group (9, 10)

Community Service	School Years	Hrs.-Per-Wk./ Wks.-Per-Yr.	Positions/Responsibilities
The Shapiro Learning Center—provides support for homeless children in Cleveland	10, 11, 12	3/40	Volunteer Art Instructor/Academic Tutor
March of Dimes Foundation	11, 12[7]	4/25	YOUNG HEARTS—Youth Leadership Council in Cleveland: President (12), Member (11), Local Health Fair Representative (11, 12)
March of Dimes Walk America	11, 12	5/1	Central Cleveland Youth Coordinator (11, 12)
MADE: Music, Art & Dance Ensemble—a Community Vis- ual and Performing Arts Show	11	6/1	Volunteer

[5] Slide numbers 1 and 2 in Art Portfolio.
[6] Unavailable to ninth and tenth graders.
[7] Unavailable to ninth and tenth graders.

Ronald Siegal
123-45-6789
Swanee High School

Summer Experiences	Summer	Hrs.-Per-Wk./ Wks.-Per-Yr.	Positions/Responsibilities
Cleveland Art Museum	2000	40/6	Paid Summer Internship in Education Department ($200 per week)[8]
Bauer Fine Art Gallery (Cleveland, Ohio)	2000	5/8	Director's Assistant and Inventory Clerk
The Art Workshop at Cleveland Comm. College	2000	10/8	Student—Projects in Painting and Advanced Drawing
Newman Art School	2000	4/8	Student—Painting and Drawing
ASA Spanish Language and Culture School—Madrid, Spain	1999	30/4	Community Volunteer and Student—Advanced Spanish Language and European Art History
Summer Discovery at Michigan	1999	20/3	Student—Tennis and Photography
Swanee High School Math Acceleration Program	1998	15/6	Student—Course II
Newman Art School	1998	20/6	Student—Studio Art, Art History

Employment	School Years	Hrs.-Per-Wk./ Wks.-Per-Yr.	Positions/Description
Bauer Fine Art Gallery	12	8/30	Director's Assistant and Inventory Clerk
Private Spanish Tutor	11, 12	2/35	Earned $60/month (savings)
Babysitting	9, 10, 11, 12	4/50	Earned $80/month (savings)

Hobbies and Interests	School Years	Hrs.-Per-Wk./ Wks.-Per-Yr.	Positions/Responsibilities
Drawing and Painting	9, 10, 11, 12	4/50	
Photography	10, 11, 12	2/20	Develop own black and white photos
Cooking	9, 10, 11, 12	4/40	Traditional Spanish dishes
Running	9, 10, 11, 12	2/40	2–3 miles outdoors
Tennis	9, 10, 11, 12	3/16	

[8] Saved earnings to pay for art supplies.

RONALD SIEGAL*
SWANEE HIGH SCHOOL
123-45-6789

- **National Art Honor Society** President/Art Historian (12), Treasurer (11), Secretary (10), 6 hrs/wk, 40 wks/yr. The club is responsible for beautifying Swanee High School by painting murals and by spreading art awareness. I organized our Dalí Day.

- **Newman Art School** (Cleveland, OH) Student (9, 10, 11, 12): Studio Art, Elements of Drawing and Painting, 4 hrs/wk, 40 wks/yr and summers 1998 and 2000. I love painting and drawing because of the freedom it gives me to express myself.

- **Outstanding Student Award** In recognition of Outstanding Character, Leadership, and Service to Swanee High School and the Cleveland Community presented by the State of Ohio, Office of the Attorney General, (11).

- **The Shapiro Learning Center** Volunteer Art Instructor/Academic Tutor (10, 11, 12), 3 hrs/wk, 40 wks/yr. The center provides support for battered women and children in Cleveland.

- **The Cleveland Art Museum** Summer 2000. Paid summer intern in the Education Department, $200 per week, 8 hrs/day, 6 wks. My experience working at the CAM was educational and inspiring.

- **Spanish Club** President (12), Vice President/Activities Coordinator (11), Secretary (10), Member (9), 4 hrs/wk, 40 wks/yr. As the Activities Coordinator, I organized many events such as scheduling an art history professor to come speak about Mexican art and arranging a Mexican dinner.

- **ASA Spanish Language and Culture School** (Madrid, Spain) Summer 1999, Student and Volunteer, 4 weeks. I was placed into the Advanced Spanish Language class, and I took European Art History. On my own, I traveled to Toledo and other small towns through Galicia.

- *MADE: Music, Art, and Dance Ensemble* A community visual and performing art show that Patrons of Music and the Arts sponsored (11). Only student art chosen to be displayed. (Slide numbers 1, 2 in portfolio.)

- **Peer Counseling** Chosen to Counsel (11, 12), Member (10, 11, 12), 3 hrs/wk, 40 wks/yr.

- *The Swan,* **school newspaper** Business Manager (11, 12), Editor (11, 12), Reporter (9, 10), 7 hrs/wk, 35 wks/yr.

- **Swanee High School Student Government Special Recognition Award** For my service to the Art Honor Society and the beautification of Swanee High School (11).

---

* This form of the brag sheet for Brown University needs to appear on one page, 8½ × 11, with a space in the upper right corner for a photo.

- **The Art Workshop at Cleveland Community College** (Cleveland, OH) Summer 2000, Student-Projects in Painting, Advanced Drawing, 7 hrs/wk, 5 wks.

- **Patrons of Music and the Arts** Student Liaison (11, 12), 3 hrs/wk, 20 wks/yr.

- *March of Dimes, Birth Defects Foundation*-**YOUNG HEARTS-Youth Leadership Council in Cleveland** President (12), Member (11), Local Health Fair Representative (11, 12), *March of Dimes Walk America* volunteer (11, 12), 4 hrs/wk, 25 wks/yr.

- **National High School Honor Society** Member (11, 12), 3 hrs/wk, 40 wks/yr.

- **Major Volunteer Service Award** The Shapiro Learning Center and March of Dimes (10, 11, 12).

- **Summer Discovery at Michigan** Summer 1999, Student—Tennis and Photography, 3 wks.

- **John Davidson Leadership Award** Only given to four students out of two hundred at Summer Discovery.

- **Group Skills** Leader (11), Member (10), 3 hrs/wk, 20 wks/yr. I helped sophomores become more adjusted to high school.

- **Cleveland Teen Center** Assistant to Executive Treasurer (11, 12), Hiring Interviewer (10) 3 hrs/wk, 40 wks/yr.

- *The Open Space Gallery* A student art show. Art chosen to be displayed in (9). (Slide number 3 in art portfolio.)

- **Class Government** Cabinet Member (9, 10, 11, 12), 2 hrs/wk, 20 wks/yr.

- **Swanee Village Window Painting Contest** Best overall for my age group (9, 10).

- **Swanee High School Math Acceleration Program** Summer 1998, 15 hrs/wk, 6 wks.

- **Exploration at Middlebury College** Summer 1997. Studio Art, Art History, Economics, Comparative Gov't. 20 hrs/wk, 6 wks.

- **Drawing and Painting** (9, 10, 11, 12), 4 hrs/wk, 50 wks/yr. At home, I continue my latest artwork.

- **Photography** (10, 11, 12), 2 hrs/wk, 20 wks/yr. I frequently develop my own photos at school facilities.

- **Student Activities Committee** Club/Society Representative (10, 11, 12), Voting Member (9, 10, 11, 12), 2 hrs/wk, 35 wks/yr.

- **Cooking** (9, 10, 11, 12), 4 hrs/wk, 40 wks/yr. I like cooking Spanish food. My family loves my paellas.

- **Running** (9, 10, 11, 12), 2 hrs/wk, 40 wks/yr. I usually run two or three miles outdoors.

- **Tennis** (9, 10, 11, 12), 3 hrs/wk, 16 wks/yr. Move over, Sampras. I wish.

William Thomas
123-04-5555
Holland Hall High School

Extracurricular Activities	School Years	Hrs.-Per-Wk./ Wks.-Per-Yr.	Positions/Responsibilities
Aikido— Martial arts training in meditation, armed and unarmed combat	9, 10, 11, 12	7/45	Go-kyu (5th Level white belt)[1]
The Hallway— School Magazine	10, 11, 12	7/40	Editor-in-Chief (12) News Editor (11) Student Writer (10)
Honor Council— Body of students and teachers; deal with students who violate the code of conduct at Holland Hall	10, 11, 12	5/40	Elected official (12, 11, 10)
Holland Hall Speech and Debate Team— Debate Team	10, 11, 12[2]	10/40	Chapter President (12) Chapter Vice President (11) State Qualifier (12, 11) Regional Qualifier (12–10) District Qualifier (12–10)
Do Lord!— Church Youth Group; organizes charity events around Tulsa[3]	9, 10, 11, 12	4/45	Youth Council Representative (12–9)
Do Lord Drama Club— Division of Youth Group; Perform musicals in the community to raise money for various charities[3]	9, 10, 11, 12	4/45	Master of Ceremonies (12, 11, 10, 9)

[1] In Aikido, there are six levels of white belt before achieving black belt.
[2] Holland Hall's debate program was recreated my sophomore year.
[3] Charities include mission trip to Nuevo Progreso, Mexico; sister schools to Boston Ave. Church, etc.

William Thomas
123-04-5555
Holland Hall High School

Student Ambassadors of Holland Hall	9, 10, 11, 12	3/40	Student Ambassador; Welcome new and prospective students; escort prospective students around campus; attend annual promotions of Holland Hall
Table Tennis Federation— Hold tournaments to raise money for charity[4]	11, 12	3/40	Co-Founder; Emperor aka President (12, 11)
Dutch for Christ— Holland Hall's Christian meeting group	10, 11, 12	3/40	DFC Officer (12, 11) Members share breakfast weekly; various acts of community service[4]
Spanish II Honors	12	10/40	Teacher's Assistant
Dutch Soccer Team	9, 10, 11, 12	15/15	Varsity Player (12, 11) 3rd Place in Conference (10, 11) Junior Varsity (10, 9)

Awards and Honors	School Years	Awards/Positions
National Merit Society	12	Semi-finalist
Cum Laude Society— Top 10% of junior and senior class is initiated	11, 12[5]	Member
Headmaster's List— Reserved for highest level of academic merit	9, 10, 11, 12	Accepted Scholar
Honor Roll	9, 10, 11, 12	High Honor Roll Inductee
National Spanish Honor Society	11, 12[5]	Inducted member
Cystic Fibrosis Foundation	11, 12	Received letter of thanks from CFF President
National Spanish Exam	9, 10, 11, 12	1st in State, 1st at HH (11) 7th in State, 2nd at HH (10) 4th in State, 3rd at HH (9)

[4] Charities include: Cystic Fibrosis Foundation; Daycenter for the Homeless.
[5] These awards are only available to juniors and seniors.

William Thomas
123-04-5555
Holland Hall High School

National Forensics League	10, 11, 12		Degree of Excellence (11)
			Degree of Honor (10)
			1st Place CX Team at following tournaments:
			Cascia Hall (11)
			Sapulpa (11)
			Broken Arrow (11)
			UCO (10)
			1st Place Speaker at following tournaments:
			Cascia Hall (11)
			Sapulpa (11)

Community Service	School Years	Hrs.-Per-Wk./ Wks.-Per-Yr.	Positions/Responsibilities
Great Strides— Annual 5K walk; Raises money for a cure for Cystic Fibrosis	9, 10, 11, 12	15/20	Council Member; Second largest fund-raiser in Oklahoma ($22,000.00)
Thirty-Hour Famine— Led by Dutch for Christ: Raise money for starving families while fasting	11, 12	30/6	Activity Leader; Fund Raiser
Do Lord Mission Trip— Build cinder block houses in Mexico	9, 10, 12	45/3	Youth Leader (12); Book runner
Book and Art Fair— Sale of donated material by Holland Hall; profits go to students on scholarship	9, 10, 11, 12	20/4	Organized the fair; donated books, magazines, etc.

Summer Experiences	Summer	Hrs.-Per-Wk./ Wks.-Per-Yr.	Description
Spartan Debate Camp (East Lansing, MI)	2001	40/3	Practiced Policy Debate
Academic Studies Abroad (Barbate, Spain)	2000	18/5	Lived with a host family; Attended classes through ASA; toured Andalucia
Holland Hall Science Trip (Australia and New Zealand)	1999	45/3	Studied natural resources of both countries

William Thomas
123-04-5555
Holland Hall High School

Jackson Hole, Wyoming	1999–2001	40/2	Visited grandparents
Boston, Massachusetts	2000	40/3	See employment

Summer Employment	Summer	Hrs.-Per-Wk./ Wks.-Per-Yr.	Positions/ Responsibilities
Readers Are Leaders[6]— Reading-writing course designed for 4–7-year-olds; Based on phonic sounds	1999–2001	30/7	Teacher (12) Teacher's Assistant (9–11)
Attention to Detail[6]— I advertise locally as a car detailer	1999–2001	5/12	Owner; I've made approximately $2000.00
Boston Coosin's Camp[6] (Boston, Massachusetts)	2000		Camp Counselor; Guided children around Boston; taught them history of the city

Hobbies and Interests	School Years	Hrs.-Per-Wk./ Wks.-Per-Yr.	Positions/ Responsibilities
Japanese Culture	9, 10, 11, 12	15/50	In addition to Aikido, I am dedicated to learning Japanese culture and history. I collect many objects, specifically chopsticks and samurai swords.
Mind Puzzles	9, 10, 11, 12	5/50	Mensa-level problems (Rubix Cube, etc.)
Reading	9, 10, 11, 12	4/52	Novels; authors include: J. D. Salinger, Paul Auster, and Aldous Huxley.

[6] Money from these jobs went to the purchase of my first, used car.

Benjamin Andrew Press
123-00-6789
Hackley School

Extracurricular Activities & Community Service	School Years	Hrs.-Per-Wk./ Wks.-Per-Yr.	Positions/ Description
The Dial— Hackley School Newspaper	9, 10, 11, 12	10/45	Editor-in-Chief (11,12) Dialogue Editor (9, 10, 11)
Krav-Maga— Israeli Military Hand-to-Hand Combat; This system is considered to be the most effective form of self-defense that exists.	9, 10, 11, 12	3/52	Student; Brown Belt
Community Council— Student Government	11	3/40	Class President
Hackley Film Club— Film Club focuses on student-financed amateur digital film production. It holds the highest membership of all the school's clubs.	9, 10, 11, 12	2/52	Founder and President
Educational Leadership Institute— Teaching of Hebrew school and Hebrew language	10/11	2/40	Teacher; Form lesson plans, keep students engaged, and lead classes
Hebrew High School— Advanced Hebrew and Judaic studies	9, 10, 11	3/40	Student/Tutor; Graduate and Post-Graduate Diplomas
Hackley Political Science Club—Princeton and Harvard Model Congresses	11, 12	4/20	Co-President (12); Prepare the school delegation Attendee (11)
Westchester Model UN Club	11, 12	4/10	Co-President (12) Attendee (11)
HackSCOT— Hackley School Citizens of Tomorrow; Supports awareness, activism, and voter registration.	12	1/40	Founder and President
Hackley Mock Trial Club	12	1/40	Member

Benjamin Andrew Press
123-00-6789
Hackley School

Honors and Awards	School Years		
National Merit Scholar Semi-Finalist	12		
AP Scholar With Honor	12		
American Scholastic Press Association Second Place Newspaper	12		
Scholastic Writing Contest Gold Key—Short Short Story	11		
Scholastic Writing Contest Gold Key—Personal Essay	11		
Academic Honor Roll Each term and for entire year	9, 10		
National Latin Examination Medalist	9, 10		

Summer Experiences & Employment	Summer	Hrs.-Per-Wk./ Wks.-Per-Yr.	Position/ Description
Bloomberg L.P. Information Systems and Broadcasting—Bloomberg is an information company that provides real-time financial news via terminals, internet, radio, and television (New York, New York)	2001	40/9	Paid intern;[1] Researched and wrote financial news stories for television broadcast, obtained filming permits from city and assisted with live location shoots
Chetz V'Keshet— Israeli Army Training and Culture Immersion, including basic training by the Israeli army (Jerusalem, Israel)	2000	FT/5	Participant
Maxime's Restaurant— A local five-star French brasserie (Granite Springs, New York)	2000	10/5	Assistant Chef; Unpaid Intern

[1] Saved earnings—about $4000

Benjamin Andrew Press
123-00-6789
Hackley School

Brandeis Hebrew Language Institute— Intensive Hebrew Language Course, equivalent to one year of college Hebrew (Brandeis University, Woltham, Massachusetts)	1999	FT/5	Student; Earned an A for the course.
Family Vacation—Israel	1999	FT/3	
Summer Enrichment Camp Academic Study (Haverford College, Haverford, Pennsylvania)	1998	FT/5	Student

Hobbies and Interests	School Years	Hrs.-Per-Wk./ Wks.-Per-Yr.	Description
Film; Amateur Screenwriting, Acting and Directing	9, 10, 11, 12	2/52	Filming done both for Film Club (see above) and independently or with friends
History/Politics/Current Events	9, 10, 11, 12	4/52	Independent research on Israeli and Middle Eastern military history and political affairs
Reading	9, 10, 11, 12	4/52	*Time, Newsweek, Popular Science,* John Irving, Tom Clancy, Stephen King
Writing	9, 10, 11, 12	4/52	Films, Screenplays, Mini-Novels, Short Stories, Poetry, Essays, Articles
Skiing	9, 10, 11, 12	25/2	
Computers	9, 10, 11, 12	3/45	Proficient in use of complex programs, including graphic design, desktop publishing and film editing, software, hardware and installation. Acted as consultant; designed and assembled systems for numerous people
Travel	9, 10, 11, 12	FT/2	USA, Canada, Europe and Middle East

SUMMARY

When it comes to selling yourself to the colleges of your choice, it is important to remember that your application will be one of thousands read by each college admissions committee in any given year. As such, it is imperative that you find a way to personalize your application and make it stand out. The secret here is to spend as much time as possible exploring yourself both as a student and as a person, assessing your strengths and weaknesses, goals and aspirations. If you can give a compelling and accurate view of who you are, making the facts and figures of your application come alive in the mind of the admissions reader, then you already have a leg up on the competition. To do this, you will need to keep detailed records of everything you do outside the classroom, ideally starting from the summer before your freshman year in high school. But remember—no school is looking for one particular type of student. You should not try to mold yourself into something you are not or spread yourself too thin among activities that neither interest nor benefit you. Take your time thinking about what truly interests you and don't be afraid of a little self-analysis. The truth is, this is what colleges want to see in your application: *you*.

INSIDER TIPS

✓ Every detail counts. Supply as much information about your nonacademic life as possible. You essentially have to account for every hour you have spent outside of school from ninth to twelfth grade, other than doing homework, eating, sleeping, shopping, and hanging out.

✓ Exercise restraint. Do not, for example, include something you do for only a few hours a year like bungee-jumping during family vacations.

✓ Focus. Keep in mind that selective universities are not looking for well-rounded students, but for well-rounded student bodies.

✓ Do what you love. Get involved with a few activities that truly interest you. Do not do things you hate just because they "look good."

✓ Stick with it. Colleges specifically look for consistency and commitment. Do not jump around from club to club year after year just to create a long list of clubs for your brag sheet.

✓ Be yourself. Make your application come alive with all those details that are so you.

7

TAKING
THE
TESTS

MYTHS AND TRUTHS

MYTH: A straight-A student should have no trouble getting a 1600 on the SAT I.

TRUTH: Your classroom ability does not necessarily correlate to your standardized test–taking ability. It is helpful to prepare for the SAT I by taking practice tests eight to ten times prior to the actual test date.

MYTH: You should keep preparing for and keep taking the SAT I until you are happy with your score.

TRUTH: Studies have shown that a student's SAT I scores tend to plateau after the third time, so there is little reason to go beyond that. In addition, too many attempts at the SAT I will look desperate to an admissions board.

MYTH: A high score on the SAT I guarantees you a spot in one of the nation's top colleges.

TRUTH: There are no guarantees when it comes to college admissions; and a high SAT I score is NOT your ticket in. Your transcript is more important than your SAT I score. The truth is, your application is comprised of both your academic and personal records, and your SAT I score is just one piece of the whole pie.

MYTH: Even if a school does not require the SAT I, you should take it anyway, as a sign that you are committed to learning.

TRUTH: If a school doesn't require the SAT I, only send your scores if they are excellent and/or better than the grades on your transcript would predict.

MYTH: Take as many SAT II exams as possible—it's the quantity of your test results that counts.

TRUTH: Take the required SAT II exams and then only take any extra exams in those areas in which you excel. In addition, you should take the SAT IIs right after you've completed course work in that subject. You can repeat these tests using score choice, and choose your best score in these subjects to send to the colleges of your choice.

COLLEGE ENTRANCE EXAMS

You know the scene: the early-morning haze over your eyes; the perfectly sharpened number-2 pencils lined neatly on your desk; the industrial clock ticking away the seconds; those little bits of eraser gathering at your feet . . .

You guessed it. It's a standardized test. The names and formats may have changed over the years, but ever since your parents were schoolchildren, standardized tests have visited the lives of American students like annoying relatives you are forced to talk to at the family reunion. To this day, most four-year colleges require applicants to take one or more of a number of standardized tests for admission, and your results play an important role in the relative strength or weakness of your college application. It is a necessary evil, one that must be conquered if you are going to get into the college of your choice. But how?

The truth is *you must be prepared*. You must know which tests to take and when to take them. You must know how to interpret the scores and understand how they fit into the larger application picture. The information and tips contained in this chapter will guide you toward this knowledge, bringing you one step closer to the college of your dreams. As you read through the following sections, keep in mind that your test scores are never the only criteria considered for admission but are nonetheless a major factor in support of your academic record. There are five major tests you will encounter; and, unless otherwise stated, they are all administered by the College Board. The five most common tests are: the PSAT/NMSQT (Preliminary Scholastic Aptitude Test/National Merit Scholarship Qualifying Test), the SAT I, the SAT II–Subject Tests (formerly Achievement Tests), the ACT (American College Test), and the AP (Advanced Placement) exams.

PSAT/NMSQT
(Preliminary Scholastic Aptitude Test/National Merit Scholarship Qualifying Test)

This exam is administered once a year in October and is excellent practice before you take the SAT I. You may take it in ninth, tenth, and/or eleventh grade. The PSAT is essentially a shortened version of the SAT I but is not required by colleges. It tests verbal, math, and writing skills scored on a 20 to 80 point scale. Students receive a printout with their answers for each question as well as the correct answers and the difficulty level of each question. The students also receive their original test booklets so they may review their results accurately. Scores for students in eleventh grade are automatically entered into the National Merit Competition. Those eleventh graders scoring high enough (fifty thousand of 1.2 million entrants) will automatically become National

Merit Semi-finalists or National Merit Commended Scholars. Go to *www.nationalmerit.org* for more details.

SAT I (Formerly SAT or Scholastic Aptitude Test)

The SAT I is a predominantly multiple-choice test that attempts to predict a student's first year college grades. Most colleges and universities require either the SAT I or the ACT, although you should read each college's application materials carefully to determine its individual requirements. The SAT I is a three-hour examination that you can take more than once. It consists of a verbal and a math section, each scored on a scale from 200 to 800, 1600 being the highest possible composite score. Colleges usually take the highest individual verbal and math scores, although they always receive your entire College Board SAT I testing history. Calculators are currently allowed and it is recommended that students bring one with them; one will not be provided at the test site and sharing is not allowed. There are some open-ended math questions that require the student to produce an answer rather than choose from multiple answers. All rules and regulations are contained in the SAT I registration booklet available from your high school's college counseling office. The SAT I will dramatically change in 2005. The test will have three sections, including a new writing section, and will be scored out of a possible 2400 points. Please see *www.collegeboard.com* for further details.

SAT I Preparation

As you are probably aware, there are numerous classes designed to prepare you for the SAT I exam. Whether or not you are interested in increasing your score—which you should be—these classes can also help by demystifying the test-taking process, breaking it down into its component parts, and making you feel more comfortable with test-taking in general. Many courses have computer programs that analyze your correct and incorrect answers, categorizing and pinpointing your weaknesses. For example, the Princeton Review offers this sort of analysis with group classes, and companies like IvyWise, Advantage Testing, and InSpirica offer one-on-one tutorials. There are also books and computer programs that you can buy to practice on your own. I myself took the Princeton Review in its first year of existence on the West Coast and improved my score by more than two hundred points.

The truth is, the more you practice, the more comfortable you will be with the test itself, and the higher score you will achieve. Probably the best preparation in this sense is simply taking practice SAT tests; they can be found contained in books such as *10 Real SATs* published by the College Board. I usually have my students take one practice test per week for eight weeks prior to the real test date. They take a practice test at 8 A.M. on Saturday morning, strictly timing themselves, under conditions similar to those they will face at the actual testing site (that is, not in their pajamas lying on the sofa). Afterward, they are responsible for scoring themselves. Inevitably, the more familiar they become with the test, the better they become at taking it.

I recommend giving yourself three opportunities to take the real SAT I exam. I believe the best test dates are March and May of the junior year, and October of your senior year. March seems to be the best test date overall because more people take the SAT I on that day than on any other. Since your score and percentile ranking are determined in relation to all the other students taking the test on that day, it is to your advantage to take it when more students are testing. Usually only the most prepared students, the ones who have their acts together early and are thinking of applying early to one of the more selective colleges, take the January test, so that tends to be a more difficult test date. If your March scores are not what you are capable of (that is, if they do not match your practice test scores) or if you simply had a bad day (were sick, distracted, depressed, or stressed), you will still have other opportunities to take the test. However, you should *not* take the SAT I more than three times because it will look like desperation to an admissions officer and your score will probably not improve much—statistics show that scores tend to level out after the third time. Remember: most colleges will take the highest verbal and highest math score, even if they occurred on different test dates.

You should start preparing intensively in December or January of your junior year and continue until the May test. Remember: just because you are a straight-A student does not mean you will breeze through the SAT I with a 1600. Nor does getting a 1600 on your SAT I guarantee you admission to a selective college. I remember one naturally gifted student who got a 1590 the first and only time he took the SAT I. Everyone expected great things from him. Unfortunately, since everything came so easily to this student, he never fully applied himself. His grades fell far below what a SAT I 1590 would indicate—not because he couldn't do the work, but because he was lazy and complacent. Subsequently, his teacher recommendations were anything but stellar: they all indicated he had a serious attitude problem. Not only was this student "asked to leave" his elite boarding school in his junior year, he was also denied admission to all his top college choices. On the other hand, I had a student who was somewhere in the top 20 percent of his class and, because nothing came very easily to him, he developed a tremendous work ethic. Through painstaking SAT I preparation he was able to raise his test score by more than two hundred points to a 1350. In addition, his teachers universally praised his hard work and dedication. This student was admitted early to the University of

Pennsylvania. The truth is clear: hard work and dedication pay off when it comes to applying to—and getting into—the nation's top colleges.

SAT II–Subject Tests (Formerly Achievement Tests)

The SAT II Subject Tests are one-hour exams in specific subject areas that measure the student's knowledge of a particular field of study. The SAT II Subject Test scores range from 200 to 800 for each test. Check the requirements of the colleges you are considering before deciding which tests to take. Some schools require certain tests—usually writing, math, and another test of your choice—while for others, SAT IIs may be optional. In 2000, the University of California school system reworked its eligibility index, giving the SAT II twice as much weight as the SAT I. But beware. In today's competitive college admissions environment, students applying to the most selective schools often send in more than three SAT II scores. I have seen as many as ten on one application. If you plan to take this many SAT IIs, you must prepare ahead of time: not all tests are available on each testing date and you may only take up to three SAT II tests on any given day. For instance, SAT IIs are not offered in March. Also keep in mind that it is impossible to take both the SAT I and SAT II tests on the same day. As of the 2001 school year, the following SAT II tests were available:

English	
Literature	Writing

History	
U.S. History	World History

Languages:	
Chinese with Listening*	Japanese with Listening*
French	Korean with Listening*
French with Listening*	Latin
German	Spanish
German with Listening*	Spanish with Listening*
Modern Hebrew	English Language Proficiency
Italian	

* The "listening" portion of the language test requires students to decipher verbal samples of the target language.

Mathematics
Mathematics Level IC   Mathematics Level IIC

Science
Biology E/M   Chemistry Physics

The best time to take the SAT IIs is right after you have finished your course work in that subject, usually in June, but also in December or January for fall semester courses. I usually have my students reserve the June date of their tenth and eleventh grades for SAT IIs. It is also a great idea to start taking the SAT IIs as early as ninth or tenth grade. For instance, if you take biology in ninth or tenth grade and are getting an A or B in the course, you should take the SAT II in June of that year. In addition, you can take Math IC and Writing (as they do not correspond to specific courses) at any time.

The College Board has now abolished score choice. A student used to be able to take as many SAT IIs as he or she wanted to take and release only the three highest scores to the colleges of their choice. The College Board got rid of score choice because they saw too many students forgetting to release any scores at all, and they thought that some students were using the score choice SAT IIs as practice tests, which promoted gamesmanship and benefited wealthier students who could afford to take multiple tests. Now, each time you take an SAT II, your score will show up on your ETS score report, like each SAT I you take. In light of this change, it is important to be truly prepared for the SAT IIs you plan on taking, because colleges will see all of your scores. What remains to be seen is how your scores will be evaluated by an admissions committee. Is the student who gets a 750 on the Writing SAT II for the first time considered "better" than the student who takes the writing test five times and ends up with a 750, with all of the lower scores showing? Most colleges have said that they will still only take your highest scores, like they do for your highest verbal and math scores on your SAT I. My advice is to be prepared before taking an SAT II, and take one subject no more than three times.

ACT (American College Test)

The ACT is a single-format test in the academic areas of English, reading, mathematics, and natural sciences. Students receive a sub-score on each of these four sections, graded on a scale of 1 to 36, as well as an overall, composite score. Most colleges will accept either the SAT I or the ACT. There is no distinct advantage to taking one test over the other, although there are many more test preparation options for the SAT I than the ACT. On the other hand, some students have found the ACT slightly easier to take. My advice is, if you have unrepresentative SAT I scores and your top colleges require one of the exams, you may want to take the ACT as well. If a school's application indicates that standardized test scores are optional, then only send scores if they are excellent. You never want to give an admissions board a reason to doubt your abilities. If you submit both scores, the college will use the one that reflects your higher achievement. Please refer to the list below comparing ACT and SAT I scores.

ACT (Composite Score)	SAT I (Combined Verbal and Math Scores)
36	1600
35	1550
34	1520
33	1470
32	1420
31	1380
30	1340
29	1300
28	1260
27	1220
26	1180
25	1140
24	1110
23	1070
22	1030
21	990
20	990
19	910
18	870
17	830
16	790
15	740
14	690
13	640
12	590
11	550
10	500
09	450

Advanced Placement Tests

The College Board also offers the Advanced Placement Program for high school students. In Advanced Placement classes, students are given the opportunity to take college-level classes in thirty-three different curricular areas. Although not all high schools participate in the program and Advanced Placement courses are by no means required for college admission, they do demonstrate an in-depth knowledge of a particular field as well as an ability to do sustained work at a college level. In May of each year, the College Board offers exams in each of the thirty-three subject areas. These exams are scheduled to avoid conflict with the May SAT I and SAT II test date. If you are successful on these exams you can earn 3, 4, or 5 units of college credit based on your score. Not all colleges, however, give college credit based on a passing mark on the exam. Either way, these classes identify the student as one who is capable of taking the most rigorous course work and is apt to be successful in college. Please also note that International Baccalaureate courses, often given in international American school curricula, are comparable to AP courses. Below is a list of the Advanced Placement courses currently available:

Art History	International English
Biology	Language
Calculus AB	Latin: Virgil
Calculus BC	Latin Literature
Chemistry	Macroeconomics
Comparative	Microeconomics
Government and	Music Theory
Politics	Physics B
Computer Science A	Physics C Mechanics
Computer Science AB	Physics C E and M
English Language	Psychology
English Literature	Spanish Language
Environmental Science	Spanish Literature
European History	Statistics
French Language	Studio Art Drawing
French Literature	Studio Art General Portfolio
German Language	U.S. Government and Politics
Human Geography	U.S. History

TOEFL (Test of English as a Foreign Language)

The TOEFL program provides English proficiency testing for international students planning to study in the United States, Canada, or other countries where English is the primary language of instruction. However, you should check whether your college of choice would accept English proficiency already on the basis of having taken the SAT I or ACT: Harvard will, for instance, but Princeton will not. The new computer-based TOEFL, introduced in 1998, features a new scoring scale, partly due to the addition of a writing section and partly due to the computer-adaptive nature of some of the test sections. The TOEFL exam consists of a mixture of fill-in-the-blank, multiple choice, and essay-style questions. Students taking the TOEFL exam will receive a total score ranging from 0 to 300 as well as three scaled section scores:

- Listening—a scaled score between 0 and 30
- Structure/Writing—a scaled score between 0 and 30
- Reading—a scaled score between 0 and 30

If you are getting answers consistently right in the listening and structure sections, the computer will automatically pitch tougher questions to you. Both the number of right answers and the questions' level of difficulty are taken into account when determining your score. A comparison table has been published to help students who take the new test in its first few years at *http://www.toefl. org*. Or you may write to:

TOEFL Services
P.O. Box 6151
Princeton, N.J. 08541-6151

FEE WAIVERS

Fee waivers are available for eligible students for all of the examinations listed above. Students can obtain a request for fee waivers from their high school college counselor. If you can demonstrate need for financial assistance, you will be exempt from payment. However, the supply of exemptions is very limited and you should apply early for consideration, as funds do not usually last throughout the school year.

REGISTRATION PROCEDURE

Test applications are available in your high school's college counseling office. Use a number-2 pencil to complete the application form. You will use the same application for both the SAT I and the SAT IIs. The ACT requires a different form. Mail the application and check, money order, or fee waiver in the envelope provided in the registration booklet. Remember to fill in the correct College Entrance Examination Board (CEEB) code for your high school on the application. Applications must be postmarked by the due date or a late fee is charged. You can also register online at *www.collegeboard.com.* Once you have registered by mail for the SAT I or SAT II tests, you may register for future tests by phone. There is an additional charge for this and you will find instructions in the registration booklet. The deadlines remain the same. You will receive an admission ticket in the mail before the test. If you fail to receive it by the Wednesday before the test, call the Educational Testing Service at *(609) 771-7600.*

It is possible to take the SAT I or SAT IIs without registering in advance by showing up on the day of the examination and either obtaining a walk-in registration or taking the test standby, filling the space of registered students who do not show up. However, taking the test standby should be a last resort, not protocol.

KEEPING TRACK

As you wade through the murky waters of standardized testing, you may find it useful to take advantage of the following chart to schedule and keep track of your college entrance exams. Even though you can have your scores sent directly to your schools, each application will ask for this information again. If you keep track of all of your examination dates and scores in an organized fashion, you will be able to transfer this information directly onto your college applications, thereby saving both time and energy.

MY COLLEGE TESTING SCHEDULE

Ninth-grade tests	Subject	Date	Score	Composite score
SAT II	Biology			

Tenth-grade tests	Subject	Date	Score	Composite score
PSAT			M	
			V	
SAT II				

Eleventh-grade tests	Subject	Date(s)	Score	Composite score
PSAT			M	
			V	
SAT I			M	
			V	
SAT I			M	
			V	
SAT II				
ACT				

Twelfth-grade tests	Subject	Date(s)	Score	Composite score
SAT I			M	
			V	
SAT II				
ACT				

NOTE ON TEST SCORES

I would like to say a few words about the accuracy and fairness of the above-mentioned college entrance exams. Although these tests have been around for a long time, helping colleges to determine the potential of countless college applicants, they are by no means perfect. As with any standardized form of general assessment, the college admissions tests we currently use in this country are limited in their ability to test true academic ability. A caring, outgoing student who listens well, asks interesting questions, and promotes stimulating classroom conversation would clearly be a bonus to any school—and would most likely perform well in a college environment. Such information, however, would have to come out in a letter of recommendation or interview because such character-based academic strengths are not tested by a standardized exam such as the SAT I.

In addition, these standardized exams are far from objective in the knowledge they test. Subjective factors such as race, gender, economic standing, and cultural upbringing play a role in one's ability to perform well. These tests, it turns out, may be skewed toward those students whose upbringing is representative of the ethical, moral, and cultural perspectives dominant in today's American society. This means, of course, that certain minority groups have a disadvantage simply walking into the test. For this reason, the University of California public school system is spearheading a movement to abolish the SAT I as an admissions criterion.

The fact that there is a crisis is evinced by the many editorials and articles that have come out in the past few years. The following is one such editorial from *The Brighton-Pittsford Post*, which I feel gets to the heart of the question. I include it because it points out the inherent absurdities of our current testing process. I also include it as encouragement to you, the student, as you face the often bewildering process of college testing. Just remember that no test is perfect. Also remember that you are not a number. We counselors do not think of you as numbers, and neither do the college admissions committees.

You may find it helpful to remember the words of John Katzman, founder of the Princeton Review, who said the following about the role of the SAT I: "It's an arbitrary, biased, somewhat pointless exam that doesn't test anything important. . . . I treat the SAT I the way a doctor does cancer. It's a disease that has to be eradicated."[1]

The SAT Defined[2]

Our national Rorschach test for high school students is getting a new name, or, to be more precise is losing its old one. This month, the SAT, long feared by students and occasionally embraced by politicians, ceased being the abbreviation of anything. The SAT is now . . . well, it's the SAT. Confused? Imagine how the kids whose futures may hinge on the thing must feel.

"SAT" used to be short for "Scholastic Aptitude Test." It was created in 1941 by a private company, the College Board of the Educational Testing Service. Since then, many colleges have used it to help determine who deserves to go to what college and, in some cases, who gets scholarships. Most college admissions departments make a point of saying that the SAT does not by itself determine which high school seniors are accepted, that it's just one of many factors admissions officers consider. But regardless of the weight it's given, the test is of presumably some importance. So what the heck does it measure?

The "Scholastic Aptitude Test" did not measure aptitude. Researchers repeatedly showed that students improved their scores after they were coached on test-taking procedures. And it would be silly to assume that aptitude could be improved through coaching. Nor was the test measuring achievement in high school, as some may have thought. The College Board produces a whole series of subject-specific tests to gauge how much students have learned in given subject areas: in math, in the sciences, in English and in other languages. Colleges often use those test scores to decide what level of courses individual freshmen should take. The SAT was something different.

So considering the SAT didn't measure aptitude and that it didn't measure achievement, the College Board decided in 1994 to change the name to the "Scholastic Assessment Test." "Assessment" is just another word for test. So the SAT, in essence, became the Scholastic Test Test. That seemed appropriate. A lot of educators had been saying for years that what the SAT really measured best was a student's ability to take tests—specifically multiple-choice tests. However, it would have been awkward for the College Board to admit that. After all, the ability to take multiple-choice tests is not a skill that will get a person very far in life, at least not beyond college. And it's a skill parents and others might balk at spending money to assess.

The College Board recently threw in the towel and issued the ultimate press release about the SAT. "Please note that SAT is not an initialism," the statement read. "It does not stand for anything."

Now we know.

While I happen to agree with this opinion about the SAT I, we unfortunately do not have a viable substitute that would equally and fairly assess all high school students. For now, we have to put up with the SAT I. Wouldn't it be

---

[1] Tony Schwarz, "The Test Under Stress," *The New York Times Magazine* © 1999.
[2] "The SAT Defined," editorial, *The Brighton-Pittsford Post.* © 1997.

a great endeavor, besides being financially lucrative, to create a new test that was not biased, that correlated to one's GPA and IQ, not to one's class or ethnicity, a test that accurately and fairly predicted how a student would perform in the first year of college?

After all, if SAT stands for nothing, then why is it still around?

For more views of authorities on intelligence and testing concerning the SAT's relation to the IQ test, its ability to predict success in school, and the debate over whether the SAT measures "aptitude" or "achievement," see: *http://www.pbs.org/wgbh/pages/frontline/shows/sats/test/views.html.*

SUMMARY

Standardized tests are a necessary evil of the college admissions process. To get into the college of your choice, you must be prepared to face a number of college entrance exams. You must know which tests to take and when to take them. You must also know how to interpret the scores and how they fit into the larger application picture. The secret to acing your exams is to practice taking them as often as possible in order to familiarize yourself with the test-taking process. There are five major sets of tests that selective colleges use as an indication of your preparation for college-level courses: the PSAT/NMSQT (Preliminary Scholastic Aptitude Test/National Merit Scholarship Qualifying Test), the SAT I, the SAT II-Subject Tests (formerly Achievement Tests), the ACT (American College Test), the AP (Advanced Placement) examinations, and the TOEFL (Test of English as a Foreign Language), for foreign students planning to study in the United States.

INSIDER TIPS

✓ Take the PSAT. It is great practice for the SAT I. Students receive a printout with their answers to each question as well as the correct answers. You can use this as a guideline for areas of improvement.

✓ Practice the SAT I. I have my students take one practice test per week for eight weeks prior to the real SAT I test date.

✓ Leave time for improvement. I recommend giving yourself three opportunities to take the SAT I, in order to allow for improvement.

✓ Start early. You should start preparing in December or January of your junior year. Just because you are a straight-A student does not mean you will get a 1600. Nothing pays off like hard work.

✓ Try the ACT. If you have low SAT I scores and your colleges require one of the exams, take the ACT. Some have found it easier to take.

✓ If all else fails. . . . You can take the SAT I or SAT IIs without registering in advance with walk-in registration or taking the test standby.

✓ Put your best foot forward. If an application says that test scores are optional, only send your scores if they are excellent. You never want to give an admissions board any reason to doubt your ability to perform.

8

WRITING AN OUTSTANDING ESSAY

MYTHS AND TRUTHS

MYTH: As a college applicant, you need to find some gimmick to make your essay stand out from the competition.

TRUTH: Never rely on gimmicks—they are usually just a transparent attempt at compensation for a bad essay. Instead, spend time getting to know yourself, probing your thoughts and wishes, and mining your past for a great story.

MYTH: These days, every college applicant gets so much help with his or her college essays, you'd be a fool not to consult with a professional writing coach before submitting your application.

TRUTH: Colleges want to hear from you. They want to get to know your dreams, desires, triumphs, and failures expressed in your own voice. Chances are a hired gun won't care as much about your application as you do and has a different voice than you anyway. If "you" emerge in a thoughtful essay that addresses both your strengths and your weaknesses in a clear yet creative manner, you will already have a huge leg up on the competition.

MYTH: In your personal essay, list as many achievements as you can from your brag sheet in order to ensure that your admissions reader is aware of all the great things you have done.

TRUTH: Choose a single incident from your past, a single moment that defines who you are, and write a clear and creative essay about it. Listing your achievements in the essay is redundant and insults the intelligence of the application reader.

MYTH: The content of your essay is what's important, not the look.

TRUTH: Presentation can make or break your college essay. Be sure to catch all typographical and grammatical errors. Also, make sure to read the instructions on each application and follow them.

ESSAY WRITING

Once you've taken the necessary standardized tests and used your brag sheet to organize and convey your extracurricular activities, it is time to start work on one of the most important components of your personal record: the personal essay. I was about to say the "dreaded" personal essay, but the truth is, there's really no reason to fear it. Advice books and educational consulting companies will try to scare you into thinking you need their services before you can crack the mystery of the college essay. Although it is an extremely important component of the college application, if you have been following the exercises, tips, and suggestions in this book, you are already halfway there. You know the truth about college applications. You know that the secret to a great application is knowing yourself.

Plus, by now, you've experienced a lot in your life. You've been involved in thousands of rewarding, disappointing, triumphant, transformational, educational, and hilarious situations. One of them will form the perfect point of departure for an excellent college essay. In this section, you will learn how to choose which one. You will also learn some insider tricks on how to turn this most telling of anecdotes into the best representation of who you are as a person and what you have to offer the colleges of your choice. I find it helps to imagine the personal essay as your handshake, as your first and most memorable impression to the admissions committee. It is your chance to stand out as a unique personality, to verbalize who you are in a compelling and effective manner, and to highlight your character and your achievements in your own voice. The trick, as always, is to be yourself.

ESSAY TOPICS

Most college admissions committees want to know something about the applicant that they cannot otherwise learn from the rest of the application (that is, from your courses, grades, test scores, recommendations, brag sheet, and interview). A good essay makes an applicant come alive for the evaluator. It transforms a candidate from a series of numbers and statistics into a living, breathing human being. Although you may write your essay on one of your brag sheet activities or experiences, you should avoid writing an essay that simply lists all of your brag sheet's contents. A specific and concise essay concentrating on *one* activity will give you the opportunity to elaborate on something important while using specific details. It will also make you sound more sympathetic and realistic than some list of impressive-sounding achievements. In order to plan your workload, it is a good idea to read through each college application that you plan to submit in order to determine the number and nature of the essays you'll have to write. Some schools ask very specific questions, others will allow you to choose from a number of questions, while still others will let you choose a topic of your own.

One of the best topics for your college essay is a story, one that only you can tell. The best stories capture just a moment in time—perhaps a day in your life, a turning point, a brief encounter—and demonstrate your originality, passion, and intelligence both as a writer and as a person. For example, if you are a varsity basketball player, you might write about a game that taught you something about yourself, perhaps a moment of struggle when you had to confront your limitations, as your father watched you from the stands. You could use italics to express your inner thoughts during the game. You might even compare the game to a battle from Greek mythology, showing your passion for that academic subject. With a strong beginning, middle, and end, this could make an excellent essay. However, you should avoid doing anything silly like sending your essay written in the shape of a basketball to illustrate your point.

Other gimmicks that will not get you into college include:

- Writing your essay backward in order to convey how "backward" you are: Do you really want an already overburdened admissions officer to have to read your essay in a mirror? Believe it or not, I heard about this fatal mistake on an application from a Brown University admissions officer.

- Writing about your first sexual experience, losing your virginity, coming out of the closet, sexual abuse or fantasies, etc. These may have been important moments in your life, but they are very intimate, so please, save them for your friends or therapist.

- Writing about the time your little puppy was hit by a car or any other heart-wrenching, sympathy-grubbing "sob" story. They always come off as insincere and desperate to make an impression.

- Writing your essay entirely in Latin or any language other than English. You may be fluent, but you don't want to force the admissions committee to hunt down a Latin translator.

- Writing in the third person because you think it sounds sophisticated, clever, or "objective." Colleges want to hear your unique voice, so write in the first person.

- Writing about a tragedy that occurred to somebody else that stresses how supportive you were in a time of need. The essay should be about something that happened to you.

Another topic that applications often ask you to address is a life-changing event or a person who has had a significant effect on your development. Many times this experience or person comes out of volunteer work or community service. If this is the case, you should be careful not to come off as patronizing when talking about volunteer experiences. Cite specific incidents that have been meaningful to you and avoid generalizing about all the "good" you have done other people. Volunteer work is by nature "good" and the admissions committee wants to know about you and your transformative moment, not about the homeless man you once fed.

In addition, as with all exercises in self-assessment, don't be afraid to write about being unsuccessful. Failure is usually a growth experience. I always say that the pillars of success are built upon the steps of failure. It is in the trying moments of our lives that we learn the most about ourselves. How we cope with our limitations and deal with disappointment form the marrow of our human experience and such moments can make excellent essay topics.

Furthermore, you may be asked in your application to select a quotation, novel, or play that has had a profound effect on your thinking or to answer a more philosophical question in the vein of "What is your definition of honor?" Schools such as the University of Chicago, Princeton, Northwestern, and Johns Hopkins are among those that have come to prefer this type of analytical question to the more traditional autobiographical essay question. When asked what she felt the two most important aspects of the college application were, Carol Lunkenheimer, Dean of Admissions at Northwestern, listed the transcript and the applicant's ability to articulate herself in writing. If you encounter this type of question, be sure to explore the more general political and philosophical implications of the work or concept in question, but also remember to relate the chosen material to your own ideas, outlooks, and aspirations. In other words, be both analytical and personal, but avoid being overly philosophical or profound—it is doubtful that at age seventeen, you are the next Friedrich Nietzsche.

Finally, you may be asked why you are applying to a particular school. In that case, the admissions committee wants to know what you hope to gain from your education as well as what you hope to bring to the institution in question. The work you have done "imagining you're there" in Chapter 5 will come in handy here. If you have done the necessary research, you will know exactly why a particular school is right for you. Don't say: "You have a great faculty and fabulous courses and the college is in a beautiful location." This is vague and unconvincing. Be detailed. Cite specific aspects of the campus, curriculum, environment, and activities that appeal to you.

SAMPLE QUESTIONS

Now have a look at some sample questions taken from actual college applications. Read them carefully and consider how you might answer them.

Please write about what is important to you and your goals, and the ways in which they are reflected in your accomplishments, challenges, or hardships. Describe them and how you have responded.

"We learn almost nothing in victory, but we learn much in defeat." Do you agree with this? Explain.

Community service can be a valuable part of the college experience. If you were to devote one year of service to a volunteer project, what would it be, and what would you hope to accomplish?

What do you think has been the most important social or political event of the twentieth century? The twenty-first? Do you share a personal identification with this cause?

Please tell the Board of Admissions about a significant event or experience that has had a profound effect on you, and why.

Recall an occasion when you took a risk that you now know was the right thing to do.

You have just completed your 300-page autobiography. Submit page 217.

State your favorite quotation and how it relates to your life.

If you could travel to any time, past or future, when would it be and why?

In applying to this college you have shown an interest in some aspect of our environment. What do you envision your future contribution to our community to be?

Who has influenced your life the most, and how have they shaped your future?

Describe one of your intellectual achievements—such as a paper, project, production, or performance. Explain not only the achievement but what you gained from it as well.

What group of people, or organization, do you admire and why? What qualities, ideologies, accomplishments, sacrifices, and/or contributions make them worthy of your admiration?

If there was one person from history whom you could meet with, who would it be and what would you discuss?

If you were given the time and resources to develop one particular skill, or talent, or area of expertise, what would you choose to pursue and why?

What sorts of thoughts go through your mind when faced with a difficult moral or ethical decision? Are there any rules of thumb, general principles, or certain questions you always ask yourself, that you find particularly helpful in reaching a conclusion?

Describe your ideal college roommate.

Describe any unusual circumstances or challenges you have faced and discuss the ways you have responded.

In what ways can you imagine yourself growing and changing as a result of spending the next four years in college?

You have been asked many questions on this application, all asked by someone else. If you yourself were in a position to ask a thought-provoking and revealing question of college applicants, what would that question be? Now answer it.

BRAINSTORMING STRATEGIES

Before you begin formulating any responses to your personal essay questions, you will need to brainstorm some topics. Below you will find detailed accounts of some IvyWise insider tips that have helped my students identify great essay topics and follow through on them. As you read through the following suggestions, please remember there is no specific formula for success. You will have to probe your past experiences on your own—no one can write your essay for you, as tempting as it may be to seek outside help either from a parent or an essay-writing service. Admissions committees are comprised of highly trained professionals who have seen it all, and they will surely be able to tell the slightest discrepancy between your writing style in one section of your application and your writing style in another. Any glaring differences will make them suspect you sought too much outside help and this will almost immediately disqualify you from contention. The truth is, there is no easy way around doing the hard work necessary to create an outstanding college essay.

The following four strategies will encourage you to examine yourself with open-mindedness and creativity, and you will arrive at an essay topic that is sure to make your application stand out from the crowd.

Personal Questions

First, I would like you to write brief responses to the following questions on a separate sheet of paper. When you are done, look at your answers carefully. Each one is a possible essay topic.

1. What makes you happy?

2. When were you most satisfied?

3. When were you saddest or most disappointed?

4. Who is your hero or heroine? Why?

5. Who has let you down?

6. Where do you see yourself in a year; four years; seven years?

7. What are your fears?

8. What are your hopes?

9. What is your favorite activity and why?

10. What is your favorite subject in school, the favorite book you have read, and the favorite paper you have written?

11. What is the funniest thing you have ever done?

12. How would you describe your personality?

13. When have you struggled in your life through something uncomfortable and how did you get through it?

14. If you had five minutes with the dean of admissions at your top choice school, what would you say about yourself? Remember: you only have five minutes, so be precise and respectful of the dean's time.

"So You" Stories

Now I would like you to do the following exercise as a way of coming up with a number of possible essay topics that express your personality and character in the form of a story that is *so* you.

1. Choose the five people who are closest to you; they could be friends, parents, siblings, boyfriend or girlfriend, etc.

2. Ask each of them to supply you with a story which they feel is *so* you. You

know what I mean: when you are telling a story about your best friend, Jeff, and you say, "Listen to this. This is *so* Jeff."

3. Take notes as you listen and come up with a master list of five stories that are *so* you.

4. Now choose one and write about it as your college essay.

5. Show the completed essay to the four people who supplied you with the stories you *didn't* choose. Does it make them feel the same way as their stories? Have you captured the "*so* you" part?

6. If not, go back to the drawing board and try again.

7. If so, then your essay will undoubtedly relay something "*so* you" to your admissions readers. This is the sign of an outstanding essay.

Personal Time Line

Next, try the following exercise as a way of pinpointing the most meaningful moments in your life. These often make great essay topics.

• On a piece of graph paper, create a personal time line of "life" moments you can remember, complete with valleys and peaks. What are the high points in your life? The low points? The turning points? The watershed moments when you first discovered something about yourself or the world around you? When you changed your opinion about something or someone? When you experienced something that has changed you forever? These are the moments that colleges want to hear about. You will most likely choose your essay topic from among these moments.

Five Adjectives

Next, do the following exercise as a way of training yourself to evoke specific characteristics of your personality without actually stating them.

1. Choose five people who are close to you. They may include friends, boyfriend/girlfriend, parents, teachers, siblings.

2. Ask each one of them to come up with three adjectives to describe your character, your personality, you. Tell them they have to be completely honest in order for the exercise to work.

3. Consider the adjectives they have chosen. Since they all know you so well, some will inevitably overlap. Create a master list of five adjectives.

4. Now, sit down to write your essay on one of the topics you have chosen

using the strategies above. Make sure that you express these five adjectives without ever using them.

5. Once the essay is done, show it to your college counselor or some other objective person—not one of the five above. Ask them to come up with five adjectives to describe the person and the events as they are described in the essay.

6. If you can get an outside reader to guess the five adjectives without knowing them beforehand, then you have succeeded. An admissions officer will draw the same conclusions.

7. If you cannot, you must go back to the drawing board, write another essay and repeat this process. Eventually, you will succeed and you will have an excellent essay for your college applications.

GUIDELINES FOR WRITING AN OUTSTANDING COLLEGE ESSAY

In my private college counseling practice, I have developed a number of guidelines to help my students improve their writing skills. Once you have chosen a topic and written some sample essays using the four brainstorming strategies above, you will want to review the following pointers to make sure you are getting the most out of your college essay.

Style and Tone: Show, Don't Tell

In your personal essay, you want to avoid making overt statements about your character such as "I'm a great person" or "I'm responsible, hard-working, intelligent, caring, creative, and a leader." Although these characteristics are certainly laudable—as well as being precisely what colleges are looking for—there needs to be more finesse in the way you get your point across. Your goal with the essay is to show your wonderful qualities and characteristics in the form of a story, not tell them dryly in the form of a list. Let the reader conclude that you are wonderful without your actually saying it.

Diction and Vocabulary: Let the Reader Hear Your Own Voice

You should use vocabulary with which you are familiar, not complex words taken from a nearby thesaurus that end up sounding not only pretentious, but uneven and stiff. Your own voice will distinguish what you have to say more effectively than an unnatural, borrowed diction. As W. T. Conley, Dean of Undergraduate Admissions at Case Western Reserve University in Cleveland, Ohio, commented: "Admissions officers want to read what you want to write, not what you think we want to read." Trying to tailor your essay to the imagined expectations of an admissions committee is a recipe for disaster. The essay is, after all, a prime opportunity to express your individuality. It is worth bearing in mind that an interview is not always granted, in which case the essay becomes even more important in distinguishing your voice from those of the other candidates.

Format and Length: Follow Instructions and Be Concise

Most colleges require the essay to be typed, whereas Brown University requires it to be handwritten. I recommend you write no more than two pages, double-spaced, in 12-point Times Roman font using standard margins. In general, no admissions officer wants to read more than two pages; their time is valuable and limited. When I was a reader for Yale's office of admissions, I was advised to spend no more than twenty minutes on an *entire* application folder—reading and evaluating it. Consider these time constraints and try to imagine that you are the admissions officer: What would you be able to read in under twenty minutes? Furthermore, if the application allows a given space such as one page or half a page, fill that space. You can type your essay on a word processor and manipulate the margins to fit the space allowed. You can even cut out your printed essay and affix it to the page with a glue stick. Just make sure you follow all directions and specifications for each application. For example, if an application allows for an extra sheet (rather than sheets) of paper beyond the space given, make sure you attach only one page.

In addition, stick to the topic at hand. Although you may not agree with their choice, boards of admissions spend a great deal of time determining their essay question(s). If they ask a specific question, then you must try to answer it.

The Catchy First Sentence

As a general strategy, it is always a good idea to have a catchy first sentence. If it grabs the reader's attention, the reader will be encouraged to read on. If it is awkward or falls flat, the admissions reader may feel frustrated at having to read yet another uninspired essay. Even if the body of your essay is brilliant, there is no point in making the reader have to work to get there. To that end, have a look at the following opening lines. These are examples of what *not* to do. They range from confusing, obvious, and dumb to arrogant, creepy, and, well, dumb. Needless to say, the essays did not help their writers with the college admissions process.

1. High school has been a really educational experience.

2. Reality is relative—each person has his own—like snowflakes.

3. Ever since I can remember, I have been bored.

4. Everyone always says how incredibly gifted I am.

5. Many interesting and important issues have played an important role in my extracurricular interests.

6. I believe that clothes say a lot about who the person is on the inside.

7. Speaking is a fundamental part of language.

8. The biggest influence on my character has been the presence of my father, habitually dressed in a housedress, a duster poised in his hand and a feather boa around his neck.

9. Many people have influenced me in my life, but not as much as I have influenced them.

10. Well, I guess I better say something about myself.

Pay close attention to the opening lines of the sample essays that follow. I think you will see the way they entice the reader to continue reading. They are bold, poignant, mysterious, full of color, dramatic, descriptive, energetic, and informative. When you sit down to write your own essay, you will want to use them as models. One word of caution, however: as you begin to craft your masterpiece, you may not want to *start* with your opening sentence. The last thing you need is to sit there pulling your hair out, desperately trying to come up with the perfect first phrase and ignoring the body of your essay completely. Write your essay first. Explore your theme. Then come back to the beginning—and nail it.

SAMPLE ESSAYS

Before you begin writing, I suggest you take a look at the following series of sample essays taken from many different sources over the course of my career as a college counselor. *These are the success stories.* These essays helped their authors gain admission to some of the most selective colleges and universities in the country. For your convenience, I have provided the questions themselves when available and have tried to include their authors' eventual places of enrollment. Please note that, as with any material of such a personal nature, some of the authors granted me permission to use their work on the condition that they remain protected from infringement.

For other sample essays, you might also take a look at one particularly good online service, IvyEssays, started in late 1996 by a Williams College graduate, Daniel Kaufman. For a minimal subscription fee, you gain access to a collection of more than one thousand essays from successful applications to the nation's top colleges. But beware. As Jill Fadule, admissions director for the Harvard M.B.A. program, has said: "You can be sure we'll be buying the essays ourselves and becoming very familiar with them." So, again, *do not be tempted to copy*. Instead, use IvyEssays as a tool to help you better convey your own experiences, thoughts, and ambitions. Use them as sources of inspiration and as particularly good examples of what admissions officers at selective colleges are looking for in a college application essay. You can visit IvyEssays at *www.ivyessays.com*

As you read the following essays, I suggest you pretend you are on the board of admissions at a selective university. Would you want these students on your campus? What do you learn about them from their essays? How have they conveyed a sense of who they are and what they value?

Early Riser

This essay came from my certification course materials at UCLA Extension. It is a general personal statement, written anonymously.

I often try to imagine what it would be like to sleep in and awaken to the smell of fresh morning coffee, the singing of birds, a cool fragrant breeze blowing across my pillow, and delicate golden sunlight filtering through the shutters onto my face. But, when one is a paperboy, one cannot enjoy such pleasures.

In reality, I must arise at 5:30 in the morning, fumble in the dark to switch off my blaring alarm clock and stumble half asleep across a cold black room to put on my clothes. My shirt is usually on backward, my hair is sticking straight up, my shoelaces are untied, and I trip down the stairs often stepping on the sleeping family dog. Thereafter, the dog lets out a painful howl that sends the neighborhood dogs into a barking frenzy and scares me half to death.

Actually, I like being a paperboy. There is something romantic about delivering heavy newspapers on an old rusty bicycle on chilly mornings. The feeling of being the first to see the morning newspaper, to actually deliver news that may have a profound effect on people's lives, is second to none.

When I first started my route more than three years ago, I was very uncoordinated. The papers would fly through the air and land on the wet grass, in a bush or flower bed, smack the side of a car, slam against a door or window, or skid into a pile of mud. I received many complaints. Over time, my arm muscles grew stronger and my aim became sharper. Now, each paper lands with a solid thunk on a porch or walkway, and complaints have become rare.

After years of riding the streets before sunrise, I have become familiar with some of the other early risers in the neighborhood. There is the birdwatcher who paces the sidewalk with binoculars in hand, the Asian man who performs Tai-Chi in his driveway, the young woman who often becomes entangled by the leashes of her six Pekinese dogs, the old woman who walks hunched over with her arms clasped behind her back, and the overweight lady with two pigtails who sings to herself while jogging. Then there are the other types of early risers such as the raccoon I see scurrying along an ivy-covered fence and the family of opossums I see crossing the street.

Yes, being a paperboy has its ups and downs, but I would never trade my alarm clock, ratty old coat, thick woolen gloves, or newspapers for an extra hour of shut-eye. Never!

Commentary on "Early Riser"

You may use the space below to discuss the merits of this essay. What characteristics or adjectives does the essay portray without actually mentioning them? What are its overall style and tone?

_____

_____

_____

_____

_____

_____

My Thoughts on "Early Riser"

The first word that comes to my mind about this boy is that he is responsible. If I lived in his neighborhood, I could rely on him to deliver my paper every day. I would extrapolate that he would be a responsible student, showing up every day to class on time and completing the requisite assignments. He has worked for his money and does not come across as lazy or spoiled either. This leads me to believe he would probably work just as hard in school. He is also diligent—he stuck with his job even though it was difficult for him at first. I imagine he would plug through his college studies with the same tenacity. And he is observant—he has not gone through life with his eyes half-shut but instead takes notice of the details of his morning route. He will bring his observations and analytical skills to the classroom. Besides all of this, he seems like a great guy who would make a wonderful roommate and have many friends. One page has convinced me to invite him to my campus. This is also an excellent example of the "Show, Don't Tell" maxim—at no point in the essay does he actually use any of the adjectives I just mentioned.

ABBA!

Question: Tell us something more about yourself that would help us toward a sense of who you are, how you think, and what issues and ideas interest you most.

On that foreboding morning of my SATs, I committed the potentially fatal mistake of allowing my parents to drive me to the test center. The ride would last approximately twenty-five minutes. I'm surprised I even survived the trip and even more shocked that the volcanic atmosphere of the ride didn't have any fatal reverberations on my boards. This is the story of that ride . . .

We, the Adelmans, had chosen to entrust our lives to the forest green Volvo 850 for reasons that illustrate our collective personality. First, it's a safe car (it's gotta be the safest); it's a station-wagon (we need space for the massive amount of luggage we carry); it's certainly not the most desirable car (what car-jacker wants a forest green Volvo station-wagon?); and it's got SRS airbags, or, for the non-Volvo owner, side airbags. Yet, the car is just the tip of my familial iceberg. The word "parents" doesn't even begin to sum up my parents; try "loving," "caring," "nurturing," "cautious," "nervous," "overbearing," "paranoid," and "quirky." Neither sleet, nor snow, nor an army of juggernauts could prevent my parents from asking me questions, ensuring my safety, or pushing me in the right direction. One might call it beloved. I call it neurotic insanity.

As we cruised down the majestic avenue, I sat in royal silence. I furrowed my brow as vocabulary and mathematical equations danced in my head. When we were not even two blocks from my house, my dad had flipped on the stereo and slipped his favorite selection into the CD player. My focus session was interrupted by ABBA—the Swedish '70s disco group. ABBA!—even the capital letters scream at you. I glanced at my watch. It was 7:15. Nobody is a "dancing queen" at that ungodly hour.

"Phonetics!" declared my proud father. "The group, ABBA? They were Swedish . . . knew not a word of English . . . sung using phonetics. Amazing." The sad thing was that he was serious. I decided to block him out. ABBA too. *"Dancing Queen . . . you're so sweet, only seventeen, yeah, yeah . . ."*

"So what are your plans for after the exam?" screeched my mother. And there it was . . . the question of all questions. It didn't even concern the SAT, like I wasn't about to sit through one of the greatest tortures known to man. My plans . . . haven't parents learned by now that we don't plan? I looked at my options for an answer to this absurd question: A) Going out to a movie with my girlfriend; B) Going out; C) Doing something; D) No idea. I chose "A," with aspirations of killing the blossoming conversation.

"Wow, wow, wow," exclaimed my easily amused father. "Where are you taking her?"

I didn't know.

"I don't know."

"What movie are you seeing?"

I didn't know.

"I don't know."

"Do you know anything?"

I didn't.

"I don't."

I really fared well on that quiz. At least, I had regained silence, save ABBA. They were now singing "Waterloo." I began quizzing myself with the flash cards I had brought along. Trenchant . . . sharp. Mattock . . . ax. Wield . . . to handle skillfully. Patricide . . .

"What are you doing tonight?" asked my dad with the utmost confidence. This is the "double question"—meaning the already asked and answered or deemed unsolved. The "double question" is a direct result of my father's listening habits. My father loves and cares, but sometimes he zones out of the conversation and when he finally emerges out of his mental coma, he feigns rapt attention with little success.

"Bill, he *said* he doesn't know," said my mother, coming to my rescue.

There was a lull in the conversation. I decided any further attempts to scrutinize my SAT knowledge would be in vain. At that second in time, I wished to be a pigeon, so I could soar out of the Volvo via the sun roof and seek refuge in a far, far away, warm and sunny spot of solace. Perhaps a tropical island where there existed no parents, no standardized tests, and only my girlfriend waiting for me, holding a thirst-quenching (virgin) Piña Colada. Behind her would be a long line of kosher butchers waiting to prepare me a dinner of *kasha varnishkes*.

"Richard! Snap out of it! Your father was engaging you in a practice multiple answer *problem* while you were zoning out. You are just like your father."

"Waterloo . . . couldn't escape if I wanted to . . . Waterloo . . ."

"Richard, who was the president of the United States before Reagan? Was it: A)," he continued, sticking out his thumb with each letter. "Gary Carter; B) Jimmy Carter; C) Teddy Roosevelt; or D) Teddy Ruxbin?"

"Is it 'B'?" I replied, feigning uncertainty. My dad's eyes lit up as he almost drove off the road with excitement.

"Ellen, the boy's a genius. Forget about this SAP nonsense, sign him up for Mensa!"

Outside, traffic seemed to operate at light speed, while inside, it seemed as if a tractor was towing the Volvo back to the apartment. My dad took a swig of his cold, congealed oatmeal, which he conveniently put into an empty *yartzeit* glass. The sound of his chewing rose and dueled with ABBA until it was victor. I felt as if I was inside a washing machine. My mind spun as fuzzy ABBA music videos replayed themselves over and over again in my mind as my dad sung along with a mouthful of oatmeal. The kosher butchers on the beach were twirling roast-pig and dousing it with milk while rabbis were devouring ham and cheese sandwiches. Just at that moment, my dad pulled up to the test center and liberated me from bondage. The SATs were no longer torture, but asylum.

"Good luck! Call us when you get out."

I gripped the soothing metallic handle of the door and pushed onto the sidewalk. I could hear ABBA tripping away behind the closed door. Then something snapped. A bubble of air escaped from my cavernous lung, which had otherwise been fraught with stress. The bubble escaped my throat and snowballed into a chuckle, eventually transforming into raucous laughter. This was ridiculous! My parents were ridiculous, but they meant no harm, only love. In this moment of clarity, nothing seemed to be looming. I could only think of my parents and the interview they would give me when I got home. Laughter painted the exterior of the school, as well as my mental mind-set. In some circuitous fashion, I had been quelled.

This nonsensical neurotic paranoia of pushy, protective parents is the reason for my distinct personality, and, while it may seem crazy, brutal, and as pet-peeving as pinched nerves in ten different parts of your body, you learn to love it, embrace it, cherish it, and God help you, pass it on to the next generation until an asteroid with the diameter of twenty million matzo balls hits New York City and everybody kicks the proverbial bucket.

I watched the Volvo putt away and took a deep breath. After all, I had a big test to ace.

© Anonymous, 1999

Commentary on "ABBA!"

You may use the space below to discuss the merits of this essay. What characteristics or adjectives does the essay portray without actually mentioning them? What are its overall style and tone?

_____

_____

_____

_____

_____

_____

My Thoughts on "ABBA!"

This is one of my favorite essays because it captures the student's character in relation to his family and their particular yet universal dynamics. In addition, he is a truly funny writer and his use of humor in this essay works. Beware, however. Humor is not for everyone. We all know there is nothing worse than that guy who thinks he's a riot but isn't. Stylistically, I also enjoyed this author's use of dialogue as well as his recourse to the many ABBA refrains. This is high quality creative writing and I could imagine the author being a lively and intelligent participant in any classroom discussion. This student was admitted to Brown University.

I Am a Christian

Columbia Question: Write an essay that conveys to the reader a sense of who you are.

University of Chicago Question: Pose an untraditional question of your own. "What is an uncommon way to deal with the stress of common experiences?"

It's 2 A.M., and I am a Christian.

City curfew has been in effect for three hours, and I have spent the remainder of my evening alone in my room. The key to understanding is patience, but today I have experienced such narrow-mindedness toward the culture of the Far East that this virtue has been taxed to its limit. I kneel comfortably on the floor and begin a meditation period to dissolve the thoughts and memories of prejudice that have kept me awake so late.

My thoughts float to Michigan, where as a child of five I am seated in the kitchen of my Chinese aunt. She is preparing dumplings by hand, and she is teaching some of the older cousins the delicate process of Chinese cuisine. I am far too young to engage in the festivities but my aunt hands me a tiny ball of dough from her batter. Even now I can almost taste the batter as I remember my first encounter with the Far East. The memory fades away as I sink deeper into a state of peace.

As I continue my meditation period, I remember the prejudiced slanders of friends and neighbors toward the East. The tiny Japanese who assumedly spend their time shouting, "Me, Samurai!" seem to be a constant gag to most Americans. This morning at my Christian breakfast group, I was told to pray for those who have turned away from the saving grace of Christ. Asians are mentioned as a portion of the fallen; apparently the entire continent of Asia is damned. I argue the request; "There are Christians in Asia," I say, "and it seems counterproductive to declare yourself superior." I argue man's inability to prove the existence of God as evidence that perhaps these "fallen" are closer to the truth than Christianity. I do not claim atheism; I simply ask that we question, for our assumptions lead not only to the bigotry that most Americans take in stride, but also to the subversion of the attitude of loving acceptance that we as Christians advocate.

I am wrong, of course; no amount of logic would win this argument. I sit back, accept defeat, and try to ignore the eyes of friends who are silently questioning my faith.

It is 2:13 A.M., and I am a Christian.

I shift my right leg and settle myself upon my hamstrings as the conflict of the morning slips from my mind. The day slides away, memory by memory, and soon I am left empty inside. All that remains is my room, Him, and me. Slowly my room grows fuzzy and seems to disappear. The Japanese flag and a collection of Samurai swords melt together in a twisting of red and black. A lava lamp fuses with track lighting and a pseudo-ancient hanging lantern; the three glow together in a shower of white light. A giant fan, sensing a sudden isolation, flaps away. A Rubic's cube sheepishly tumbles after a miniature, wooden version of the city of Kyoto. My grandparents amble away in a cedar picture frame. Books seem to fall forever as the floor below me disappears into a sea of glowing white. *The Art of Meditation* collides with other books regarding Japanese swordplay, J. D. Salinger, and a study of Aikido by a renowned British practitioner. Finally, the Holy Bible glides away from my nightstand into the white. I am left with my body, and soon I forget it is even there. My mind walks freely in the white.

I arouse from my meditation feeling relaxed and tranquil. The stresses from today's events have become distant lessons of tolerance. As the room slowly returns, I close my meditation by saying a short prayer to Him. Shaking the blood back into my legs, I crawl into bed, and drift off to sleep. My Bible has found its way back to the nightstand, and is nestled comfortably next to a smiling Samurai's mask.

It is 2:27 A.M., and make no mistake. I am a Christian.

© Will Thomas, 2001

Commentary on "I Am a Christian"

You may use the space below to discuss the merits of this essay. What characteristics or adjectives does the essay portray without actually mentioning them? What are its overall tone and style?

_____

_____

_____

_____

_____

_____

My Thoughts on "I Am a Christian"

This essay was written by a student of mine from Oklahoma who applied early decision to Columbia University and early action to the University of Chicago. What I love about his writing is the careful, intimate detail he reveals while discussing his inner thoughts and private space. We are privy to only a few minutes in the writer's life—a moment of meditation—and yet we feel as though we have experienced a lifetime of questions, anxieties, and beliefs with him. Thematically, it is a breathtaking exploration of the kind of peaceful equilibrium that can be reached despite a seemingly contradictory existence. His Christianity and his Far Eastern interests clash, and yet he is able to negotiate this difficult dichotomy in a truly creative and reflective manner. In addition, this essay topic is off the beaten track, treating a potentially sensitive issue with maturity and individuality. Finally, it is the symbolic quality of the objects that surround him in his room that anchors this speculative essay in the here and now. We can see and feel the internal contradictions of his situation in the very objects that adorn his room. Yet, like his dual systems of belief, both Christian and Far Eastern objects coexist peacefully within the walls of his room. This student was admitted early decision to Columbia and early action to the University of Chicago.

The Gift of In-Sight

Question: Tell us about a person who has had an important influence on you. What qualities in that person do you most admire, and how have you grown from knowing that person.

> She is gazing at me with ardor and admiration. Her delicate face exposes a perfect set of pearly-whites, which are reflecting the sun's glare as she laughs. I feel her little palm in mine and her fingers are clutching mine instinctively with an innocent need for security. I almost wish that I did not have to take her to the starting line of the obstacle course. I reluctantly tell her that we are about to begin. She abruptly turns to me with an anguished look. Her blank, colorless eyes seem to stare at me, pleading with me to help her. I know where this look of fear comes from: Gabrielle is blind. And she is about to embark on a daunting journey by climbing over walls, running through tires, and swinging on monkey bars.
>
> Gabrielle is seven. The only two English words that she speaks are "Hello" and "What?"; her native tongue is French. I met her earlier this morning here at the Blind Olympics. I am here to assist one child through all of the events. When I was first assigned to Gabrielle

I was presented with a challenge: we would necessarily communicate in French for an entire day. I had studied French for ten years, longer than Gabrielle was alive, but my French seems sophomoric compared to her extensive vocabulary and impeccable pronunciation.

After getting through our first obstacle course, the language barrier, Gabrielle and I are both pleased until we approach the next obstacle course. As we stand here, her voice chokes up and she tells me why she is so frightened. The year before, her chaperone had been aloof and had not been paying attention when Gabrielle crashed into one of the walls of the course. I empathize with her because I too have counted on others who have led me astray. I have my doubts and I am tempted to let her sit this one out, but the director of the program suddenly signals me to guide her out to the dark green line of tape: the starting line. *I* have butterflies in *my* stomach. Gabrielle's hand is sweaty and she is clutching my hand so tightly that I feel needles begin to prick the tips of my fingers. Her fear is running through me. I only hope that I can help her through this course without her getting hurt in any way.

Silence hangs in the air until a sharp splitting noise . . . the whistle . . . , pierces the stillness. I find myself urging Gabrielle on with the most soothing words I can muster in French: *"Ne t'inquiète pas. Je suis là."* She conquers the first wall. We're doing well. She crosses the monkey bars and runs through the tires with amazing agility and speed. Gabrielle finishes with a competitive time. I am somewhat shocked because she ran the course as if she could see exactly what lay ahead. As I congratulate her in French, *"Très bien ma petite amie. Très bien!,"* her tear-stained cheeks break into a cherubic smile of delight. She did it. She has conquered her fears. I too feel a sense of accomplishment and I am proud of her. I shamefully begin to wonder how I ever doubted that she would complete the obstacle course.

Two hours later, I am sitting on the bus returning home. Gabrielle and I have said our *"au revoirs"* and I promised her that I would return next year. As we drive under an overpass of the freeway I begin to recount today's events. It occurs to me that I am the one who is blind and that it is Gabrielle who has helped me to see . . . something about myself. Clearly I see that I need to take challenges presented to me, even when there are obstacles blocking my path. Gabrielle has helped me see that I am blessed and that I often take what I have for granted.

When I finally get home, I take out my cello, which has been sitting collecting dust for quite some time. I sit down on the cool black leather stool and grip my bow with a certain enthusiasm and determination. I find the worn page of music that I have long been practicing, but never able to play well. I sit here for an hour and play it over and over, until the rosin flies off my bow. I play until I get it. And I feel content with myself, with playing the song and with having been able to help a child realize her own inner strength. Or did she teach me these things?

I understand now that Gabrielle does not see with her eyes, but with her heart. This in-sight gives her courage to conquer her fears. And she has given all of this to me.

© Lauren Kilroy, 1998

Commentary on "The Gift of In-Sight"

You may use the space below to discuss the merits of this essay. What characteristics or adjectives does the essay portray without actually mentioning them? What are its overall tone and style?

_____

_____

_____

_____

_____

_____

My Thoughts on "The Gift of In-Sight"

This essay was written by one of my former students who chose to write about a person who influenced her through her most rewarding volunteer activity. As I warned above, community service essays can be trite and patronizing, but this essay is compelling and genuine. She paints a vivid picture of both her external and internal circumstances, and also finds a completely natural way to mention her French and cello-playing abilities. The writer comes across as a caring, thoughtful, and dedicated person who would make a fine contribution to any college campus. To make the essay unique, I suggested that she write about a single day with this person and that she use the present tense to make the action come alive, thus conveying her emotions more powerfully and making the reader a witness. It worked well, and she was admitted to Boston University.

Animal Free

Question: Describe a situation where your values or beliefs were challenged. How did you react?

Once again I find myself in a situation I have never enjoyed: walking through the mall with my parents trying to find a nice suit I can wear for the holidays. This time, however, shopping is difficult. Unlike the relatively easy preteen days of the ubiquitous and obnoxious cookie-cutter blue blazers with gold buttons on the sleeves, I am looking for an *animal free* formal suit.

With no influence from peers or family, I adopted the vegan lifestyle during the first month of my junior year. After picking up a pamphlet on vegetarianism at a concert, I researched on the web the impact consuming animal products has on the environment and animals. I decided to rid my diet of all animal by-products including milk, eggs, meat, even honey. As restricting as that sounds, I didn't stop there. I stopped purchasing and wearing leather, silk, and wool. Wool is the material that causes the problem in this suit mission.

My parents, lovingly supportive of my lifestyle change, take it upon themselves to help me shop. After several unsuccessful attempts, disappointment and frustration begin to set in. I, on the other hand, am not in the least bit concerned, considering I can't stand dressing up in uncomfortable clothes in the first place. But, halfway through our pilgrimage at the mall, after my parents have spoken with a dozen sales representatives explaining our desire for wool-free suits, I take a step back and observe my parents. The irony of our situation becomes blatantly clear to me once I realize that my father is wearing leather shoes, wool slacks, a leather belt, and a leather jacket. Not to be outdone, my mother is in head to toe leather: pants, jacket, shoes, and purse. An acre of the rain forest, a 10-mile wide gap in the ozone, and an entire family of cows adorning my parents appears to belie their requests for a non-silk tie and a wool-free sport coat. I laugh out loud. We eventually leave the mall with a polyester suit and I ultimately find the accessories on the Internet. My parents are relieved.

A revolution has taken place within my family because of my decision to be vegan. Initially, my concerned mother sent me to a nutritionist to find out how incredibly deficient I am in all necessary nutrients and vitamins. But, I had done so much research on being a vegan and the health issues that go along with that lifestyle, that I was not worried in the least. I showed the nutritionist my daily diet and vitamin consumption, and she responded with a thumbs up. My parents again were relieved until the car incident.

I decided it was finally time to talk my dad into letting me get rid of my new Dodge Durango, a gas-guzzling, leather-interior, sports utility vehicle. I researched cars to find out which car was the least damaging to the environment while still being practical and safe. I found the new Volvo had an extremely low emissions rating, used large amounts of recycled products, environmentally friendly paints, and was available with a nonleather "pleather" interior. So I made the proposal to my father. He agreed on the grounds that he wouldn't have to spend any more money during the exchange. We test drove, and traded the environmental massacre of the Durango for the friendly flower of the Volvo.

Cut to several months down the road, I am riding my bike instead of driving whenever possible and limiting my material purchases to environmentally friendly and cruelty-free products only. I walk into my kitchen, which was once a haven for chocoholics with brownies and cookies and milk. But this time, I peek over my mother's shoulder and see a tofu stir-fry on the pan and soy milk in the refrigerator. I hear my dad say, "What's for dinner tonight?" My mother replies brightly, "Tofu and vegetable stir fry." And with all the sincerity in the world my father's response is, "Perfect, that is just what I am in the mood for." A smile graces my face as I sit down for dinner.

It is still difficult to get my parents to think about recycling during their routine "junk mail throw away" spree. I find myself picking out papers and water bottles from their trash. But, all in all, my dedication to living a cruelty-free, environmentally supportive and healthy existence has worked well within my supportive household. Thanksgiving at Grandma's however (her hairstyle hasn't changed since 1942) is not such a smooth experience.

© Jack Dolgen, 1999

Commentary on "Animal Free"

You may use the space below to discuss the merits of this essay. What characteristics or adjectives does the essay portray without actually mentioning them? What are its overall tone and style?

_____

_____

_____

_____

_____

_____

My Thoughts on "Animal Free"

This essay was written by a former student of mine who was a truly unique individual. A strict vegan, much of his philosophy about life stemmed from his veganism. We would never have learned this about him through his transcript, test scores, or brag sheet; therefore, it is an excellent topic to address in his personal essay. I especially enjoy the way he paints a clear picture of his family dynamics and gives us a powerful sense of his commitment to an issue of global importance. Clearly someone with this sense of humor and awareness of the not-so-funny sides of life would make a great addition to any freshman class. He was admitted to NYU.

Sandy

Question: Please use the space on this page to let us know something about you that we might not learn from the rest of your application. We ask that you limit your response to the space provided. In the past, applicants have used this space in a great variety of ways. They have written about family situations, ethnicity or culture, school or community events to which they have had strong reactions, people who have influenced them, a significant experience, intellectual interests, personal aspirations, or— more generally—topics that spring from the life of the imagination. There is no "correct" way to respond to the essay request. In writing about something that matters to you, you will convey to us a sense of yourself.

I remember the house perfectly; it was, after all, a child's dream. Big and ranch-like, the house was surrounded by a swimming pool and though the net was never up, and probably hadn't been for years, a tennis court which primarily served as a parking lot for bikes, skateboards, and those miniature cars that drive on a battery. There were winding paths with overhanging branches and secret forts behind the tennis court gates. In the front there lay an underground tunnel, lined with ripped-up Hefty bags, and an oversized trampoline, complete with a treehouse just close enough from which to jump.

The gates would open to a torrent of barks, interrupting the usually calm and peaceful ambiance of the surrounding neighborhood. Sandy's father, Mr. Burke, would then run toward me, chasing after their two black Labs and an overexcited mutt they still called "the puppy." I would prepare to defend myself from the oncoming canines, their thrusting paws and slobbery kisses leaving me, more than once, huddled on the sun-kissed driveway. "Sandy!" Mr. Burke would yell as he held on to the collars of the panting dogs. "Tina's here!"

Sandy would then appear, running from inside the house, careful not to trip on his untied shoelaces. He would greet me still in his school uniform—rather drab attire, consisting of a collared navy shirt and a pair of Sue Mills khaki pants. He always managed to make his uniform his own though—his pants stained from his Squeezit at lunch and his knees marked with green battle wounds from the Frisbee game during PE. His black oversized hightops were loose and clumsy, catching the cuffs of his pants as he scampered across the driveway. Though he often stopped to retie his sneakers, his neatly tied bows almost always resulted in a tangled mess—the laces cascading over the overstuffed and overdecorated tongue of his black shoes.

I stood in the driveway, a scrawny ten-year-old, and leaned against my bike. It was my brother's—an old, red ten-speed—and although it was too big for me, and my father had only taught me to use the back derailer, I rode it like a champ. A short tomboy with legs like string beans, I defended myself against the overpowering canines. My stringy hair was loose, whirling over my freckled face like wild blades of grass, though unlike Sandy, I had changed from my plaid jumper into more appropriate attire—more appropriate meaning the more holes the better, and today was no exception. I wore my favorite shorts, a pair with blue and white Hawaiian flowers and a *Go Ride a Wave* logo that even my brothers would call "cool." Miniature holes ripped at the already tattered seam; a gray backpack was slung over my shoulders carrying a bike lock and a crumpled sweatshirt. I had five dollars with me and a handful of coins—enough to buy an Orange Bang, a bag of candy, and to split a large basket of french fries.

Removing his palms from the handlebars and throwing them in the air, Sandy sped ahead of me: "Hey Tina, look at this!" he shouted as his bike quickly swerved toward the curb. "Whoa, that was close." Laughing, I attempted my own stunts, my hands leaving and returning to the handlebars in a fast clapping motion. Riding our bikes gave Sandy and me a freedom we didn't get in school; there was no set course, no definite schedule. We had the whole afternoon to waste, and our bikes gave us the means to do so.

The Country Mart is a group of one-story buildings, a collection of shops and eateries with a large central patio. Sandy and I were convinced that the central chicken stand sold the best french fries in Santa Monica. Sandy and I could talk about everything over an Orange Bang and french fries. The crisp Mart fries and sherbet-colored drinks always kept us going; they were like a prerequisite to our afternoon, a comfort, a tradition. Though sometimes we might enter the Country Mart unhappy with a test score or with a friend's remark, we'd always leave happily stuffed with fries, forgetting the day's tribulations.

Though it has been many years since Sandy and I have spent afternoons together on our bikes or in his backyard, I still see him on occasion. I no longer see a clumsy boy of ten with clothing stains and dirty hair, a boy who jumps at me from behind a tree or gets his hands dirty fixing the chain on his bike. Instead, I see a grown young man of six feet who shaves weekly and rides with pretty girls, not on a bike but in a car—one who'll never have to count quarters again, his leather wallet always stocked with crisp five-dollar bills. Like Sandy, I too have shed my awkward ten-year-old appearance and stand five feet eight, my lips glossed, my hair pulled back, although the freckles of a little girl remain. Though I sometimes put on a skirt or a pair of high heels, I always look to my bike for solace. It stands, leaning up against the garage wall, a symbol of youth and freedom, a reminder of what has brought me here. I know my bike will be safe in the refuge of my garage, as I must leave it behind on my next adventure—college.

© Anonymous, 1998

Commentary on "Sandy"

You may use the space below to discuss the merits of this essay. What characteristics or adjectives does the essay portray without actually mentioning them? What are its overall style and tone?

_____

_____

_____

_____

_____

My Thoughts on "Sandy"

This essay was also written by a former student of mine who chose to write an autobiographical piece in response to Yale's general essay question. I like the essay because it is a simple and well-written description of her childhood. There is a nostalgic tone to it, one that is evocative of times past and full of vivid detail. In addition, it says a lot about the writer and her relationship to her own childhood, capturing a particular period in American culture, a way of life that is slowly disappearing—both for the writer and for us. On top of it all, she has produced a very personal story of growth and maturity as told through the foil of a deep childhood relationship. We see how the author has graduated to other worlds, yet she still retains the verve and originality of this magical childhood place. She was admitted to Yale.

Worth Fighting For

Question: First experiences can be defining. Cite a first experience that you have had and explain its impact on you.

I kicked it as hard as I could with exactly the right part of my foot. I remembered my first coach telling me when I was a small agile six-year-old, "Sara, use the inside of your laces when you want to kick the ball hard." I ran to the other end of the field to retrieve my "dying" soccer ball, "dying" because I had played with it so much it was on the verge of being deflated and useless. I remembered all the adulation I used to get about my soccer skills, and I wondered where I had gone wrong. I used to be one of the best, revered by my coach and known to all the other coaches as "someone to look out for."

From the time I was eight to the time I was twelve, the perception of my soccer skills, and the skills themselves I admit, slowly atrophied. Other players were flourishing and pushing me off my pedestal of glory and recognition. I landed upon unfamiliar territory: the once familiar field seemed foreign and unruly. I couldn't maneuver as I used to, but nevertheless, I put aside my growing frustration and concentrated on enjoying the game. I received adequate playing time because the American Youth Soccer Organization (AYSO) supports the motto, "Everyone Plays." Although I was working hard to improve and succeed, I wasn't moving up in the ranks. When I got to high school, I realized that the AYSO motto, "Everyone Plays," no longer pertained. I learned that I couldn't earn playing time just by working hard and having a good relationship with the coach; if I wasn't good enough, I wasn't going to play. What really irked me were my good friends on the team. It seemed that their nonchalant attitude was rewarded, while my love of soccer was quashed. They had a penchant for joking around and ignoring the coach. While they got starting positions, I sat on the bench.

I decided not to take this sitting down . . . on the bench. Subsequently, I picked myself up and explored other avenues through which I could satisfy my love of soccer. I applied to AYSO and was approved to coach a team of ten- and eleven-year-old girls. The parents on the team were skeptical of me—they were not convinced that a sixteen-year-old girl was responsible enough to take care of their children. After all, I was up against seven middle-aged men who had been coaching since I was born. I struggled and am still struggling to find the balance between being a friend, role model, authority figure, and entertainer. I spent the season teaching my team everything I knew about soccer. We made it all the way to the single elimination round in the semifinals. I watched the girls on my team moving to the open space to support each other, calling for the ball, and giving 100 percent effort. They had actually listened to me and were doing all the things I had spent the entire season nagging them to do. They were using the skills I had taught them and playing their hearts out. Of course, they wanted to win, but I explained a very important lesson to them that I had just learned: playing itself was the most significant goal. After having been benched in high school, for me just getting to play was winning.

My coaching experience fulfilled my needs temporarily, but I was now both mentally and physically ready to focus on myself as a player. I went through fall training at high school with the attitude that I had put in the work and was ready to make Varsity in November. Unfortunately, the coach didn't agree with me and he told me I would do a great job as captain on JV. I tried to make the most of JV and to use all the feedback I could get to better myself both as a person and a soccer player, but I was devastated that I was working so hard and not succeeding. Toward the end of the season in February, I got a call from the Varsity coach saying that he wanted me to move up and join Varsity in CIF. The best things in life don't come easy, but they are the things worth fighting for.

© Sara Kramer, 1998

Commentary on "Worth Fighting For"

You may use the space below to discuss the merits of this essay. What characteristics or adjectives does the essay portray without actually mentioning them? What are its overall style and tone?

_____

_____

_____

_____

_____

My Thoughts on "Worth Fighting For"

This essay is about dealing with failure in a mature way. This student came to me with an incredible list of accomplishments yet was having trouble finding a good essay topic. When we spoke at length, she referred to a moment of frustration amid all her success. I encouraged her to explore her frustration and soon enough she had developed her challenging moment into a compelling and insightful essay. She makes a virtue of her approach to disappointment by turning a negative situation into an opportunity to reveal her character. She also demonstrates her commitment to a particular achievement—soccer—as well as her newfound passion for teaching others. Throughout the piece, her voice is adult and clear and never falls into any sports clichés or whiny bids for sympathy. She knows it is her life and that she is ultimately responsible for it. This combination of self-awareness, affable writing style, and athletic ability makes her a very attractive applicant for a selective college. She was ultimately admitted to the University of Pennsylvania, early decision.

Different Heart

Question: Evaluate a significant experience, achievement, or risk that you have taken and its impact on you.

It was going to be a busy day. At 8:30 A.M., I had my annual cardiac check-up to evaluate the status of my faulty valve that, along with my bumpy scar, is the only remainder of the heart surgery I underwent when I was two years old. At 12:30 P.M., I was attending a Debutante Ball luncheon with my childhood friend, Daniella. The seriousness of the morning ECHO exam was the polar opposite of the "display" of the debutantes over a lunch of salmon and cucumbers.

As a possible "debutante prospect," all eyes were on me as I was questioned about my school and volunteer experiences. But to my surprise, the greatest significance was placed on my family's history. My mom's accent, not British, created some confusion, but all was remedied when Daniella's mom explained my dad's Mayflower background and association with the "right" charitable groups and clubs.

I wanted to throw up. The salmon with the "extra tangy dill sauce" got caught in my throat. But just then, the harpist began strumming and the debutantes embarked on their parade. Some wore dresses with puffed sleeves so large I thought they were going to fly away. Some bowed so awkwardly I thought they were going to tip over as they curtsied. I thought I was an extra in an episode of "Saturday

Night Live" as I observed this tragic comedy of superficiality. Listening to the vapid conversation over the dresses made me think about an issue my cardiologist brought up a few hours before, which put everything into perspective.

Usually, following the annual exams, Dr. Victor, my cardiologist, briefs me on the strength of my pulse and status of my valve. I often approach these conversations with lightheartedness. But today's visit was different. Dr. Victor continued, "Now that you are seventeen, it is appropriate to inform you that women with your type of heart defect have a much higher than average chance of giving birth to a child with more complex anomalies. Consequently, you will be confronted with one of the following scenarios: a first trimester termination of pregnancy, fetal surgery, genetic alteration, or you could give birth to a child as naturally created."

Dr. Victor's comments about my future stunned me. I am only seventeen and not planning to have children for a long time. Sure, I read about the most philosophized animal, Dolly, but never saw its connection to me. For the first time, I encountered my inevitable adulthood. Now difficult ethical questions have permeated my reality.

I know that I would never change my child's sex, hair, or eye color. But if it would be advantageous to alter DNA to protect my child from severe heart deformities, I believe that I would consider it. I would wonder if I was abusing the power that was dictated to mankind. Should I play God or should I let destiny take its part in mapping out my child's future? I continue to ponder, struggle, and hope to make a compassionate decision.

Clapping hands awoke me from my deep thought when the audience was asked to rise and applaud the debutantes. And as I stood up, bringing my hands together in support of my friend, I realized that I could never "come out." Come out from where to where? To some, entry to a certain charity or debutante society means the world. To me, it means nothing, even though traditions play a big role in my world. It became very clear that I experience life with a different heart.

© Anonymous, 2000

Commentary on "Different Heart"

You may use the space below to discuss the merits of this essay. What characteristics or adjectives does the essay portray without actually mentioning them? What are its overall style and tone?

_____

_____

_____

_____

_____

_____

My Thoughts on "Different Heart"

This essay was written by a former student of mine for her Harvard application. I especially like the way it sets up a strong dichotomy between the polite superficialities of the debutante world and the intense reality of the author's physical condition. Instead of merely bashing her debutante friend, the author is actually very sympathetic to her aspirations, even though she clearly does not share them. That the author is able to touch on issues like genetic manipulation in such a natural and personal way is truly remarkable. This is the trick with such "big" themes: you must find the personal connection that makes them come alive as subjective stories, and not just state them as objective facts. In addition, each sentence of this essay is clear and concise and carries us through to the final word with conviction and grace. The author was admitted to Harvard, early action.

Strawberries

Question: Recall an occasion when you took a risk that you now know was the right thing to do.

How can I give someone a sense of who I am? Well, I am a person who likes to play in the rain, especially if I have nice clothes on. I do not do so just because I'm not supposed to, or because I hate nice clothes, or because I am an aquaphile. I do not do so because I am unable to understand the consequences; on the contrary—I understand the consequences very well. So, while others hide under doorways and awnings, I play. If only they knew that this could be their last chance to play in the rain.

I remember one summer, my father and I had driven to Chicago to visit relatives. We were at a Walgreens when it began to rain so hard that puddles became small lakes. Everyone huddled inside the glass doors to wait for a chance to run to his or her vehicle in the parking lot.

Why? Water doesn't hurt. Just as I began to feel afraid like the others— afraid of nothing, I ran for the doors. This of course, was not easy, as I had to squeeze through an area packed with people shoulder to shoulder. As I reached the doors, I felt like I was coming up for air from the depths of the oceans. I burst outside, danced, jumped, sang. I looked back at the throng of people jammed in the doorway, and they were all laughing. I am sure some were laughing at the crazy kid who didn't know any better than to play in the rain; but I am also just as sure that some were laughing because they wanted to be out in the rain with me.

The rain finally stopped, the huddled masses poured out of the store, and my father and I got in the car. I was sitting on a bunch of plastic bags, soaking wet, but completely comfortable. The world looked prettier that day as I stared out the window of our yellow, 1986 Toyota Corolla, and I did not regret what I had done. That, more than anything is what I remember, and what I dream about—living with no regrets. I want to enjoy every second I have, to know everything, to feel everything and to live life. The world is not perfect and never will be. Those wishing the world to be anything that it is not are missing out on life. I don't mean to say that a difference can't be made. In fact, when people ask me what I want to do with my life, the only response I have is "to make a difference." But, you don't make a difference by wishing, and especially not lamenting.

Some years later, I heard a Zen story that reminded me of that day in the rain. A man was chased by a tiger. Coming to a precipice, the man grabbed a vine and swung himself over the edge. As the tiger sniffed at him from above, and a rocky death awaited the man below, two mice began to nibble at the vine. Seeing a strawberry, the man reached over and picked it. How sweet the strawberry was. Life is too short to spend worrying. I eat strawberries. I play in the rain.

© Jack Schneider, 1998

Commentary on "Strawberries"

You may use the space below to discuss the merits of this essay. What characteristics or adjectives does the essay portray without actually mentioning them? What are its overall style and tone?

_____

_____

_____

_____

_____

_____

My Thoughts on "Strawberries"

This candidate chose to answer the question by highlighting a single, meaningful moment in his life, which shows that he generally takes risks. What I like so much about this essay is its small, almost intimate scope. The author has not chosen a moment of "global" importance—it is doubtful that many teenagers have experienced moments of global importance in their short lives anyway. But there is something universal about his depiction of this seemingly insignificant event. He has taken a rainstorm and turned it into a profoundly meaningful expression of his independent and creative spirit. We can also see firsthand the kind of effect he has on his immediate surroundings. Finally, by relating this small event in his life to a Zen story, the author gives the entire essay punch and scope. He was admitted to the University of Pennsylvania.

Some Take I95, I Take the Inca Trail

Question: Tell us something more about yourself that would help us toward a sense of who you are, how you think, and what issues and ideas interest you most.

As I travel the winding road to school, I begin to examine the creases between the exhausted cobblestones. My eyes squint as the sunlight reflects strongly off the round stones and I feel the unique equatorial burn on my right arm resting on the lowered car window. I gaze outward and lose consciousness in the seemingly endless scenery. In the distance, the Cotopaxi volcano stands proudly as it hugs the valley of Cumbaya. The royal blue sky contrasts dramatically with the pristine whiteness of the volcano's snow-covered peak, creating a peaceful canopy over the city of Quito. It is under this majestic canopy deep in the lush green valleys of the Andes that my life unfolds.

The car takes a sharp turn and my thoughts move beyond the sheer beauty of the scenery to travelers on this road prior to me. The late fifteenth century brought the Chasquis, efficient Inca mailmen who ran swiftly through this mountain range recognizing no boundaries (now there are many!) and extending the glory of the Inca Empire. It is hard to imagine that only fifty years later these mountains witnessed Orellana, the Spanish conquistador, marching down this trail in search of the Amazon River. The remoteness of these mountains also attracted Sephardic Jews and Basque peasants for different reasons: some sought respite from the Spanish inquisition, others economic improvement from a tired continent.

The beauty that touches me so and its history is not only my way to school, but a centrifugal part of my personal tapestry: seeds from these travelers reside within me, a late-twentieth-century teenager wearing the universal uniform of faded jeans and Nikes.

The jeep speeds up as if to warn me that the school bell might soon ring, but I still feel I have time to reflect upon how these surroundings tie all my loose ends together. These visions and thoughts visit me frequently at immigration lines, as I fumble through my beat-up book bag searching for the "right" passport (among 3!). My accent does not match any of these passports but rather represents a very Latin American trait: hybridness. I have noticed that my maternal Colombia has left inside me the rhythm, flavor, and folklore of the "cumbia" and "vallenato." I feel Colombian gusto is there when I tell a story or simply crack a joke. Ecuador has produced a more conventional and somber side that at times makes its appearance to which I must bow respectfully. Helpless submission to nature's beauty and a need for a spontaneous setting are my Brazilian birthplace sentiments. These are no stronger than the North American innovative, entrepreneurial dreams that a great-grandfather seems to have left in me. He came as a member of the teams of engineers who carved roads in the Andes, allowing the twentieth century to step in.

Simple character traits and three formal documents (Ecuadorian, Colombian, and Brazilian passports) create a feeling of warmth and belonging for an entire region that goes beyond one felt for a particular country whose boundaries are but imaginary lines.

The school bell faintly rings (which means I am late!) but my mind disregards it and begins to picture Simon Bolivar, our "libertador"—a hybrid like myself. My roots lie deeply in his dream; a joint region named "La Gran Colombia." I like to think that he and I are citizens of this region. As did Bolivar (and my parents and grandparents), I wish to leave these mountains to fill my mind with global and innovative ideas but only to come back and make my significant passage across the Andes.

As I cross the street to enter the school gates, I encounter a group of Indians. Hunchbacked and walking slowly, they stare downward at the cobblestones. A gust of dust hides the beauty of their features and the splendor of their clothing. It saddens me that this is what remains of the once proud kings of the Andes. But they too are an integral part of my patchwork, for their seed also lies within me. At the door, a paper placed in my hand interrupts my daydreaming. The global village kid roaming the Andes is given an unexcused tardy slip.

© Alejandro Landes, 1999

Commentary on "Some Take I95, I Take the Inca Trail"

You may use the space below to discuss the merits of this essay. What characteristics or adjectives does the essay portray without actually mentioning them? What are its overall theme and tone?

_____

_____

_____

_____

_____

_____

My Thoughts on "Some Take I95, I Take the Inca Trail"

This essay was written by a former student of mine from Ecuador who applied to Brown University. He describes his hometown, his place in the history of his country, and his multinationality. These are potentially large and difficult themes, yet he is able to ground them in his particular experience and offer us some truly unique details and insights. Each step on the way to school is imbued with meaning and portrayed in rich, descriptive language. To me, that is the sign of a gifted writer. In addition, he is clearly self-reflective and observant, as well as acutely aware of his place in the bigger picture. These qualities would make him an excellent candidate for a top school and I would have no doubt that he could succeed in a foreign culture under rigorous conditions. This student was admitted to Brown.

I Wish to Write

Question: If you were given the time and resources to develop one particular skill, talent, or area of expertise, what would you choose to pursue and why?

I woke up from a dream in which I was flying. I thought of what it would be like to be one of Da Vinci's primary sketches, where man (or woman) with the help of artificial wings actually flew. Propelled by strength, stamina, and courage, he or she defies gravity. Amidst my serene vision, I remember a Greek myth in which the central character, Icarus, attempts to fly off the island of Crete. Recalling his fate, I then reconsider this thought and the possibility of a watery grave. I stumbled into my kitchen in a slumbered stupor and glanced at my microwave. It glared back at me flashing a menacing grin . . . 12:00, 12:00, 12:00. As if it were to say, "Quoth the raven nevermore." I pondered the convenience of having a proclivity toward fixing household appliances. Is it even imaginable to ascertain the talent of one who can set up a VCR or microwave, refrigerator, and clock-radio all in one, thus making the entire concept of the kitchen obsolete. With all of this time spent taking measurements and crunching numbers, my life would take place in my kitchen. I was then reminded of Gregor Samsa in Kafka's *The Metamorphosis*. He lead an unfulfilling life confined in one room and the prospect of transmuting into a monstrous vermin did not suit me at all. I opened the refrigerator door, its cool breeze and quiet hum embraced me. I reached for a carton of eggs. After opening it, I was greeted with the most cruel surprise. There were no eggs left. Atop this horror, I did not possess the capability to buy eggs. Inevitably, I thought about being rich . . . filthy, stinking rich. I thought of being so rich that my backyard would be the size of a small third world country. So rich that every day I would be forced to choose between driving my Rolls Royce or my Bentley. Only then to realize that "It is my driver's order of business and what am I doing out of bed at 11:30 A.M. on a Tuesday. I don't work. Bring me some more caviar!" Upon slamming the refrigerator door, I recalled a biblical passage stating, "It is easier for a camel to pass through the eye of the needle than for a rich man to get into heaven." Thinking it was silly to wonder if this statement held true for both sexes, I resolved to see that not even Daisy and Tom Buchanan lived so "happily ever after" in West Egg. I slowly progressed toward my couch and upon reaching it, I curled into the fetal position. It was then I witnessed my calling. A tiny ivory figure enveloped in a poofy taglioni. There she stood in an *attitude derriere* on an advertisement in the Arts section of *The New York Times*. Alessandera Feri, the perfection of the human form. How exhilarating to be what Martha Graham once called "an acrobat of God," a dancer. I peeled myself off the couch wanting to get a closer look at the photograph. I sprang off of the floor, and midway into my *jete*, my ankle caught a piece of my protruding coffee table. My face hit the floor, convincing me that my coordination and motor skills were not up to par with anyone in American Ballet Theater. I grabbed my nose while wincing, contemplated the avenues of medical science but then decided to pass. Half a league, half a league, half a league onward. Into the kitchen for ice I charged. I retreated to my room and laid on the floor staring at the bookshelf. The names of Nietzsche, Shakespeare, Kafka, Dowd, Twain, Joyce, Morrison, Salinger, Fitzgerald, and the Holy Bible stared back at me. It was this moment I knew. I wish to write, to write well. I wish to write in a style expressing my individuality while simultaneously helping shape the individuality and identity of another. My work would not be sold at Barnes and Noble. I would not discuss it on Imus. I am not sure if I would even sign it. Rather, my dream is not one of fame, fortune, or defying the laws of classical physics, but to merely fulfill myself while helping to inspire meaning and substance in the lives of others.

© Christine Nealy, 1998

Commentary on "I Wish to Write"

You may use the space below to discuss the merits of this essay. What characteristics or adjectives does the essay portray without actually mentioning them? What are its overall tone and style?

_____

_____

_____

_____

_____

My Thoughts on "I Wish to Write"

This essay was written by a former student of mine. More than just talking about her love of reading and her skill with the pen, she chose to demonstrate her writing abilities in a beautifully crafted and highly creative essay. We understand immediately where her inspiration comes from: the many books she has read play a profound role in the way she thinks and feels, and when she says she wants to write, we have no doubt she will eventually succeed. In fact, she already seems to be on her way, relating to the great writers of the past as though they were fellow thinkers and discussion-partners. Although this essay was initially written for Princeton, the author ended up attending Holy Cross, where her writing career is currently thriving.

Night

For the same Princeton application, the above author wrote the following compelling essay on a book that had influenced her. I have included it because it is an excellent answer to a type of question that appears on many college applications. When answering this type of question, remember to:

- Stick to the book at hand.

- Cite specific passages and respond to them critically and analytically.

- Comment on how and why those passages have been meaningful to you personally.

- Conclude with a statement or two about what you plan on doing with the knowledge gained from reading this book or how the book has influenced or changed you.

Question: What book that you've read in the past couple of years left the greatest impression on you? Explain why.

In *Night*, Elie Weisel recounts his struggle for survival as a concentration camp prisoner during the Holocaust. At the opening of the novel, Weisel and his family lived as the typical Jewish-Hungarian family. They minded their own business and resided peacefully among their fellow townspeople. As the story line progresses, and Nazi power increases, basic rights Weisel and his family once took for granted were now, at best, privileges. Forced to stay inside their homes during certain hours of the day and adhere to a strict curfew degraded them not only to second-class citizens, but likened their position in society to animals held in captivity. Inevitably, Weisel is separated from his family, taken from his home in Hungary, and deported to Auschwitz. Upon arrival, Weisel and his father are forced to work as slaves and to wallow in their own filth. Weisel's graphic and horrific description of life inside the camps is nothing short of grotesque and disturbing. I could not comprehend or even imagine the sense of both anguish and desperation that the prisoners must have felt. At times, feelings of nausea, shock and disgust would be so overwhelming that I could barely continue to read.

After closing the book, the feelings would be assuaged only then to be changed into an overbearing sense of compunction. As a reader and human being, I owed to all those who perished and to those who suffered and survived, the sacrifice of my own comfort and read on. Near the close of the novel, Weisel, his father, and multitudinous camp refugees are forced to seek asylum in a shed. Weisel meets an old friend, Juliek, who has with him his violin. Weisel recounts, "The sound of a violin, in this dark shed, where the bodies of the dead were heaped upon the living . . . I could only hear the violin and it was as though Juliek's soul were the bow . . . He played as he would never play again." Indeed, he did not. Weisel woke up the next morning to see Juliek dead and "his violin smashed, trampled." Weisel clung to every breath as Juliek played each note, the two united in their quest for survival.

Shared experiences often bring out an intangible and indestructible bond between human beings. Weisel's incomprehensible strength was exhibited not only when things seemed at their bleakest, but when the everyday became intensely perplexing. "Yom Kippur. . . . to fast would mean a surer, swifter death. We fasted here the whole year round. The whole year was Yom Kippur." Eli's attempt to make light of this life or death conundrum exemplifies the perseverance of his sanity in the face of mass destruction. Throughout the novel, Elie, while concerned with his own survival, was primarily focused on the well-being of his father, always placing him out of harm's way. Elie even remained with him for several hours on the eve of his death.

I now fully understand the precarious nature of life. I consume each day and attempt to live without regrets. A new awareness of the miniature holocausts plagues my mind. Ethnic cleansing in Bosnia, tribal warfare between the Hutus and the Tutsis, the dilapidated condition of race relations in America, and the plight of the quality of inner-city life for urban youth, prompt me to change various injustices around me. I am working to start an extension of Amnesty International at my high school. One day I hope to join an organization such as UNICEF or the Peace Corps. Perhaps my contributions toward ending violence and hatred by educating others will impact another to do the same.

© Christine Nealy, 1998

Commentary on "Night"

You may use the space below to discuss the merits of this essay. How does the author relate the events in the book to the events in her life?

_____

_____

_____

_____

_____

_____

My Thoughts on "Night"

This is an excellent interpretive essay. Certainly the subject matter of the Holocaust is a tricky one—and her conclusions risk falling into the "avoid talking about world peace" category—but ultimately the author handles her interpretation of Weisel's moving text with care and intelligence. This essay tells me she is clearly capable of contributing to a college-level discussion. It also displays her passion for humanitarian causes, indicating a direction she might take once she gets to college. But it is ultimately her ability to draw conclusions of universal importance from Weisel's work that makes this essay so memorable.

A Typical Freshman Day at the University of Pennsylvania

Question: What characteristics of Penn, and yourself, make the University a particularly good match for you? Briefly describe how you envision your first year in college. How will your presence be known on campus?

Leaving Professor Poggi's course, Twentieth-Century Art: 1900–1945, on a cool fall morning, I envision an independent study next semester focusing on World War I and its influences on art. After speaking with Professor Poggi, we agree I should take Professor Bokovoy's course, Twentieth-Century American Culture, because it will help me with my research concerning cultural influences on art during the early 1900s. Both professors' courses will allow me to link two of my favorite subjects, art and history. I know I will have dialogues through e-mail with Professor Poggi and Professor Bokovoy discussing how World War I shaped art in the 1920s. Both professors told me they would assist me in determining the locations for primary sources and meeting other knowledgeable professors at the University of Pennsylvania.

Later in the day, I visit the Institute of Contemporary Art and confirm my internship in the Education Department for next semester. I know the paintings there will provide the basis for part of my research. In addition, the university's urban setting allows me to go to many museums on a regular basis.

I have asked my professors about arranging more art-related community service activities on and off campus like I did in high school. Last week, I organized a Cubist Day and invited a guest speaker from a nearby museum to speak about Picasso's influences on art in the twenty-first century. This was similar to many of my high school activities with the National Art Honor Society. I provide information about art, such as museum exhibitions or gallery openings to Penn students through an interactive website that I personally designed. I know I will have to retain my excellent time management skills because in addition to my schoolwork, I am a member of the Artist Guild and DART. I also joined the Skydiving Club, much to my parents' chagrin. But hey, you're only young once.

After I return from the museum, I head straight to the library to do research on a paper analyzing Ionesco's *Rhinoceros* due in a few weeks. A few hours later, in the early evening, I recruit classmates for my new community-wide art club. Having received permission from the University of Pennsylvania, the School District of Philadelphia, and the Philadelphia Federation of Teachers, we assist in the development of the new PreK-8 University-assisted public school in West Philadelphia. We enjoy painting murals in the school and at the playgrounds, and holding art classes after school for the students. I have asked local businesses to donate supplies, in addition to organizing our own fund-raising events.

Finally to relax, I meet my friends at a nearby coffee shop to have dinner and discuss Saturday's amazing Penn-Princeton football game.

© Anonymous, 2000

Commentary on "A Typical Freshman Day . . ."

You may use the space below to discuss the merits of this essay. What characteristics or adjectives does the essay portray without actually mentioning them? How does this student's campus research pay off?

―――――――――――――――――――――――――――――――

―――――――――――――――――――――――――――――――

―――――――――――――――――――――――――――――――

―――――――――――――――――――――――――――――――

―――――――――――――――――――――――――――――――

My Thoughts on "A Typical Freshman Day . . ."

This essay was written for the University of Pennsylvania. I have chosen to include it because its question—"Why this school?"—is typical of many college applications and interview situations. The answer is a particularly good one because we gain an immediate awareness of all the research the author has done on Penn. It is easy to envision him discussing art in a college-level class, participating in campus life, and contributing to the surrounding community. This is a superb result of what happens when you follow my suggestions for "imagining you're there" (see Chapter 5). We understand immediately where this student's interests lie and glimpse the ways in which he will be an enthusiastic member of a college community. Again, a little hard work early on in the process has paid great dividends: this student was admitted early decision to the University of Pennsylvania.

Reading

Question: You are about to begin reading Italo Calvino's new novel, *If on a winter's night a traveler*. Relax. Concentrate. Dispel every other thought. Let the world around you fade. Best to close the door; the TV is always on in the next room. Tell the others right away, "No I don't want to watch TV!" Raise your voice—they won't hear you otherwise—"I'm reading! I don't want to be disturbed!" Maybe they haven't heard you, with all that racket; speak louder, yell: "I'm beginning to read Italo Calvino's new novel!" Or if you prefer, don't say anything; just hope they'll leave you alone.

Finally, I can start reading. As I turn the first page, I remember that my English paper is due the first week of December, and I need to gather my secondary sources. In the background, despite my pleas, I can hear the television's volume rising. I storm into the den, across the hall, "Can you guys please keep it down? I'm trying to read!" I shout. "Joey, it's not that loud," my sister happily adds. "Sure, we'll make it lower," my parents quickly say, not wanting to miss a word of their TV program. *Don't they understand that I'm reading a new novel?* I lie back down on my bed and continue to read. "Adjust the light so you won't strain your eyes. Do it now, because once you're absorbed in reading there will be no budging you."

I heed the book's suggestion and settle my reading light over my shoulder just enough to keep out the shadows. I follow Calvino's assumption of what I probably did in the bookstore like Calvino's hypothetical book-buyer scanning the shelves of the bookstore. As I rub my eye, I gaze up at the shelves above my desk filled with books I've read and some I've been planning to read. Kafka's *The Meta-morphosis* attracts my eye because of its golden cover. I lift my legs and arms and try to feel like Gregor for a moment, alien to the rest of my family in the other room. Rocking back and forth on my back, my "bug" eyes notice *Madame Bovary* by Gustave Flaubert resting comfortably next to Harper Lee's *To Kill a Mockingbird. To Kill a Mockingbird* is the only book that always makes me rethink my value system and the society in which I live every time I read it. As if its title is drooping, a sorrowful *Pride and Prejudice* stares at me, pleading to be read. I relax and metamorphose back into a high school senior, worrying about college admissions but still aspiring to become a true academic scholar, and the Robertson family's academic recluse.

I continue reading to the middle of chapter three of *If on a winter's night a traveler*, but stop because of uproarious laughter from the den. I stand up to open the door, and listen to my parents and sister guffawing; it must be another Thursday night sitcom. Apparently, they take "must see TV" literally. I crawl back into bed hoping the noise will abate, as I try to ingest chapter three. The main reader in the novel goes to a university searching for answers to one of the stories, making me think of my own future quests for knowledge. In college, I want to discuss with my professors great works of literature and examine topics as arcane as the influence of the Cimmerian language on plot.

As I finally finish chapter three, I have a revelation about the novel: "one thing is immediately clear to you: namely that this book has nothing in common with the one you had begun." I have just set off on a literary adventure. In the middle of *Without fear of wind or vertigo,* I stop and reread a line: "in a distress that lasts an instant, I seem to be feeling what she feels: that every void continues in the void, every gap, even a short one, opens into another gap, every chasm empties into the infinite abyss." I often reread passages from books. I close my eyes and envision a deep ravine emptying into a large crevasse, attempting to imagine what the author is describing.

As I am sinking into the mattress, my dream is abruptly cut short by the "Friends" theme song; I trudge into the den, hopefully for the last time, to plead for serenity.

© Anonymous, 2000

Commentary on "Reading"

You may use the space below to discuss the merits of this essay. What characteristics or adjectives does the essay portray without actually mentioning them? What are its overall style and tone?

_____

_____

_____

_____

_____

_____

My Thoughts on "Reading"

This essay was written in answer to an Amherst College essay question, one of the least answered essay questions, because it requires the student to read a book. This can be a great choice, however, because it shows an admissions officer that you are eager to learn, unafraid to challenge yourself, and truly interested in their school. One of the great things about this particular essay is its tone. It adopts and mimics the language of both the question and the novel. It also gives us a creative and lively view into the author's family dynamics. This student was admitted early decision to the University of Pennsylvania and therefore withdrew his application to Amherst.

Dynamic Figure

Question: In order for the admissions staff of our college to get to know you, the applicant, better, we ask that you answer the following question: Are there any significant experiences or accomplishments you have had that have helped to define you as a person?

I am a dynamic figure, often seen scaling walls and crushing ice. I have been known to remodel train stations on my lunch breaks, making them more efficient in the area of heat retention. I translate ethnic slurs for Cuban refugees, I write award-winning operas, I manage time efficiently. Occasionally, I tread water for three days in a row. I woo women with my sensuous and god-like trombone playing, I can pilot bicycles up severe inclines with unflagging speed, and I cook Thirty-Minute Brownies in twenty minutes. I am an expert in stucco, a veteran in love, and an outlaw in Peru.

Using only a hoe and a large glass of water, I once single-handedly defended a small village in the Amazon Basin from a horde of ferocious army ants. I play bluegrass cello, I was scouted by the Mets, I am the subject of numerous documentaries. When I'm bored, I build large suspension bridges in my yard. I enjoy urban hang gliding. On Wednesdays, after school, I repair electrical appliances free of charge. I am an abstract artist, a concrete analyst, and a ruthless bookie. Critics worldwide swoon over my original line of corduroy evening wear. I don't perspire. I am a private citizen, yet I receive fan mail. I have been caller number nine and have won the weekend passes. Last summer I toured New Jersey with a traveling centrifugal-force demonstration. I bat 400. My deft floral arrangements have earned me fame in international botany circles. Children trust me.

I can hurl tennis rackets at small moving objects with deadly accuracy. I once read *Paradise Lost, Moby Dick*, and *David Copperfield* in one day and still had time to refurbish an entire dining room that evening. I know the exact location of every food item in the supermarket. I have performed several covert operations for the CIA. I sleep once a week; when I do sleep, I sleep in a chair. While on vacation in Canada, I successfully negotiated with a group of separatist terrorists who had seized a small bakery. The laws of physics do not apply to me. I balance, I weave, I dodge, I frolic, and my bills are all paid. On weekends, to let off steam, I participate in full-contact origami. Years ago I discovered the meaning of life but forgot to write it down. I have made extraordinary four-course meals using only a mouli and a toaster oven. I breed prize-winning clams. I have won bullfights in San Juan, cliff-diving competitions in Sri Lanka, and spelling bees at the Kremlin. I have played Hamlet, I have performed open-heart surgery, and I have spoken with Elvis.

But I have not yet gone to college.

© Anonymous

Commentary on "Dynamic Figure"

You may use the space below to discuss the merits of this essay. What characteristics or adjectives does the essay portray without actually mentioning them? What are its overall style and tone?

_____

_____

_____

_____

My Thoughts on "Dynamic Figure"

This is one of the better known essays to have made the rounds on the Internet, because it takes significant risks by trying to be smart and funny. You should not attempt to copy this style, because every admissions officer has read this. Nevertheless, I have chosen to include the essay because of its unique approach to the question. It is clearly meant to poke fun at the entire application/brag sheet/"show don't tell" process. It also offers admissions readers who may have spent hundreds of hours sifting through tedious lists of identical achievements a little levity. Again, I do not recommend going this far afield—the danger that you will not be funny is too great. Nonetheless, there is a certain brilliance at work here, one that evidently made an admissions officer stand up and take notice. Clearly the author is a gifted writer and perhaps that talent alone got him into college. I would suggest using it as an example of humorous writing, and nothing more.

Ski Bum

Warning: The following essay serves as an example of what *not to do*. Afterward, in the "Commentary" section, you will have a chance to critique it based on what you have learned so far about essay writing.

Question: Ask, and then answer, an important question you would have liked us to ask.

"How have your summer experiences changed who you are?"

These past two summers, I have been lucky enough to attend summer programs in both France and Switzerland. Seeing Paris at sunset from the top of the Eiffel Tower and skiing down a double black diamond run on a Swiss glacier in the middle of July are definitely some of my best memories. But what I got most out of those programs was the experience of being removed from my home, and my country, and placed in a completely different environment. I was immersed in a different language, different food, and most importantly, different people. In Switzerland, for the first time in my life, I was thrown into a dormitory situation with a hundred teenagers where 30 percent were American and maybe 50 percent spoke English. As for my two roommates, one was Palestinian, and the other was from Kazakhstan. At the time, I had no idea where Kazakhstan was and he didn't know enough English so that I could ask him. I experienced many new things in Europe and learned a lot too.

What remains from those trips is about fifteen close friends. Some of those friends that I met live as close as just a few minutes by car and others live five thousand miles away. Needless to say, I don't see most of them too often and I don't even speak with them much. I have kept in contact with them by writing letters every so often. This experience of keeping in contact with so many people has been particularly rewarding for me. I know some of those friends as well as even some of my best friends here, which I see daily. Now that almost everyone has access to the internet, I could communicate with them every day if I wanted to.

When the program in Switzerland ended, I never would have thought that I would still know some of them today. I still love receiving an actual letter from someone and feel confident that I will know at least a few of them ten years from now.

© Anonymous, 1997

Commentary on "Ski Bum"

The student who wrote this essay was a legacy at an Ivy League school. He went to a competitive private high school with a history of sending students to Ivy League schools. He got mainly B's and his SAT I scores were in the upper 1400s. He was rejected from the school. Why?

_____

_____

_____

_____

_____

_____

My Thoughts on "Ski Bum"

I would explain the failure of this essay by looking first and foremost at the question the student chose to ask himself. It is utterly uncreative. If the admissions committee had wanted to ask this question, they would have included it in the short-answer essay section, not as the major personal essay. Moreover, the writing never moves beyond the superficial—there doesn't seem to be anything especially inspirational or transformational about this student's experience in Europe. In addition, a certain immaturity is conveyed in the subject matter as well—to say one is "immersed" in a different culture simply because one is living in a different culture is redundant and not particularly informative. Finally, the student comes off as lazy and unresponsive, admitting that he could communicate with his friends if he wanted to, but chooses not to. Based on this essay alone, I would say this student lacks inner voice and spirit, making him an undesirable candidate for selective college admission.

What he also lacks is any clear sense of the personal and/or philosophical importance of his experience in Europe. For instance, for my own college essay, I chose to use a central motif—my camera—to unite the personal and philosophical by bringing together the various experiences and impressions I had the summer of 1984, when I attended the Olympic Games in Los Angles and lived in Argentina. I tried to paint a clear picture of who I was at the time, how I thought about what I encountered, and what I was feeling as I photographed the Olympics and people and places in Argentina. But I also tried to offer a commentary on the function of the camera—its role in "capturing" moments, in both distancing its subjects and bringing them closer. In other words, I tried to make it both personal and philosophical. That is, I believe, a great strategy for coming up with both a topic and a tone that are sure to grab the attention of your readers.

This reminds me of another essay writing experience I went through recently with one of my students. This student had wanted to write about a number of different experiences, none of which had any immediate relationship to the others. We contemplated focusing on a single episode, but she was reluctant to give any of them up. Finally she happened to mention that she couldn't believe she was still wearing the same pair of shoes she had been wearing during so many of the experiences in question. Eureka! She decided to write her essay about this pair of shoes, to chart their changing appearance as she progressed through her life experiences. This unifying object gave the essay a definite structure and strengthened its thematic backbone. If you can find this thematic structure early on, the rest of the essay will fall into place.

SUMMARY

The personal essay is an extremely important part of the college application. A good essay can make the applicant come alive in the mind of the evaluator, transforming a candidate from a series of numbers and statistics into a living, breathing human being. By reflecting carefully on the transformative people, places and events in your life, you can arrive at an essay topic that is specific in detail yet universal in theme, attention-grabbing in tone yet methodical in structure. The secret is to make it a story, one that reads dramatically and with a solid, clear structure. It should communicate the five most important characteristics of your personality (see pp. 137–138) without mentioning them directly. By reading a number of sample college essays, you can better acquaint yourself with the strategies that have worked for former applicants. But do not be tempted to plagiarize or seek too much outside counsel. Ultimately, colleges are looking to hear your unique voice, not that of your parents, your counselor, or another student. Write from the truth of your experiences and people will want to read what you have written. Create a lively, probing, and well-structured portrait of who you are as a person, and you will be one step closer to getting into the college of your dreams.

INSIDER TIPS

Consider the following tips as you sit down to write your personal essay.

✓ Write a story. Avoid listing all your brag sheet activities. Colleges want to hear a personal story about a moment that was meaningful to you. How did it change you? What did you learn? How is it *so* you?

✓ Show, don't tell. Try to evoke your personality and character without actually stating your specific attributes.

✓ Do not delay. Begin writing at least a month before the application is due. Write multiple drafts and edit them carefully.

✓ Revise. Double-space your first draft, even if it's handwritten. This will allow room for revisions.

✓ Share your work. Read your draft out loud to someone and make sure each sentence is clearly written and properly punctuated. Put your draft aside for twenty-four hours and then read it again.

✓ Proofread. Make an appointment with your English teacher for proofreading. Allow him or her to edit for typographical errors that you might have missed.

✓ Present tense. Even if you are writing about a past experience, try using the present tense, which will make your readers witnesses of the action.

✓ Beware of humor. Only use it if you are truly funny. There's nothing worse than being the only one who laughs at your own jokes.

✓ Keep it short. When I was a reader at Yale, I was advised to spend no more than twenty minutes on an entire application folder.

✓ Follow directions. If an application allows for *one* extra sheet of paper beyond the given space, make sure you attach only one page. In addition to everything else, the application is a test of your ability to complete an application. Follow directions and pass the test.

9

GETTING GLOWING LETTERS OF RECOMMENDATION

MYTHS AND TRUTHS

MYTH: Getting a well-known personality or your father's influential friend to write a letter on your behalf can significantly boost your admissions profile.

TRUTH: Any recommendation from a writer who doesn't know you well can actually work against you. Stick to people who know you well and can address your particular strengths, both academic and extracurricular.

MYTH: You want to get recommendations from teachers who have given you A's, even if they were easy A's.

TRUTH: Not necessarily. You want to get recommendations from those teachers who know you best. Hopefully, you also did well in their classes.

MYTH: You only need to meet with your high school college counselor the couple of times he or she requires it.

TRUTH: In order to stand out from the crowd of students who throng your high school's college counseling office, you must develop a strong relationship with your counselor by visiting as often as you can, supplying him or her with evidence of your achievements, and relaying any salient anecdotes that might provide invaluable insight into your character.

MYTH: Writing recommendations is part of a teacher's job, so they'll do it well no matter what—why else do we pay them?

TRUTH: Teachers are by no means required to write letters of recommendation. You must take time to cultivate your relationships with them and make their lives easy by getting them everything they need in a timely and orderly fashion, and thanking them wholeheartedly for their time and effort.

LETTERS OF RECOMMENDATION

Most selective colleges require one to three letters of recommendation to accompany your college application: usually two from teachers and one from your high school college counselor. Some students, however, choose to include extra letters of recommendation from mentors and associates such as coaches or employers. Above all, letters should come from people who know you well, particularly as a student. The truth is, colleges place a lot of importance on these letters, especially the teacher recommendations, as your teachers often spend more time with you than your own parents and are the representatives of the adult world who know you best as a student. Colleges therefore trust them to give an honest and clear picture of who you are. Bad recommendations can seriously hinder your chances of gaining admission to the college of your choice. Beware, however, that letters from noted individuals, family friends, or generous alumni seldom mean anything unless you have worked closely with them over time. If they are only endorsing your application with bland praise and the prestige of their name, it can actually work against you. Too many references only add to the weight of the folder and reduce the enthusiasm of the admissions officer to look at it objectively. As with the length of your personal essay, you should always be mindful of the admissions officer reading your application. What would you want to read in the short time allotted to each application?

HELP YOUR TEACHERS

It is important to select your teacher recommendation writers carefully and properly, asking them ahead of time if they will write on your behalf, providing them with the proper forms in a timely manner, and including a stamped, addressed envelope. Eleventh-grade teachers are good people to approach first. Whomever you choose, it is essential to ask a teacher who knows you well, perhaps someone who has taught you over several years or who knows you in multiple capacities such as a longtime teacher who is also faculty advisor to the debate team you are captain of. Beware of the teacher who hastily gives you an A but has no real idea who you are—his recommendation will necessarily sound generic. This is yet another reason to cultivate good relationships with teachers as early in high school as you can!

The more you speak up in class and the more you get involved in all aspects of high school life, the better chance you have of getting great teachers to write glowing recommendations on your behalf. Arrive to class on time; do all of the required assignments as well as extra work; be polite and helpful to your peers; participate often without taking over the class; go to your teachers during office hours; get to know them and let them get to know you—all of these strategies are very effective when it comes to shoring up support for your application. If you have done your job well, your teachers will actually volunteer to write letters for you. It is also a good idea to request your recommendations from one teacher in the humanities and one in math or science since colleges like to see you have proven yourself in a broad array of academic areas and developed strong ties to teachers in various disciplines.

You should make it clear to your teachers and your high school college counselor that you are waiving your right to see their work. Very few students actually ask to see their teacher recommendations before they go out; the teachers usually send them directly to the college admissions offices in the envelopes you provide. Requesting to see their letters can put your teachers in an awkward position, potentially curtailing their creativity and honesty. Students also tend to harp on even the smallest bit of criticism if they happen to find any in a teacher recommendation. Just remember that nobody is perfect. If your teachers were to say you were, the admissions committees would not believe them. Put it this way: if you are worried enough about a certain teacher to want to see the letter before it's sent out, then you should probably not be asking that teacher for a letter of recommendation in the first place.

One essential difference between teachers and college counselors is that college counselors are required to write letters of recommendation for every one of their college-bound seniors while teachers have the option to refuse. If a teacher tells you that she does not have time to write a letter, she might be politely telling you that she is not the best person to sing your praises honestly and wholeheartedly. If a teacher appears reluctant to write you a letter, do not insist on it. Find someone else, someone who knows you well, someone who can really go to bat for you.

As they are constantly telling you, teachers are very busy and will be happier to deal with all your applications at once rather than piecemeal and/or late. You may want to give them a copy of your brag sheet along with a copy of the best project, paper, or assignment you did in their class. To ensure that recommendations are written and sent off in good time, I recommend that you label each form clearly with the due date, include addressed stamped envelopes, and request that your teachers get a proof of mailing from the post office in case any letters get lost in the mail. Also, be sure to write your teachers thank-you notes for their time and effort—remember, they are *not* required to write letters of recommendation. Because your college counselor is required to write a letter on your behalf, it is a good idea to get to know your counselor well. Set up extra meetings with your counselor and inform him or her about what you are doing with yourself both in and out of school. You might even want to present your counselor with your answers to some of the question-naires in this book. That way they have your strengths, weaknesses, achievements, and aspirations gathered together in one convenient format. It is easier for a counselor to write a good letter about someone he knows than someone he has met with only once or twice.

NOTES FOR TEACHERS AND COUNSELORS

I have found that in some cases teachers and counselors are open to suggestions as to the format and style of the recommendation letter—they may have fifty or more letters to write and any extra information you can provide might lighten their task. In addition, new and/or foreign teachers may not be aware of the requirements of the recommendation letter. If that seems to be the case, you may want to approach them and ask if they would be open to receiving some of the following advice. If they say yes, you might find it helpful to photocopy the next few pages and turn them in with your request for a recommendation. Of course, many colleges and universities will give more specific guidelines as to what they expect in the letters of recommendation and you should always follow their rules and formats first.

1. Introduce yourself at the beginning of your recommendation letter. State the subject you teach, the duration of instruction in that subject, and the duration of instruction of the student in question.

2. Discuss the student's distinguishing or unusual intellectual traits (positive and/or negative), such as reasoning ability, curiosity, creativity, or extra effort. What was the significance of the student's involvement in classroom discussion? What was his/her impact on the intellectual life of the classroom?

3. Comment on the contribution of the student to the class in terms of effort, interest, responsibility, and reliability.

4. Cite evidence of accomplishments, special talents, creativity, or leadership in academic area(s).

5. Discuss distinguishing or unusual personality traits other than intellectual (positive and/or negative), such as character, morality, integrity, that go to make up the kind of person he or she is.

6. Cite evidence of accomplishments, special talents, creativity, or leadership in nonacademic area(s); include awards, honors, and volunteer work. Out-

side jobs are especially useful if they reinforce student maturity, responsibility, or are supplementary to a student's field of study.

7. Discuss unusual circumstances, background data, obstacles that have been overcome, linguistic and cultural factors that contributed to or inhibited the student's performance in your class, or other information regarding this student.

8. As you may have to write many letters of recommendation at once, try to vary your style and word choice to avoid sounding prerecorded.

9. For the less able student whom you nonetheless wish to support, diplomatic wording of his or her weaknesses and/or areas for improvement is essential. Anything negative can always be made into a positive by stressing that the student is actively engaged in the processes of learning and growing.

10. Try to give an indication as to the student's overall character.

11. Try to make the student stand out. Keep in mind that good colleges have many highly qualified applicants with similar profiles of accomplishment and distinction. They will choose the candidate who has reached beyond the usual, the typical, the expected, the one who has demonstrated real initiative, independence, tenacity, or growth. It is your job to convey any areas in which you believe the student truly stands out.

12. Strive for a direct and concise letter of approximately one page. There is no need to overburden the readers with redundant praise.

13. Consider quoting directly from the student. This makes the candidate come alive in the mind of the reader.

14. Give examples rather than lists of adjectives. If the student demonstrates a particular characteristic, provide a story that illustrates it in action. Admissions officers always prefer a good story.

SAMPLE TEACHER RECOMMENDATIONS

Your teachers may also find it useful to look through the following examples of particularly good recommendation letters.

Letter 1

I have been a teacher of U.S. History for over twenty-five years and never have I encountered a student with as much verve, dynamism, intellectual curiosity, and willingness to tackle the deeper issues of history as Amanda Decker. I can vividly recall the first day she came into my classroom for what many students consider to be the most grueling class they will face in their junior year. She wore her signature orange sweater and purple pants, her clothes lighting up the room the way her mind would light up our discussion all year long. It was no surprise when she ventured the first answer to my lead-in question about the Constitution. She eloquently argued that our founding fathers' true legacy was right here in our very classroom, "where we are free to discuss ideas without fear of being censored—it's such a privilege."

To say I thoroughly enjoyed the opportunity to work with Amanda would be an understatement. I will deeply miss her contributions to our classroom discussion and I know her fellow students will miss her as well. Amanda never ceased to amaze me with her willingness to help others through the more challenging aspects of our historical material, always ready with an encouraging smile and an insightful question. In our mock presidential debates, her fellow students awarded her the "Spirit of Thomas Jefferson Award" for her love of learning, her eloquence in speech-making, and her defense of democratic principles—characteristics she demonstrates outside the classroom as well where Amanda is co-president of our High School Debate Team, of which I am faculty sponsor. I have seldom seen such a poised, considerate, unflinching young woman in my many years with the team. Her performance in our "High School Violence" debate earned her an academic gold star and she dramatically carried the team to victory in the final round of debating.

To think that Amanda has done all this while suffering through the divorce of her parents is truly incredible. The compassion she shows others remains undaunted by the difficulties of her home life, where she must literally care for two younger brothers and an infant sister during this time of turmoil. Her grades dipped slightly in the middle of the semester as the divorce took its toll, scoring uncharacteristically low on her first semester final paper, a study of the root economic causes of the Civil War. By the middle of our second semester (the course I teach lasts the entire junior year), Amanda was back on top. Her test scores were consistently high and her writing returned to its normal clarity, grace and logic. She has consistently demonstrated an enviable ability to observe historical facts, arrive at a conclusion, and support that conclusion with accurate, historical speculation. Never have these skills been more present than in her final research paper analyzing the countercultural revolution of the sixties in relation to American foreign policy in Southeast Asia. At my urging, she submitted this research paper to the *Concord Review* for which I am proud to say she was awarded a Ralph Waldo Emerson Prize in history.

Amanda's success is a reflection of her commitment to excellence, her solid work ethic, and her bold intellectual drive. Along with her natural compassion, her sensitivity to the nuances of both her fellow students and the historical material at hand, these traits will make her an outstanding college student wherever she chooses to go. Amanda has demonstrated over and over that she cares deeply about her academic success and her personal growth, and I am proud to be able to offer her my highest recommendation. A student like this comes around only once.

Regards, etc.,

Letter 2

I want you to know right off the bat that I unequivocally support William Smithers in whatever he chooses to do. I even offered to write this letter of recommendation on his behalf before he had the opportunity to ask me. That is the kind of student William is. That is the kind of person he is too.

I have taught American Literature for the past twelve years and rarely in my career have I had the privilege of meeting an intellectual equal in the mind of a student. William's intellectual apparatus is entirely in place—now he just needs to indulge his passion for reading and gain more knowledge. I predict—if I may be so bold—that he will make a fine professor some day.

Wheelchair bound since birth, William had to learn at a young age that life is mutable and that setting your own priorities and goals is of the utmost importance. He does this miraculously well. He is curious, creative, and independent in his learning, but does not work hard for grades alone. I can remember an incident during my Nineteenth-Century American Literature course when William came up with a strikingly courageous interpretation of a Melville short story. The other students in the class were clearly spellbound, yet confused. I could tell that because of his disability, no one felt comfortable questioning his words. Finally, one of my braver students ventured a comment. Silence. Then a smile broke out on William's face and he said, "My gosh, you're right. What I just said was completely unfounded. Let me try to back it up." In the course of his attempt to self-analyze what he had just come up with, we were all privy to one of the more outstanding extemporaneous expositions of a text that I have ever heard. What honest probing. What willingness to put himself on the line. What humor.

Whether in the classroom or in the editing room of our high school's literary journal, William's thoughtful, engaging intellect is always just a microsecond away. His essay on Hawthorne last year gave clear voice to the Puritan heart and the transcendental head of a conflicted writer. Both intuitive and concise, it was a writer's view of another writer. This is what makes him such a great leader on the editorial staff of the journal as well. He immediately senses what needs to be done to bring out the crux of an otherwise jumbled short story or poem. It's just too bad more students don't submit their work to the journal, as everyone could benefit from William's level-headed yet passionate readings. Early in the year, I was already so astonished at the sensitive style and thought of this assertive young man, that I initiated a peer referral program in my classroom whereby students are required to read each other's work and critique it before submitting it to me. I thank William for the great results this exercise has produced.

As a person, I adore William. His myriad conflicting parts fit together into a complex and delightful whole. He loves fairness and justice and loyalty in himself and others, and is often called on by his peers to mediate an argument or discussion. He is ingenious and ingenuous at the same time. He makes mistakes and says, "I'm sorry" so openly and earnestly that there is no question of intent, thus motivating others to be as self-aware as he is. Despite his handicap, William is seen by his peers as a leader, full of fun and good humor, but serious and committed when the going gets rough. He leads by example and is the first to begin when work is needed. William has an integrity that belies his age and I know he will make an excellent contribution to even the most rigorous postsecondary institution. I recommend William Smithers wholeheartedly—he is well worth all that we can do for him.

Sincerely, etc.,

In contrast to the previous examples, the following teacher recommendation is an example of what *not* to do. First of all, it is suspiciously short and nothing distinguishes this student from his peers. Although no disparaging words are used, the recommendation does not praise the student either. Clearly, the teacher does not feel confident about recommending this student or perhaps the teacher was coerced into writing the letter or was simply too polite to refuse the request. Ultimately the student should have known better than to request a recommendation from someone capable of writing this.

> Robert proved to be a good student, with an appropriate appreciation for the subject. He functioned well in the context of the group, and seemed to take advantage of the opportunities presented to him in the group.

SAMPLE COLLEGE COUNSELOR LETTERS[1]

Your college counselor may find it useful to look over the following examples of excellent college counselor recommendations.

Letter 1

It is with the greatest pleasure that I write this letter of recommendation for Abby. As an educator for twenty-four years, I have encountered thousands of students who vary in every way possible; physical appearance, temperament, intelligence, goals, motivation, etc. I can truly say that never before in my career have I encountered a student like Abby. She is, by far, the most intellectually gifted and at the same time so incredibly unaffected, insightful, truly genuine student I have ever worked with. I have to constantly remind myself that she is a teenager, a high school student.

I first met Abby when she enrolled here in the fall of her junior year. We discussed her courses, educational plans and goals, and the best way we could meet her needs. To say she is extremely bright is an understatement. What makes Abby so unusual is the combination of her brilliance and her character, her ravenous appetite for knowledge and her humility, her genuine appreciation for learning and her genuine desire to give of herself to others. As I discussed possible college-level courses she could take while in high school, Abby's eyes lit up more and more with each possibility. It was an educator's dream of ideal: to see an adolescent who wanted to learn because the subject

---

[1] These letters were written by Linda Zimring, former college counselor at Taft High School in Los Angeles, currently director for College and Gifted/Talented Programs for the Los Angeles Unified School District C. She taught one of my courses at UCLA Extension for certification in college admissions counseling and provided copies of her excellent letters for us.

sounded truly exciting, not because it would be an easy grade or the teacher was "cool."

When Abby undertakes something, be it a hobby, a project, or a competition, she gives it 100 percent—always. Her most problematic dilemma is that there are only twenty-four hours in a day. The hardest lesson she is learning is that she cannot do everything she would like to and has had to make difficult choices. She is currently in a new role as a peer college counselor with the responsibility of helping her peers through the maze and confusion of the college admission process. As I watch her work with her counselees, her level of maturity amazes me. She treats each student as if he/she were the only student in the senior class. If time were not a factor, she would spend hours working with each student. When parents call with questions, her answers are thorough and her manner is quite polished.

The one commitment Abby has made since a very early age is to her violin playing. Where most teens would be satisfied with daily practices of perhaps one hour, Abby gets upset when her time is limited to less than two hours. She has competed for many years and even considered, for a short time, a career in music. Now, she accepts that although music will always be a very central part of her life, it will be an avocation rather than a vocation.

Abby's true desire for her future is yet to be discovered. As soon as she thinks she knows what she wants to pursue, she discovers another possibility. Her insatiable thirst for learning will again be frustrated once she arrives on a college campus and finds that she cannot take ten courses each semester. I'm sure that is the kind of frustration colleges love.

Each of Abby's teachers has come to me within weeks of knowing her with raves about her abilities. All have also stated, without knowledge of the others, that she is, without a doubt, the brightest student they have ever had. Special, unique, one of a kind—these are words that don't come close to describing this remarkable young lady. I promise you that you will agree with me, should you have the privilege of meeting her.

Sincerely, etc.,

Letter 2

A typical day in the life of Mimi goes as follows: *Get up at 6:00 A.M.* and run a mile. Leave for school. After school go to tennis from 3:00 to 7:00. Come home, eat dinner, and stay up very late doing homework and studying for tests. This is how she is able to manage her time between her serious commitment to tennis and her outstanding academic performance. Somehow Mimi can accomplish in twenty-four hours what most people would need many more hours to achieve.

Since the age of ten, Mimi has played tennis. Her school coach describes her as "superb, outstanding, exceptional, dedicated, diligent, and the best of the best." Within the tennis team, Mimi assumes the leadership role and sets an excellent example for the others on the team. Her accomplishments on the team include many tournament victories and awards and the Most Valuable Player for the past three years. Outside of school, Mimi plays in many national and sectional tournaments. Her strong self-discipline has carried her to the high level she is at today.

Academically, Mimi could not have taken a more rigorous course of study throughout her years here. With only one exception, she has taken every academic class at either honors or advanced placement level. Last year she took AP history and AP chemistry and earned 4's on both exams. Her grades here, again with one exception, are straight A's. The teacher who gave her a C complained about the number of days she missed due to school tennis tournaments.

Mimi's achievements are even more amazing when one considers that she and her family are from Russia. Her sister is a national rhythmic gymnast and has been her motivation. The teachers who have had Mimi rave about her. Some of their comments are: "Mimi is determined, confident, genuine, focused, persistent . . . She has a very high level of intellectual curiosity . . . and is excited about learning . . . She has a solid sense of who she is and where she is going—an achiever."

The college she attends will be lucky to have her. Her contributions, academically, athletically, and personally, make her truly special. She is without a doubt, one of the top few individuals in our senior class. I recommend her with the greatest enthusiasm and without any reservation whatsoever for your scholarship.

Sincerely etc.,

Letter 3

I am pleased to write this letter on behalf of Jeremy, because he is a special young man who has given an inordinate amount of himself to this school. In doing so, Jeremy has paid the price. He had decisions to make about how to divide himself between all the demanding forces that pulled at him. He reached his limit this semester as he learned the true meaning of "spreading yourself too thin." But then, youth is learning experience after learning experience.

Jeremy has grown up with an ongoing family crisis—his sister's brain cancer. She has been in and out of remission and has had numerous surgeries. Each time, Jeremy is affected—emotionally. Most recently, he traveled with his parents to Atlanta, where his sister is attending college. She had her last surgery there during the fall of his junior year. (A big drop of grades is evident at that period of time.) Despite the constant gnawing of his sister's serious illness and the effect it has had on the entire family, Jeremy has tried to maintain his academic progress. At the same time, he has been involved in several significant activities at school, including speech and debate, play production, and government.

Jeremy began his involvement in student government in tenth grade when he joined sophomore steering and student senate. He was also selected as one of the student representatives in our school's Local School Leadership Council, the governing body for the entire school community. Every change in policy was discussed and decided by this group of people. The students were part of the governance for the first time in the school's history. It was a difficult position for these students, who wanted to be heard and who represented the entire student body. It was also difficult for the faculty to listen to the students as equals. Jeremy took his role as a student member appointed by the Board of Education of the Los Angeles Unified School District quite seriously and had strong feelings and opinions about the key issues they dealt with. Jeremy is not a superficial individual, rather he assumes his responsibilities with sincerity and earnestness. At times, the large number of committee and council meetings usurped much of his study time. Rather than bow out because of his academic responsibilities, Jeremy tried to do it all. Again, I repeat youth is a learning experience. Jeremy has learned that he has limits and that he can't please everyone.

Many freshmen learn the lessons Jeremy did once they begin college. Since he has passed that point in his life, he will not have those hurdles once he begins his university experience. He is a good risk—a highly capable, intelligent, bright, ambitious, personable individual who will be a vital factor on campus. He will be involved and active and will make his mark on his institution—I am confident of that. I recommend Jeremy with utmost sincerity and enthusiasm, and without reservation.

Sincerely, etc.

SAMPLE EMPLOYER RECOMMENDATION

If you choose to have an employer write a letter of recommendation on your behalf, you may want to show him or her the following example.

I heartily endorse Jane Brane's candidacy for Harvard class of 2004.

I first met Jane last summer when she worked as a summer intern at HBO headquarters in New York City. I am a producer for the HBO Family channel, and, although Jane was interning in the Original Programming department, Jane quickly became well-known, not only because she was willing to be helpful in any and every way, but because she was actually helpful. Her knowledge of film and her feel for the art form were surpassed only by her creative ability and charm, so she quickly became very popular. My colleagues and I at HBO Family were so impressed with Jane's input that, after viewing all her films, including the film that she made in the last semester of her senior year at high school, we quickly recognized Jane as a talent to be respected and taken seriously. In fact, we have chosen this film to air as part of our HBO Kid Flicks series. Jane created a wholly unique score, by collaborating with a very talented Harvard freshman.

My colleagues and I have kept up with Jane over her first semester of her senior year in high school as Jane was editing her film to fit within our program guidelines. (We will use fifteen minutes of the film and use our interview with Jane for fifteen minutes.) We have seen her use film skills in many of her classes as she finds creative ways to express her ideas as she produces class assignments.

Jane has a unique talent, deep understanding and appreciation of film, and a very refreshing perspective. She can make the ordinary quite extraordinary with her ability to see things in a unique way, and make it thought provoking and meaningful. She did this with her film and essays that won national prizes in the National Scholastic Arts and Writing Awards contest as well as with the film we chose. With such talent, most young people would want to go directly to film school and get on a fast track. Not Jane. Her goal is to get the broadest education possible, a strong foundation in the humanities. I recommend Jane to any school requiring super intelligence and a devotion to learning, unique accomplishments, someone who will one day be a great reflection of the institution and someone who will thrive in the intellectual atmosphere. I think Jane would be perfect for Harvard in these regards, and I think Harvard would be perfect for Jane.

Sincerely, etc.

SUMMARY

The letters of recommendation accompanying your application play a vital role in giving the admissions committee a sense of how you relate to both your academic and your extended communities. They are considered objective, third-person assessments of your personality and character. Ideally they will highlight the same characteristics you have been promoting in your other application materials such as your brag sheet and your personal essay. Most selective colleges require two teacher recommendations and one college counselor recommendation. To that end, it is essential that you start cultivating strong relationships with your teachers and high school college counselor early on in your high school career. The better they know you, the more substantial evidence they will be able to provide on your behalf. The harder you work in their classes, the more likely they are to write glowing recommendations. It is also imperative that you make this process as effortless as possible for your teachers and counselor by providing them with all the necessary forms and envelopes well in advance of the application deadlines. In addition, as a courtesy to your teachers and your counselor, you may want to provide them with a copy of the "Notes for Teachers and Counselors" contained in this chapter, along with some sample letters for inspiration.

INSIDER TIPS

✓ Choose wisely. Find writers who know you well and in multiple capacities, people who can really go to bat for you.

✓ Let them be. Tell your teachers and counselor you are waiving your right to see their recommendations. You do not want to put them in an awkward position, potentially curtailing their creativity and honesty.

✓ Give them evidence. Offer them copies of your transcript and brag sheet, along with the best project or paper you did for them. Help them remember the invaluable contributions you made to their class.

✓   Go the extra mile. Set up extra meetings with your teachers and counselor. Tell them everything you are doing, both in and out of school.

✓   Do not insist. If a teacher appears reluctant to write on your behalf, *do not insist*. Chances are they are politely telling you they would not be able to write the most supportive letter.

✓   Be thankful. Be sure to write your teachers thank-you notes. After all, they are *not* required to write you a letter of recommendation.

10

ACING
THE
INTERVIEW

MYTHS AND TRUTHS

MYTH: The interview is nothing more than an opportunity for the school to get to know you better.

TRUTH: The interview is also an excellent opportunity for you to get to know more about the school—so ask questions.

MYTH: It is important to dress as formally as possible and speak as "academically" as you can.

TRUTH: Dress as you would in normal life, but with extra attention to neatness and presentation. Avoid colloquialisms when you speak, but by no means make some ridiculous attempt to speak the Queen's English.

MYTH: Just answer the questions—then get out of there.

TRUTH: The interview is a two-way street. You should always "interview the interviewer," then maintain contact with him or her throughout the application process.

MYTH: You don't really need to have an interview—in fact, many schools don't even require one.

TRUTH: If you have the chance, *always* schedule an interview—and schedule it on campus if you can. This shows genuine interest on your part and allows you to make a potentially valuable contact "on the inside."

THE INTERVIEW ITSELF

The prospect can be terrifying. The previous candidate staggers out of the door, hair ruffled, clutching desperately at his stomach, and running for the bathroom. Your name is called. You exchange a final, nervous glance with the other anxious faces in the room and walk through the door. Inside, you glimpse a row of interviewers, silhouetted against bright sunlight. Your vision is blinded but for a few suspicious-looking implements of torture against the wall. Your palms sweat. Your impossibly tight collar constricts your breath. And the questions begin . . .

Sounds horrifying, right? The truth is, it doesn't have to be. By this stage in the application process, you have already given considerable thought to many of the questions that might be asked in your college interview. If you go the extra step and familiarize yourself with the interviewing strategies contained in this chapter, there is really nothing to hold you back from making a lasting, positive impression.

To begin with, I recommend you look through all the notes you have taken about each university, the questionnaires you have answered about yourself, and your personal essays. You should also reread your brag sheet and your transcript to remind yourself of the courses you have taken in high school, your extracurricular interests and your volunteer activities. Finally, you will want to recall any conversations you have had with counselors, parents, and other seniors regarding your college choices. Now there are two ways to go about it: you can arrange for an on-campus interview through the college's admissions office; or you may be asked for an alumni interview with someone in your general geographic vicinity. If you can, it is preferable to schedule an on-campus interview, as it guarantees you a chance to visit the school and makes the admissions office aware that you have done so. In addition, you will probably be granted an interview with someone from the admissions office itself. That person is likely to be a reader or some other member of the decision-making process, whereas an alumni interviewer simply makes a recommendation to the admissions committee and will not be reading your application. Either way, the interview will be conducted one-on-one without the presence of your parents.

Throughout your interview preparation, you should think carefully about the kind of image you want to portray and about the kinds of questions the interviewer is likely to ask given your background. Most important, ask yourself if there are any positive areas of your life that have not been adequately covered in the rest of your application materials. If the essay is your handshake, the interview is your personal greeting. It offers you a great opportunity to add a personal touch to your academic statistics and gives the admissions officer a chance to hear you speak in your own voice.

In my capacity as an alumni interviewer for Brown University, I cannot tell you how many times I have encountered students who do more harm than good to their applications simply because they haven't prepared adequately for the interview. These students come to see me in my office, answer a few questions, and think that's enough to get them a good write-up. They never once ask me what I do for a living; they never once ask me about Brown. If they actually took the time to look around my office, they might notice a lot of the same college admissions books they have been poring over for the last few months. Does it occur to them I might be in the college admissions business? No, because they are too nervous or bored or depressed to notice much of anything. They don't ask for my card; they don't keep in touch. Some even go so far as to admit that their counselor told them to apply to Brown, that they know nothing of its curriculum, and that they have never even visited the school. By displaying such lack of interest in my time and the school I represent, they are bound to receive a negative write-up.

In other words, if you think the interview is a one-way street with little to no bearing on your application, you are wrong. *The interview is a dialogue.* It is a chance for you to learn about the school, either from somebody who works there or from somebody who went there.

It is also a chance for you to shine. Normally, an interview will not make or break your case. Usually, it will merely reinforce the opinion the admissions committee has already formed about your application. In rare cases, however, it can actually upset your chances of getting in. I remember one student who was a legacy at the University of Pennsylvania. He had straight A's in all AP courses and over 1500 on his SAT I exam. He should have been a shoo-in. But he went to a special "legacy" on-campus interview and remained reticent. He didn't show any enthusiasm about the school, nor did he have any questions for the interviewer. He didn't relay how much he knew about the school, and didn't let them know how much he wanted to go there. They could see in his eyes and hear in his voice that he wasn't interested. According to his college counselor, he was not admitted, largely because of this poor interview.

If you spend an adequate amount of time preparing for your interview, and you show the interviewer that you take both the admissions process and the school very seriously, you have a golden chance to bolster your application and give your target colleges a vibrant sense of all the great character traits you possess. Elaborating on your answers to the following twenty preliminary questions will begin to put you in a good position to give the best impression you can—not to mention help you to avoid those pre-interview jitters!

1. What three adjectives would your best friend use to describe you? Why?

2. What have you enjoyed most about your high school years?

3. How have you changed or grown?

4. What activities have you found most satisfying?

5. What things do you do well? What are your strengths and talents?

6. Which weaknesses would you like to improve?

7. Which of your courses challenged you? How?

8. What have been your most stimulating intellectual experiences?

9. Are you satisfied with your accomplishments so far?

10. How do you respond to academic competition and pressure?

11. What would you change about your school if you had the chance?

12. What do you do for relaxation? For fun?

13. How do you define success?

14. What do you want from life?

15. How would you describe your family? Your community?

16. What issues concern you?

17. Which authors, books, or articles have had a profound effect on you?

18. Which activities or fields have you explored in depth?

19. How do you spend your summers?

20. If you could take a year off, how would you spend it?

Now that you have done some preliminary work for the interview, you should run through the suggestions below. Some of the points may seem obvious, but it's always good to have reminders since common sense can fly out the window in the heat of the moment.

INTERVIEWING GUIDELINES

Come as you are. Don't put on airs. Be relaxed. You're not chilling out with your friends, but you're not meeting the President either. Dress as you would if you were going to school or perhaps a bit more polished. Be natural. If you wear a nose-ring, for example, leave it in. Girls, there is no reason to get your hair blown out or get a French manicure. Boys, no need for blazers and ties unless this is your school uniform and you are going to the interview straight from school. Basically, be clean and presentable. Wear the style of clothing that you like and makes you feel comfortable—not necessarily what your parents would like to see you in.

Arrive early. For an on-campus interview, if you have time or are staying overnight, you may want to check exactly where the interview is taking place and how long it will take you to get there from your accommodations. A walk around campus may also inspire you with some interesting questions to ask at the end of your interview.

Leave parents at a distance. By this stage, you have had ample opportunity to discuss all you want with your parents. They will only fluster you at this point. In any case, the interviewer wants to interview you, not your parents.

Manners. Shake hands firmly with the interviewer when you enter the room. Look him or her in the eye when you speak. Try not to fidget or bite your nails. Speak in complete sentences avoiding colloquial expressions such as "like," "you know," "and what not," and "sort of." Be properly comfortable but not too casual—putting your feet on the table is a definite no-no.

Interview the interviewer. If you participate in the conversation by asking questions, it will demonstrate interest, initiative, and maturity. Everyone likes to talk about themselves, including the interviewer. It may also guide the conversation to areas where you feel most confident. But don't be pushy and don't show off, even if you think you know something the interviewer doesn't. Find out what he or she does for a living, what experience he or she has had at that university, how the university has changed since then, etc. Be as interested in them as they are in you: this is a good indication of how you will act in a college classroom setting.

First choice last. If possible, schedule your interview with your first-choice school last. This will help you gain experience before you meet with your preferred school. If this is not possible, ask a relative, teacher, or friend of the family—preferably someone whom you respect but do not know intimately—to give you a practice run-through. It is good for confidence and may raise points you have overlooked.

Don't be shy. If you are reluctant to talk about yourself, how is the interviewer supposed to get to know you? If you had a bad day, you should try to put your problems aside and come across as an upbeat person, ready to tackle anything. I once asked a student what she liked to do and she burst into tears, too embarrassed to tell me anything about herself. Getting you to talk about what you like should not be like pulling teeth. The truth is, if you are planning on attending college, it is time to get over your shyness. If you won't answer personal questions, the colleges have no way of getting to know you. If they don't get a sense of who you are, they will skip right over you. If you find you are shy in an interview, you should attempt as many mock interviews as possible with friends and family. Make them put you on the spot. Get comfortable with the process.

PREPARING FOR THE INTERVIEW

What do interviewers want to know? The phrasing, tone, style, and, of course, content of the questions will vary from interviewer to interviewer. However, you can assume that there will be a broad mixture of the direct and indirect, the formulaic and the unexpected. Remember that the main purpose of the interview is to get to know you better, and questions are just a way of breaking the ice. Interviewers essentially want to know:

- what events and experiences in your life have shaped you as an individual, have made you truly unique or special.

- to what extent you have been active in the process of your own development.

- what inspires you intellectually.

- what your major interests are.

- where you want to go from here, what you want to achieve.

- why you want to go to college and why you selected this particular college.

- what you can offer the school, and what the school can offer you (remember, it is a two-way street).

After starting the interview preparation process by answering the twenty questions on page 201, write answers to the following questions, which require more precise responses. These questions, divided into categories, will help you think about yourself and how you might express who you are to someone who does not know you. As you write out your responses, keep in mind that the interview is entirely verbal. Formulate your responses and practice saying them out loud, but don't try to memorize them. The point of the interview is to get a sense of how you think on your feet and how you perform and speak directly with another person. Also, as you answer the questions, think about the *why*s of your responses—your purpose in interviewing is to clarify your thoughts about why certain things have been significant to you, why you continue to think about them, and why they represent who you are.

Your Academic Background and High School Experience

- Tell me something about your courses.
- Which course(s) have your enjoyed the most?
- Which course(s) have you found most difficult/ challenging/ easiest?
- How did you overcome difficulties in your most challenging class?
- What kind of student have you been? How would you change your approach if you had a second opportunity?
- Do you feel that you have fulfilled your potential?
- Is your academic record an accurate gauge of your abilities and potential?
- Are there any outside circumstances that interfered with your academic performance?
- Do you like your high school? What would you have done to improve it?
- Describe the range of students at your school. Where do you place yourself?
- Do you like your teachers? Describe your favorite teacher.
- What was the most controversial issue in your school? What was your reaction to it?
- Have you been a leader in your school/community?

Extracurricular Activities

- Which of your extracurricular activities has been most satisfying?
- What is the most significant contribution you have made at your school?
- Do you have any hobbies or special interests?
- Have you worked or been a volunteer? What did you do?
- Have you ever been employed? What were your responsibilities?
- How would you have done things differently given a second opportunity?
- What do you most enjoy doing for fun? For relaxation? For stimulation?
- How do you spend a typical day after school?
- How did you spend your last few summer vacations?
- What have you done with any money you have earned?

Your Community

- How would you describe your hometown?

- Tell me how you have engaged in the life of your community?

- What has been a controversial issue in your community? What is your position on it?

College Hopes and Aspirations

It is worth giving some careful thought to the most obvious question here—"Why do you want to go to college?" Try to dig a little deeper than "I want to have a good career" or "It's just what people do." Examine your reasons carefully and formulate a genuine response. You should certainly articulate your desire for a higher education as well as your interest in being a member of a particular school's extended community.

- Why do you want to go to college?

- What do you hope to accomplish in the next four years?

- What kind of education/knowledge are you seeking?

- What interests do you want to pursue in college?

- What do you hope to major in and why?

- What self-development do you see for yourself in college?

- What are some of your criteria or considerations in choosing a college?

- Why have you chosen this particular college for admission?

- What is of most interest to you on campus?

- What other colleges are you considering?

- What do you expect to be doing seven years from now? Twelve years?

- Have you ever thought of not going to college? What would you do instead?

- Do you have any questions for us? (Always have a list of five questions prepared about the college to ask the interviewer, even if you already know the answers. Do not refer to notes, however. Remember them as best you can—that's why you've done so much research: so you will be prepared, no matter what.)

You and the World Around You

In my experience as an interviewer, I have encountered many students who knew a lot about their academic subjects but very little about the world around them. That is not acceptable. If you can't answer questions about the world at large in an actual interview situation, you will appear sheltered and uninformed. We live today in a global society and it is your duty as a college applicant—let alone as a citizen—to know about current events. Although the general nature of these questions is designed to provoke a more spontaneous response, if you keep up with current affairs and read newspapers in your spare time, you should have little problem answering them. I suggest carefully reading the newspaper every day for at least three weeks before the interview. Don't be afraid to voice your honest political opinion. You may have been told to avoid any overt expression of your political beliefs or your party affiliation, but college interviewers want to hear your opinion as a way of getting to know you better. Of course, you don't want to appear dogmatic or intolerant either, but remember: opinions are the basis of character and interviewers want to glimpse your character in action. The following list should help by giving you an indication of what to expect, keeping you from drawing a blank, as can often happen in pressure situations.

- What political or social issues should a young person be interested in?

- What do you think about: drug and alcohol use, gun control, nuclear proliferation and disarmament, nuclear power, cosmetic surgery, human cloning, marijuana laws, feminism/equal opportunity, air pollution, the strategic defense initiative, Presidential pardoning, bee keeping, free speech and the Internet, terrorism, today's headline?

- Do you ever become indignant about anything happening in the world? If you were President of the United States, what would you do about it?

- What historical event had the biggest impact on the twentieth century in your opinion and why? How about the twenty-first century?

- If you had the political power to do anything, what would you do?

Book and Media Questions

- What are you reading now that is of interest?

- Are there any books you've read in the last year that have significantly affected you?

- What is the best book you've ever read? Why?

- Which three books would you take to a desert island? Why?

- Who are your favorite two authors?

- Who is your favorite fictional character?

- Which magazines do you read regularly?

- What TV shows do you watch?

- What are your favorite movies?

- What play/concert/museum exhibit/dance recital have you recently attended? What did you think?

Heroes and Heroines

- Do you have any contemporary heroes?

- Do you have any historical heroes?

- What person, living or dead, would you most like to have dinner with? What would you discuss with him or her?

- Which person had the biggest impact on the twentieth century in your opinion?

- Which President would you most like to meet and why?

Personal Questions

- At what do you excel? Where do your talents lie?

- Tell me something about your family.

- Tell me about your upbringing. What things are important to your parents? On what issues do you have differences?

- What are some good decisions you've made for yourself recently?

- How would you describe your friendships?

- Who has influenced you the most?

- What pressures do you feel you must conform to? How have you gone your own way?

- What do you think sets you apart as an individual in your school?

- What difficult situation have you been in and how did you resolve it?

- When have you been most happy? Most sad?

The Unexpected and Provocative

Interviewers may feel that they need to get a little bit more out of you, that there is a spark waiting to fly, or they may have done fifteen interviews that day and need something more than a regular question to stimulate their interest in you as a candidate. During an on-campus interview, one of my students was asked "What makes you angry?" This is a question clearly meant to elicit an impassioned response. Should you be thrown a curveball question such as this, try to bear in mind the following points.

- Keep your responses honest. Don't try to fake anything.

- Keep cool. Take a deep breath and remain composed. Stressful questions reveal the interviewer's personality more than yours.

- If you don't understand the question, ask what the interviewer means. Be courteous and tactful when asking for elaboration.

- Don't pose as an expert on matters you know little about.

- Instead of saying, "I don't know," you can say, "That's a good question. I'll have to think that over. If you give me your e-mail address, I will contact you tomorrow with a response."

- Think before you speak. There is nothing wrong with a little silence.

- Avoid physical violence at all costs.

CONCLUDING THE INTERVIEW

As I mentioned earlier, it is essential that you prepare four or five questions to ask the interviewer at the end of the interview. Your choice of questions should provide further insight into your character as well as arm you with something to say should there be a lull in the conversation. You might ask about the interviewer's role at the university or his or her views on a specific campus topic. You might ask him or her to elaborate on something that came up during the interview, which you feel you didn't understand fully. Or you may ask about life at the college, the availability of special facilities, or something that you read in the college prospectus that was not adequately covered in your campus tour.

At the end of the interview, I suggest putting the interviewer on the spot by asking if he or she thinks you are a good match for the school. By asking this question point-blank, you are likely to get an honest answer, and it forces the interviewer to formulate an opinion of you right then and there. In response, they may ask you the same question. You are under no obligation to tell them that you would attend the school if accepted, *unless this is definitely the case*. It is not a good idea, however, to go around telling every school they are your first choice in an attempt to strengthen your profile—this is dishonest and the interviewers will know it. But you can say that a particular school is one of your top choices. You are also under no obligation to tell them where else you are applying, nor to supply any other general application information such as your GPA, your SAT I scores, or your class rank. The interview is meant to be about you and your personality, not numbers.

Follow Up

In general, the better interviews last more than thirty minutes. An hour-long conversation shows real interest on the part of the interviewer and will provide him or her with great material to report back to the school with. In the end, thank the interviewer, shake his or her hand, ask for a business card and e-mail address, and leave the room as cheerfully as you entered. Write a short hand-written note or e-mail thanking the interviewer for his or her time and information, referencing a specific aspect of the interview or subject you talked about as a way of keeping the interview fresh in the interviewer's mind. Then keep in touch. Along with your campus tour guide, your information session leader, college representatives who have come to your high school, and your area application reader, the interviewer is another person "on the inside" who can go to bat for your application, provided you have successfully followed the suggestions contained in this chapter. Of course, don't go overboard with your correspondence by sending flowers and champagne. It was an interview, not Valentine's Day.

SUMMARY

If the essay is your handshake, then the interview is your personal greeting. It is a great opportunity for you to add a personal touch to your academic statistics and to provide an admissions officer with firsthand evidence of your passion for the school. With the thorough preparation provided by this chapter's exercises, you will be able to effectively communicate the great personality and character traits you have been promoting in the rest of your application. Before you go into your interview, look through all the notes you have taken about the university, the questionnaires you have answered about yourself, your personal essay, your brag sheet, and your transcript to remind yourself of anything and everything that might come up during the discussion. Finally, you will want to research and answer as many sample questions as you can in mock interview situations—the last thing you need is nerves keeping you from making a positive, lasting impression.

INSIDER TIPS

✓ Get out there. Try to schedule an on-campus interview. You will most likely be granted an interview with someone from the admissions office itself, someone directly involved in the decision-making process.

✓ Come as you are. If you wear a nose-ring, leave it in. Wear the style of clothing that you like—not necessarily what your parents would like to see you in. But, of course, be neat and clean at the same time.

✓ Arrive early. Tardiness shows disrespect.

✓ Leave parents at a distance. They may fluster you at this point. In any case, the interviewer wants to interview you and not your parents.

✓ Watch your manners. Shake hands firmly with the interviewer. Look him or her in the eye when you speak. Do not fidget. Speak in complete sentences, without colloquial expressions.

✓ Be honest. Don't pose as an expert on matters you know little about.

✓ Keep cool. Should you be thrown a curveball question, take a deep breath and remain composed.

✓ Interview the interviewer. Find out what he or she does for a living. Put him or her on the spot by asking point-blank if you are a good match for the school—the interviewer will give you an honest response.

✓ First choice last. Schedule your interview with your first-choice school last so you can gain experience before interviewing with your top choice.

✓ Practice practice practice. Ask a relative, teacher, or friend of the family to give you a practice run-through. It's great for confidence and may raise points you have overlooked.

11

SECURING FINANCIAL AID

MYTHS AND TRUTHS

MYTH: Since most schools will offer you an aid package based on your need, there's little reason to shop around.

TRUTH: Colleges have very different ways of dealing with your "need." They can manipulate their offers based on how much they want you to attend their school, offering more in grants and less in loans, for example. If you receive a better offer of aid from one of your schools, you should by all means let the other schools know and see if they might try to outbid one another.

MYTH: College costs consist of room, board, and tuition.

TRUTH: When calculating college costs, do not forget the 10 percent rule—take whatever you think a year will cost and add 10 percent to cover the numerous unexpected costs associated with college attendance, as well as inflation.

MYTH: Once you get a financial aid package from your chosen school, you can't change it.

TRUTH: Actually, you will be renewing your financial aid package each year, and it's not unheard-of for more money to become available, especially for high-achieving students.

MYTH: All scholarships are all more-or-less legitimate, so it's a good idea to apply to as many as fit your profile.

TRUTH: There are many scholarship scams out there, so beware.

FINANCIAL AID FOR COLLEGE

Once a college or university evaluates your application, it may or may not offer you a financial aid package to help meet college expenses including tuition, fees, books, food, housing, and transportation. It is very important for all students who plan on postsecondary education (community college, four-year college, or vocational school) to explore all financial aid options. The colleges to which you are applying will of course supply this information to you, but you should make sure to inquire in good time. Most colleges will provide information for the following year's applicants in December of each year. However, you can also save valuable time by undertaking a little research to determine college costs and what you and your parents can afford. You and your parents should not be discouraged if you find there is a considerable shortfall or if you have not begun to invest or save for college by the time you enter high school. There is a wide variety of sources of financial aid available to you. First of all, let's take a look at the costs themselves.

UNDERSTANDING COLLEGE COSTS

Tuition: the cost for attending the school for one year.

Books: the cost for purchasing books for classes during the year. Books are expensive and can cost hundreds of dollars per semester or more.

Fees: the student may be charged a variety of fees related to the instructional program of the school, including registration, parking, student body card, etc.

Room and board: the cost of housing the student on campus for a year and providing three meals a day. If the student elects to live off campus and provide his or her own food, then that cost needs to be evaluated. Colleges will give you an estimate of these costs.

Transportation: the cost of commuting to campus daily. If the student lives on campus, this becomes the cost of traveling home at least three times a year.

The 10 percent rule: total the costs of a particular college and then add 10 percent to that figure to account for unexpected expenses and inflation. You will then have a more realistic figure of what that year in college will cost.

College Cost Log

You will find Chart 11.1 useful in calculating possible college costs.

Chart 11.1
COLLEGE COST LOG

College	Tuition	Out-of-state tuition	Fees	Room & board	Books	Transport	Additional 10%	Total

DETERMINING YOUR FINANCIAL RESOURCES FOR COLLEGE

The costs associated with a college education may seem prohibitively high, but it is important to calculate exactly what your available funds are before you jump to any conclusions. In some cases, families may have very limited resources. In other cases, families may have significant resources but have conflicting demands on those resources that could include retirement, other children's needs, or support of elderly family members. Students should be sure to research their own resources as well, including savings, investments, or personal income. The Chart 11.2, Financial Resources Log, will help you determine just how much is available. Use the totals from Charts 11.1 and 11.2 to complete Chart 11.3. It will give you a useful comparative cost table for all the colleges to which you are applying.

Chart 11.2
FINANCIAL RESOURCES LOG

Parent resources (annual)		Student resources (annual)	
Savings	$	Savings	$
Trusts	$	Trusts	$
Home equity available	$	Annual income for education	$
Business equity available	$	Summer and holiday employment for education	$
Annual income to be dedicated to education	$	Other	$
Other	$		
Total	$	Total	$

Chart 11.3
CALCULATING FINANCIAL NEED

College	Total annual college cost (from Chart 11.1)		Total family and student resources (From Chart 11.2)		Total financial need
		minus		equals	
		minus		equals	
		minus		equals	
		minus		equals	
		minus		equals	
		minus		equals	
		minus		equals	
		minus		equals	
		minus		equals	

HOW DO I APPLY?

Your first step in applying for federal financial aid to attend college is filling out a Free Application for Federal Student Aid (FAFSA). This form requests financial information for the calendar year prior to high school graduation. Postsecondary institutions use the FAFSA to determine eligibility for financial aid. The state and federal government will use the FAFSA to determine eligibility for grants. To qualify for financial aid, you must:

- be a U.S. citizen, national, permanent resident, or eligible nonresident
- have completed U.S. Selective Service requirements
- be a resident of the state for which you are applying for aid
- have been accepted to and enrolled at a college or university on at least a half-time basis
- not be in default for any loan program
- be making satisfactory academic progress
- have demonstrated financial need

"Need" is defined as the difference between the total cost of attending a postsecondary institution and the amount of money that you and your family can contribute as determined on your FAFSA form. As you have already assessed this number on Chart 11.3, you will be in a good position to fill out the FAFSA quickly. The family contribution is the same amount whether you choose a college with high or low cost. You could, therefore, be eligible for differing amounts of aid at different colleges, depending on their individual costs.

Your parents will need to have the following information available when applying for financial aid:

- U.S. Income Tax return for the past year (if applying in January 2003, you will need a 2002 U.S. Income Tax Return)
- State (local) Income Tax return
- W-2 forms for money earned in the past year
- Current bank statements
- Records of untaxed income
- Current mortgage information

- Business and farm records (if applicable)

- Records of stock, bonds, and other investments

- Student's driver's license and Social Security card

Some private schools also require additional information before making an offer of financial aid. These schools may have their own forms, or they may ask students to submit a profile, a two-part form that should be filed early. There is a charge for submitting this form, and students should check whether the colleges to which they are applying require it. If you are applying for federal aid to attend a private institution, you should also fill out the FAFSA form. Students whose family income is too high to qualify for state grant programs may still qualify for financial aid from colleges, especially the private colleges.

The most important advice for completing the financial aid forms correctly is to read all instructions carefully.

When Should I File?

The truth is, students seeking college-based financial aid should start working with the college's financial aid office even before being offered admission to the college. Colleges have a limited amount of financial aid and the money is awarded to qualified students on a first-come, first-served basis. It is even more difficult to receive financial aid if you are applying from another country and are not a U.S. citizen, because most colleges have little to no funds available for such students. Contact the financial aid office at each university to obtain information concerning all types of aid, grant, and loan programs in which they participate.

Both FAFSA and profile forms will be available in your college counseling office by December or January of each year. Your high school should hold financial aid meetings in December or January to assist you in completing the forms and to offer detailed advice for the colleges to which you have applied. While background research and preparation can be started well before this, you should not mail these forms before January 1. The filing deadline to receive maximum awards is in early March, but you should aim to mail forms by February 1. You must also reapply for aid each year you are in school because a family's financial situation can change from year to year.

COMPOSITION OF FINANCIAL AID PACKAGE

Details of financial aid packages will begin to arrive in April or early May of your senior year. An offer of financial aid from a college or university may include all or some of the following:

- State grants: Most states offer grants to students who are residents of the state and plan on attending one of that state's public institutions.

- Federal grants: The federal government offers a variety of grants to students based on financial need. These include federal Pell Grants.

- Work-Study Programs: The federal government, many state governments, and many universities will offer students an opportunity to work while in school in order to earn money for college expenses.

- Loans: Federal and state governments have a variety of loan programs for students. Unlike grants, loans must be repaid. These loans include federal Stafford Loans and are repayable at variable rates depending on the current prime rate. Each university's financial aid office will be able to give you a clearer picture of limits, repayment schedules, and other related information concerning these types of loans. There are also private loans that function very much like car or home loans. Sallie Mae is the largest provider, currently offering school loans up to a certain percentage of your need, usually repayable at a low, invariable interest rate. But beware— many students find themselves in debt many years after college. You will want to consult with experts in your institution's financial aid office as well as with your parents before entering any loan program.

- Scholarships: Colleges to which you are applying, alumni groups, corporations, your local high school, local business, and community service organizations as well as many other sources offer scholarships. You should start researching scholarship information in the summer before your senior year. Scholarships do not have to be repaid. They address special student abilities, affirmative action issues, achievement in scholarship, personal achievement, and other related issues.

If, after careful consideration, you think you are going to have insufficient funds, do not despair. First of all, imagine the situation in reverse. If a selective college has offered you a place to study, it means they think their college would benefit from your presence. As you know only too well, you have been through a rigorous selection process and have been chosen out of a huge admissions pool. The college should therefore be willing to help.

You should first contact the financial aid office at the relevant college, explain what the shortfall is, and ask that they review your application. It is unlikely that you will receive a bigger scholarship, but you might easily receive a loan on more generous terms or better on-campus employment.

There are also many opportunities for regular employment on campus, ranging from waiting tables to more lucrative library or research assistant positions. Even a few extra hours of work per week can add up to a substantial amount over a year and make the difference between attending the college of your choice and settling for another school.

BEWARE OF SCHOLARSHIP SCAMS

You may not know it, but every year there are a number of scams based on imitations of legitimate foundations, scholarship sponsors, lenders, and scholarship search companies. They may even have official-sounding names, using such words as "national," "federal," "foundation," and "administration" to fool unwary students and parents into thinking that they are federal agencies or grant-giving foundations. While looking for creative ways to pay for school, students and their families often fall prey to such scams. The lure of "free money" can fool even the most skeptical of people. Listed below is some advice on identifying scams, including a list of suspicious scholarship opportunities.

Warning Signs

Application Fees: Beware of any "scholarship" that requests an application fee, even an innocuously low one such as $10 or $20. Most legitimate scholarship sponsors do not require an application fee.

Other Fees: If you pay money to get information about an award, apply for the award, or receive the award, it might be a scam. Beware of 900-number telephone services, which charge you a fee of several dollars per minute for the call. There are, however, many legitimate scholarship *search* services that charge students a fee to compare the student's profile against a database of scholarships. It is sometimes very difficult to distinguish between these legitimate services and scam imitators, because the services are often small operations that pay fees to search one of a handful of national databases. In any event, charging more than $50 to search a database is excessive, especially since you can search the FastWeb database through Monster.com for free.

Guaranteed Winnings: No legitimate scholarship can guarantee that you will win an award or promise you a minimum sum for a particular award.

Unsolicited Opportunities: Most scholarship sponsors will only contact you in response to your inquiry.

Mail Drop or Residence for a Return Address: If the return address is a box number or a residential address, it is probably a scam. Major nonprofit corporations do not operate out of homes or apartments. If it is legitimate, the scholarship program will almost always include a street address and telephone number on its stationery.

How the Scams Work

Scams are hard to uncover because the operations are usually small, change location and name frequently, and can continue for years before being discovered. Thinking that their child simply didn't win the scholarship, parents often won't realize they've been scammed. Even when you feel cheated, it is only the most stubborn who will try to take advantage of the supposed "guarantees."

Scholarship with Application Fee: If the "foundation" receives a few thousand applications, they can pay out a few $1,000 scholarships and still pocket a hefty profit. It is likely that the average scholarship scam receives five to six thousand responses, so fees can represent a significant amount of money.

The Low Interest Loan: In return for an initial fee, you might be offered a low interest educational loan. Take note that real student loans require origination and insurance fees upon disbursement, not application. If the loan is not issued by a bank, it may well be a scam.

Name Recognition: Scam scholarships have names that sound extremely similar to genuine award programs. Beware, and do not get confused.

Following are some scholarship scams:

- National Science Federation
- Guilford Scholarship
- Olin L. Livesey Scholarship (a.k.a. Winch Scholarship, the OneCard Co., or the Theta Nu Epsilon Society)
- Student Aid Incorporated

- Higher Education Scholarship Program (HESP)

- R. C. Easley Foundation/National Academy of American Scholars/ National Science Program (a.k.a. National Science Scholarship Program, National Health Scholarship Program, National Humanities Scholarship Program, National Management Scholarship)

WORLDWIDE WEB RESOURCES FOR FINANCIAL AID AND SCHOLARSHIPS

Financial Aid: http://www.finaid.org

Top-quality homepage of links to many financial aid related sites. The expected family contribution estimator is a highlight of this site.

FastWeb: http://www.monster.com

Free scholarship search database recently acquired by Monster.com. This service saves your profile and e-mails new sources of private merit aid to your mailbox online.

Financial Aid Library: http://www.nt.scbbs.com/finaid

A variety of useful links serve as a financial aid "desk reference set."

Loan Repayment Estimator: http://www.student-loans.com/Repay.html

Estimates monthly payments for various college loan programs/amounts.

Nellie Mae: http://www.nelliemae.org
Sallie Mae: http://www.salliemae.org

Information on Nellie Mae and Sallie Mae college loans.

GLOSSARY OF FINANCIAL TERMS

Academic Year: The measure of the academic work to be completed by the student in a given year of college (usually September to May).

Award Letter: Letter sent to the student that indicates the type(s) of financial aid being offered by the school, including state and federal sources.

Award Year: The school year during which financial aid is given (begins July 1 and runs through June 30).

Base Year: The calendar year preceding the award year.

Central Processing System (CPS): Where the data from the financial aid forms is processed, currently in Iowa.

Cost of Attendance (a.k.a. Cost of Education): Includes tuition, fees, and living expenses.

Expected Family Contribution (EFC): The amount the student's family is expected to pay toward the cost of attendance.

Financial Aid: Assistance with expenses for postsecondary education.

Financial Aid Package: The financial aid offer made by the college consisting of grants, scholarships, loans, and/or work-study.

Financial Need: The difference between the Cost of Attendance and the Expected Family Contribution.

Free Application for Federal Student Aid (FAFSA): The financial aid application that collects household and financial information used to calculate the Expected Family Contribution.

Parents' Contribution: A quantitative estimate of the parents' ability to contribute to postsecondary educational expenses.

Pell Grant: A grant from the federal government awarded to students from low-income families. To apply students must submit the FAFSA.

Profile: Form required by many private colleges.

Promissory Note: A legal document that the borrower signs to get a loan. By signing this note, the borrower promises to repay the loan, with interest, in specified installments.

Scholarship: Money awarded to the student on the basis of grades or other achievements. Not necessarily dependent on financial aid.

Student Aid Report (SAR): The output document sent to the student by the application processor. The SAR contains the financial and other information reported by the student on the FAFSA.

Verification: A procedure whereby the postsecondary school checks the information that the student reported on the financial aid application. Colleges often request a copy of tax returns filed by the student and the parents. Many schools conduct their own form of verification.

SUMMARY

Once a college or university evaluates your application, it may or may not offer you a financial aid package to help meet college expenses, including tuition, fees, books, food, housing, and transportation. It is very important for all students who plan on postsecondary education (community college, four-year college, or vocational school) to explore all financial aid options. The main criterion for determining eligibility is what is referred to as "need." "Need" is defined as the difference between the total cost of attending a postsecondary institution and the amount of money that you and your family can contribute as determined on your financial aid forms. You and your parents should not be discouraged if you find there is a considerable shortfall or if you have not begun to invest or save for college by the time you enter high school. If you are accepted to a school, it means they want you to attend, and they will be willing to try everything in their power to help get you there.

INSIDER TIPS

✓ The 10 percent rule. Total the costs of a college, then add 10 percent to account for unexpected expenses and inflation. Don't be caught by surprise.

✓ Start early. Start working with the financial aid office even before being admitted. Money is awarded on a first-come, first-served basis.

✓ Noncitizens be prepared. It is even more difficult to receive financial aid if you are not a U.S. citizen because most colleges have little to no funds available for such students.

✓ Ask and ask again. If your financial aid package will not cover your costs, contact the financial aid office and ask them to review your application.

You may not receive a bigger scholarship, but you might receive a loan on more generous terms or better on-campus employment.

✓   Beware of scams. Any "scholarship" funds that request an application fee, operate out of a residence, guarantee you a return, or have a name suspiciously close to an organization you know to be legitimate, is probably a scam. Research funds thoroughly before sending money.

12

APPLYING FOR COLLEGE CHECKLIST

MYTHS AND TRUTHS

MYTH: The high school college counselor will put all of the application information together and will make sure it is complete and accurate.

TRUTH: The high school counselor is responsible for things like sending the transcript, writing a letter of recommendation, and verifying class rank. One should not expect the high school college counselor to track down and compile all of the application materials. The student must put the final application together in full.

MYTH: If a step is missed through the college admissions process, parents will be expected to step in and take over.

TRUTH: The process is in the student's hands. Colleges know when a parent puts together or writes part of the application. The application needs to be the student's work in the voice of the student.

APPLYING FOR COLLEGE CHECKLIST

Congratulations! You have officially learned *The Truth About Getting In*. Now it's time to relax, enjoy the coming spring, hang out with your friends, go to your prom—all the while maintaining your grades and activities so you don't give colleges any reason to question their decision. Soon enough that fateful day will come when you will find your mailbox stuffed with acceptance letters from the colleges of your choice. Then you are on your way.

To help keep track of your college application materials, you may find the following section useful as a summary of the college application process. It can be used as a checklist in conjunction with the timelines from Chapter 1 and Chart 12.1. Please refer to the other relevant sections cited for more detail.

1. The selection process should begin no later than the junior year of high school (see Chapter 2), although it is never too early to start gathering information about colleges. The truth is, the more research you do, the better your chances are of getting in.

2. Actual application should be made during the first semester of the senior year. Most colleges have application deadlines between November and February for admission in September of the following year.

3. Plan to take any required tests prior to the end of the first semester of your senior year. You may start as early as ninth or tenth grade with SAT IIs and APs, depending on your course work. Begin SAT I testing in the junior year (see Chapter 7).

4. Obtain an unofficial copy of your transcript from your high school counseling office or registrar. This information will be needed to complete many of the applications, although your high school will be sending an official copy separately to each college.

5. Note application deadlines for each university so that test scores and transcripts can be secured and sent before their deadlines.

6. The appearance of your application will influence the admissions committee, so be sure to complete the application neatly, carefully, and thoroughly. Typing is preferable (unless you are applying to Brown University, which requires its personal essay to be handwritten).

7. Write all necessary essays and have them checked and double-checked by people whose opinion you trust. This may include parents, teachers, older siblings, or your high school college counselor (see Chapter 8).

8. Make copies of all paperwork sent to any college, including applications, financial aid forms, and correspondence. Send everything from the post office and keep your dated proof of mailing receipts. College admissions offices can lose items because of the sheer number of applications they process. You may even want to include a self-addressed and stamped card with your application and request that it be returned upon receipt. Also, double-check anything sent electronically—like online applications, which have been known to disappear into thin air.

9. Apply early decision or early action to your number-one choice, if you are ready. This may increase your chances of admission.

10. Contact teachers and your high school college counselor well in advance of any deadlines to ensure that letters of recommendation are submitted in a timely fashion. Remember to thank writers for their efforts (see Chapter 9).

11. File early for financial aid (see Chapter 11).

12. Check requirements for on-campus housing registration in the college admissions brochure.

13. Follow up on all documents requested for the application or for financial aid. Also check that every college has a complete file on you. *They must have all your data assembled before they can make a decision about your admissions status.* Be sure to check in with the admissions office at each school approximately once every three weeks. You should also be keeping in touch with your tour guide, your information session leader, the college representatives who visited your high school, and your interviewer. Showing colleges your interest as often as possible is a proven method for increasing your application profile.

Additional Tips on Applying

1. To save money in nonrefundable application fees, apply only to those schools you have investigated and that you would attend.

2. You may mail college applications even though you do not have SAT I or ACT scores yet. However, you must send colleges the scores once you take the tests. Let the college know in writing that the scores are pending.

3. An application fee of $30 or more is required for most colleges. Fee waivers for eligible students are often available. Check with your high school college counselor or with the college itself.

COLLEGE TRACKER

While applying to college, you may find the following tracker very helpful in ensuring that no important information is omitted. Fill out this form, keeping track of each college to which you are applying. (You may want to request that your high school college counselor and teachers get a proof of mailing from the post office for everything they send.)

Chart 12.1
COLLEGE TRACKER

Date	College name	Application sent	Due date	Transcript sent	Counselor recommendation sent	Teacher recommendation sent	Midyear report sent

13

SPECIAL ISSUES IN COLLEGE ADMISSIONS

MYTHS AND TRUTHS

MYTH: If you are a gifted athlete, you'll easily get a free ride through college.

TRUTH: No matter how gifted you are or how much a coach wants you, the coach is not the Dean of Admissions and cannot guarantee admission. And, you must prepare yourself sufficiently so as not to jeopardize your NCAA eligibility.

MYTH: Legacy students are a shoo-in.

TRUTH: While legacy status improves your chances for admission, it by no means guarantees you admission to a college. In fact, the onus is on you to show how much you really want to go to the school in question—and not just because a parent went there. As a legacy, you should apply early, ace the interview, and let the school know how interested you are.

MYTH: You should not self-report any learning disabilities or differences because schools don't really want students with learning disabilities or differences.

TRUTH: It is always in your best interest to self-report a learning disability or difference—it shows maturity and could clear up any possible inconsistencies in your record. Most schools gladly accept students with disabilities or differences because most have support services on campus geared to these students.

MYTH: Since affirmative action is basically dead, there is no distinct advantage to reporting your race or ethnicity on your application.

TRUTH: Now more than ever, you should self-report your race or ethnicity. Colleges want a diverse student body and your particular perspective may be precisely what a college is looking for.

MYTH: Transferring is an easy alternative to regular admissions if you don't feel like working hard to get into your number-one college.

TRUTH: If you want even the slightest chance of transferring to your favorite college, you have to perform exceptionally well at your current school, taking advantage of everything they have to offer in order to make yourself the most desirable candidate for the few transfer spots open at each selective college.

MYTH: If you don't get into college, you're screwed.

TRUTH: If you don't get in anywhere the first time around, fear not. There's always another strategy, including a number of year-off options that can drastically increase your chances of admission the second time around.

This final chapter is devoted to the needs of students who find themselves in special college application circumstances. It presents in a general fashion the trade secrets and industry truths with which they can maximize their chances of getting into the selective college of their choice.

STUDENT-ATHLETES AND THE NCAA

The National Collegiate Athletic Association (NCAA), founded in 1906, regulates most college athletic programs. If you are planning on playing sports in college, you must familiarize yourself with the rules on eligibility, recruiting, and financial aid established by the NCAA. There are three membership divisions of the NCAA: I, II, and III. Division I institutions have to sponsor at least seven sports for men and women and meet minimum financial aid awards for their athletic programs. Division II institutions are required to sponsor four sports for men and women and cannot exceed the maximum financial aid awards for each sport. Division III differs only in that it does not award financial aid on the basis of athletic ability, but on the basis of need alone. For further information, visit the NCAA at *http://www.ncaa.org/about/ div criteria.*

If you are planning to enroll in college as a freshman and you want to participate in Division I or II athletics, you must be certified by the NCAA Initial-Eligibility Clearinghouse. The Clearinghouse was established as a separate organization by the NCAA member institutions in 1993. The Clearinghouse ensures consistent interpretation of NCAA initial-eligibility requirements for all prospective student-athletes at all member institutions.

Clearinghouse Registration Materials

You will need to supply the following documents to make sure the Clearinghouse can certify you:

- Your completed and signed Student Release Form and fee.

- Your ACT or SAT I scores.

- Your official transcript mailed directly from your high school, documenting a GPA of at least 2.0 (on a scale of 4.0) in a core curriculum of at least thirteen courses from grades nine through twelve.

Make sure that you start the certification process early, generally at the end of your junior year in high school.

Student Release Form

Your high school college counselor should provide you with a student-release form and the brochure "Making Sure You Are Eligible to Participate in College Sports." Registration materials can also be obtained at no cost by calling the Clearinghouse at (319) 337-1492.

You must complete the student-release form and mail the top (white) copy of the form to the Clearinghouse along with the $25 registration fee. Give the yellow and pink copies to your college counselor, who will then send the yellow copy, along with an official copy of your high school transcript, to the Clearinghouse. Your high school will keep the pink copy for its files. After graduation and before the school closes for the summer, your school must also send the Clearinghouse a copy of your final transcript that confirms graduation from high school.

Filling in the Student Release Form

- Follow the instructions on the form closely. You may want to photocopy it first and fill out a rough draft. If you have attended more than one high school, complete Section C.

- Read and sign the entire authorization statement. If you are under eighteen, your parent or guardian must also sign.

- Permission to release to colleges/universities: If you only want the Clearinghouse to release to specific universities, you must list your choices on the student release form.

- Personal Identification Number: Choose an easily memorable number and keep a record of it. After you submit your form you can check the status of your file by calling (319) 339-3003.

- Payment: Your form cannot be processed without the correct payment or a fee waiver. You are eligible for a waiver only if you have already received one for the ACT or SAT I.

Test Scores

To be certified, you also must submit your ACT or SAT I scores to the Clearinghouse. You may either have your scores sent directly from the testing agency or have your test scores reported on your high school transcript. You can have your scores sent directly to the Clearinghouse by marking code 9999 on your ACT or SAT I registration form or by submitting a request for an Additional Score Report to the appropriate testing agency.

All prospective student-athletes, including natives of foreign countries, must achieve the minimum required test score on a national testing date. Foreign prospective student-athletes should contact the appropriate testing agency for more information about registering to take the test on a national testing date.

The following interpretations apply to the combination of test scores from more than one national testing date:

- If you take the SAT I, the highest scores achieved on the verbal and math sections from two different national testing dates may be combined in determining whether you have met the minimum test-score requirements.

- If you take the ACT, the highest scores achieved on the individual subtests from more than one national testing date may be combined in determining whether your sum score meets minimum test-score requirements.

Qualifier Index

Students must earn a composite score of at least seventeen on the ACT or combined score of at least 700 on the SAT I. The minimum GPA in the thirteen core subjects varies; see Table 13.1.

Table 13.1 NCAA Qualifier Index

GPA	ACT	SAT I
2.000	21	900
2.025	21	890
2.050	21	880
2.075	21	870
2.100	21	860
2.125	20	850
2.150	20	840
2.175	20	830
2.200	20	820
2.225	20	810
2.250	19	800
2.275	19	790
2.300	19	780
2.325	19	770
2.350	19	760
2.375	18	750
2.400	18	740
2.425	18	730

GPA	ACT	SAT I
2.450	18	720
2.475	17	710
2.500	17	700
2.500+	17	700

Core Course Requirements

The list of NCAA-approved core courses (formerly Form 48-H) identifies courses that may be used in meeting NCAA core-course requirements. Be sure that all courses that you are taking for core-course purposes are listed on your high school's confirmation list of NCAA-approved core courses. (CO8 is the required two years of additional academic core courses in English, math, or natural/physical science.)

Table 13.2 NCAA CORE COURSE REQUIREMENTS

	Division I	Division II
English core	4 years	3 years
Math core	2 years	2 years
Science core	2 years	2 years
Social science core	2 years	2 years
From English, math, or science (additional CO8 core)	1 year	2 years
Additional core (English, math, science, social science, foreign languages, computer sciences, philosophy, or nondoctrinal religion)	2 years	2 years
TOTAL CORE UNITS	13	13

NCAA Initial Eligibility

If you are planning on playing sports in college, you should look over the following list of regulations to ensure that you are eligible to play.

- Independent study or correspondence courses may *not* be used to satisfy the core-curriculum requirements.

- Courses taken in the eighth grade may *not* be used to satisfy the core-curriculum requirements regardless of the course content or level.

- The NCAA core-course grade point average is calculated using only NCAA approved core courses in the required thirteen core units.

- A school's normal practice of weighting honors or advanced placement courses may be used as long as the weighting is used for computing grade point averages at that high school.

- Students who do not meet the initial-eligibility standards may be granted an NCAA initial-eligibility waiver. Contact the NCAA for details.

- Students should register with the Clearinghouse after the completion of their junior year in high school.

- For student-athletes with learning disabilities, the following is required: (a) a signed copy of a professional evaluation report that states the diagnosis of the student's disability; and (b) a copy of the student's Individualized Education Plan (IEP), Individual Transition Plan (ITP) or Section 504 Plan or statement that relates to accommodations received by the student with the disability. The NCAA national office, not the Clearinghouse, processes this information. Students with appropriately diagnosed disabilities may use courses for students with disabilities for the purpose of meeting NCAA core-course requirements if they appear on the high school's list of NCAA Approved Core Courses (formerly Form 48-H).

This is not a complete list of NCAA regulations regarding initial eligibility. Please call, write, or visit the NCAA website if you have specific questions:

NCAA Membership Services
6201 College Boulevard
Overland Park, Kansas 66211-2422
319/339-1906 (phone), 319/339-0032 (fax)
800/638-3731 (NCAA Hotline)
www.ncaa.org

STUDENTS WITH LEARNING DISABILITIES/ DIFFERENCES OR MEDICAL CONDITIONS

If you have been diagnosed with what I prefer to call a learning "difference" (for example, ADD, ADHD, OCD, Aspergers, etc.) or a medical condition that has affected your performance in school (for example, mononucleosis, lupus, etc.), you should write to the admissions office at each college to which you are applying and inform them of your condition. If you have been awarded special accommodations in high school because of your condition (for example, untimed or doubletime testing),[1] tell them which accommodations you normally receive as well as which medications you are currently taking. You should also send all supporting documents such as doctors' reports directly to the Learning Disability Support Center on each campus. *You have absolutely nothing to lose by offering this information.* In fact, you have everything to gain. By self-reporting, you open a channel of communication with the admissions office and a file will be started on you immediately. In this way, admissions officers will have all the pertinent information at their fingertips when your application materials begin to arrive. Your documented learning difference or medical condition will help to explain any sporadic grade dips on your transcript such as when you were changing medications or going off them completely. If you do not currently receive any accommodation, this is also significant because it shows that you have achieved a high level of academic success without the benefit of any special aid and against the odds of your difference or condition. Self-reporting is the *mature* thing to do and it can only help you in your bid for admission to the college of your choice.

LEGACY STUDENTS

If one or both of your parents attended a college as an undergraduate, then you are a legacy applicant at that school. You are not a legacy applicant if any other family member attended the school or your parents attended graduate or professional school there. Legacy applicants are given special consideration in the college admissions process because it is assumed they know more about the school than nonlegacy applicants and because schools rely on alumni for donations. Legacy students have grown up with parents who talk about their alma mater, attend reunions and fund-raisers, give money and/or are involved with the school in some other fashion. Legacy students are therefore assumed to be making a more educated decision when they apply, and if accepted, are more likely to attend based on the strong family connection. If you are think-

---

[1] ETS and the College Board no longer flag your SAT scores if you took them untimed or with double time. You must show valid documentation for a learning disability in order to receive this accomodation. Do not abuse this now that scores are not flagged. I have heard of students—juniors in high school—running to psychologists to get or "buy" a diagnosis of LD. This is unethical and certainly unfair for all of the students out there who really need this accommodation.

ing of applying to a college as a legacy applicant, you should definitely apply early. Not applying early may appear like a snub to the school. You should therefore decide beforehand if you are truly interested in attending the school and not treat it as a backup. The advantages, once you decide, are clear: while Yale accepted a mere 13 percent of its general applicant pool in 2000, it accepted around 30 percent of its legacy applicants. For Princeton, the number is even higher, closer to 50 percent. Take advantage of these odds if you are a legacy applicant and you have decided on your own that the school is right for you.

MINORITY STUDENTS

Most college applications allow space in the personal information section for you to self-report your race or ethnicity. It is always a good idea to report yourself as a minority or multinational student if you are one. Schools, after all, are looking for diverse student bodies. It also gives the impression of pride in your cultural heritage and it may be something you wish to write about in your personal essay. Furthermore, given the hardships faced by minority groups in this country, self-reporting also lets the colleges know that you may have overcome certain odds to get where you are today. Finally, if you are a first-generation college applicant, colleges need to know this. They look at first-generation applications in a different light, giving special consideration to the added obstacles such a person has faced.

STUDENT ARTISTS

If you have taken a number of art classes in high school and have demonstrated special talent in a particular area, it might be a good idea to include a portfolio of your work along with your application. There is no guarantee that anyone will actually look at it, but sometimes it can help an admissions officer make that crucial final decision about your file. Keep in mind that you are asking them to do extra work in assessing your application, so keep your portfolio short and user-friendly. You may send audiotapes of your singing group, band, or recital; video footage of your dance, acting, or musical performance; slides of your paintings, photographs, or sculptures. Be sure to attach a note requesting that the materials be forwarded to the head of the relevant department. Admissions officers are not experts in these fields, but may pass the materials on to the appropriate person for evaluation. Be sure to read the instructions on each college application before you prepare a portfolio: some school will categorically reject any supplementary material. Also be mindful not to send originals, as they will not be returned. One final note: only do this if you have been urged to do so by your high school teachers and are planning on pursuing your artistic work in college.

WAIT-LISTED STUDENTS

In order not to undershoot or overshoot their desired yield, most selective colleges will maintain a wait-list of qualified applicants who fall just under the application criteria needed for admission. In the event that they need a few more students to round out their freshman class profile, they will draw from this list, usually in the beginning of the summer, after students have responded to their offers of admissions. If, after doing your best to produce a great application to your first-choice college, you are put on the wait-list, do not despair. Although your situation is difficult, there are a number of strategies you can employ to increase your chances of gaining admission.

First and foremost, you should inform the admissions office in writing that their school is still your number-one choice and that you would attend their institution if admitted. Again, colleges want to know your intentions because they remain constantly wary of their yield. Next, you should contact anyone you have met or spoken with during the application process and remind them of your strong desire to attend their institution, updating them with any and all relevant information (new grades, projects, test scores, awards). Finally, you may want to take a fine-tooth comb to your actual application and make sure you have produced the best possible representation of who you are and what you can contribute to a potential college. Often you will find hastily written or underdeveloped sections that may have forced an application reader to assume a lack of interest or effort on your part.

As an inspiration, let me recount the story of a student who had applied to a number of selective schools with SAT I scores above 1500 and straight A's in all AP courses. Shockingly, he was rejected by all of his top-choice schools and was wait-listed at one school. When I took him on as a client (after April of his senior year) and had a look at his applications, I understood immediately why—you could tell he had done no research into the schools in question; his essays were generic, not once revealing anything about himself; he had submitted the common application, not bothering to obtain the schools' actual applications; and his brag sheet was incomplete. Here was an obviously gifted student pursuing a dual curriculum (AP courses and the Talmud) at a Jewish Yeshiva, who listened to Hebrew radio each night and composed music for the piano in his spare time—and he's being wait-listed? I had him call the admissions office in question, find out who his area reader was, and make an appointment to go to the campus for a meeting. He brought with him a brand-new application, one that he had produced after doing the necessary research and following all the tips, suggestions, and exercises contained in this book. A shy person by nature, I even put him through a rigorous series of mock interviews so that he could impress the area reader with his personality as much as his new application. His persistence and effort paid off—after doing the work he should have done to begin with, the school called three days later and admitted him.

TRANSFER STUDENTS

The first thing you must understand if you want to transfer into a selective school is that it is extremely difficult. Harvard accepts only 5 percent of its transfer applicants while Princeton accepted none until 2002. This does not mean it is impossible. You must simply work twice as hard as the normal student to get the best possible grades at your current institution. You must maintain a consistently high level of participation in extracurricular activities and community service organizations. And you must go through the entire application process over again, this time stressing the reasons you want to transfer to that particular school. I am often asked if it is any easier to transfer into a selective school in any given year—it is probably easier to transfer as a college sophomore (when more students are transferring) than as a junior or senior. In addition, the rules and regulations pertaining to transfer applicants differ from college to college, so you will have to do some serious research before you begin.

One word of advice: *transfer for the right reasons*. Be absolutely sure that your target college is the only place for you. Look around at the school you are currently attending and make sure you aren't overlooking any potential opportunities it has to offer. If, after careful consideration, you still have your heart set on transferring to a particular school, then good luck and go for it. Applications usually are not due until March, so you have more time than as a senior in high school.

TAKING A YEAR OFF

There are a number of options available for students who feel they might need a year off in between high school and college. For those students, I recommend going through the normal application process during your senior year, getting into the school of your choice, and requesting a deferral. Most colleges will grant you a deferral for up to a year with the assumption that you will be doing something during that year to further prepare you for college. If you have not been accepted by any colleges you wish to attend, you can take a year off and reapply to the same schools. In that case, you must find something to do during your year off that demonstrates a strong desire to improve whatever weaknesses made you less attractive as an applicant in the first place. This may include a job where you learn responsibility and teamwork, an adventure where you learn independence and self-reliance, a research opportunity where you hone your analytic and study skills, or a community service position where you learn to help others and give back to your community. The bottom line is: make it something that makes you more attractive in the eyes of an admissions committee. Other students may opt for a post graduate, or PG, year, either abroad— Switzerland is a popular destination—or at a boarding school. For instance, if your initial application would have been weakened by some sort of trauma, a drug or alcohol problem, a disciplinary problem or a late-diagnosed learning "difference" and difficulty with new medication, you may opt for a PG year to demonstrate to colleges that you are dedicated to both your academic career and your personal growth. Provided you excel, an extra year of development and learning is often all that stands between you and the college of your dreams. See *www.studyabroad.com*, *www.GoAbroad.com*, and *www.gapyear.com* for more information.

SUMMARY

The truth is, many students apply to college under special circumstances. Some are student-athletes vying for lucrative sports scholarships. Others have learning "differences" and might need special support or accommodation on campus. Still others are legacies, artists, minorities, or transfer students whose special circumstances can affect, positively or negatively, their ability to get into college. Finally, there are those students who are initially wait-listed at the school of their choice as well as those who simply aren't ready for college at the end of high school and who would benefit from a year off before attending school. Whichever category you fall under, there are specific strategies you should employ to maximize your chances of getting into the college of your dreams.

INSIDER TIPS

✓ Know the rules. As a student-athlete, it is up to you to stay abreast of the requirements for NCAA eligibility—don't ruin your athletic dreams!

✓ Be proud. If you are a minority student, you should self-report your race or ethnicity—after all, colleges are looking for a diverse student body. If you have a learning difference, do the same—colleges want to know everything you have overcome to get to where you are today. If you are an artist, offer examples of your work to your prospective colleges—if your artwork means something to you, it will mean something to them.

✓ Show you care. Especially if you are a legacy applicant, you should stop at nothing to let your college know how much you want to attend. But first make sure the college in question is best for you—just because a parent went there does *not* mean it is a right fit.

✓ Take a look around. If you are thinking of transferring, take a look around at your current institution before you apply for transfer. There may be hidden benefits you are overlooking—the grass isn't always greener.

✓ Try and try again. If you are wait-listed at the school of your dreams, take another look at your application and make sure it is as solid as can be. If not, resubmit it after doing some serious reworking.

✓ Life isn't over. If you don't get into any of the colleges on your list, take a year off, do something challenging and worthwhile, then reapply with a fresh perspective and new experiences to draw on.

APPENDIX

FORTY ELITE U.S. COLLEGES AND UNIVERSITIES

Other than the established Ivy League, this list is based on selectivity (low admittance rates) and Howard Greene's book *The Select*, as well as my own research.

Ivy League (listed alphabetically)

1. Brown University
2. Columbia University
3. Cornell University
4. Dartmouth College
5. Harvard University
6. University of Pennsylvania
7. Princeton University
8. Yale University

Private Colleges and Universities (listed alphabetically)

1. Amherst
2. Bowdoin
3. California Institute of Technology
4. Carleton College
5. Carnegie Mellon University
6. University of Chicago
7. Cooper Union
8. Davidson College
9. Duke University
10. Emory University
11. Georgetown University
12. Haverford College
13. Johns Hopkins University
14. Massachusetts Institute of Technology
15. Middlebury College
16. New York University
17. Northwestern University

18. University of Notre Dame

19. Pomona College

20. Rice University

21. Stanford University

22. Swarthmore College

23. Tufts University

24. Washington University / St. Louis

25. Wellesley College

26. Wesleyan College

27. Williams College

Public Universities (listed alphabetically)

1. University of California, Berkeley

2. University of California, Los Angeles

3. University of Michigan, Ann Arbor

4. University of North Carolina, Chapel Hill

5. University of Virginia, Charlottesville

GLOSSARY OF TERMS

AA (Associate of Arts): a two-year community college degree.

Academic Calendar: breaks the school year into one of the following: two semesters of seventeen to eighteen weeks or three quarters of ten to eleven weeks (fourth quarter optional).

ACT (American College Test): a four-year college admissions test covering English language, reading, science reasoning, and mathematics.

AP (Advanced Placement): a system by which high school students can earn college credit by achieving a certain score on a specially designed College Board exam at the conclusion of an AP course.

Audit: to attend a class for the purpose of reviewing the information. No tests, grades, or credits are given.

Bachelor's Degree: a diploma earned after successfully completing a required course of study in a college or university. It usually takes four years. Abbreviated B.A. (Bachelor of Arts) or B.S. (Bachelor of Science).

Candidates' Reply Date: May 1 is the date when students must inform each college at which they were accepted whether or not they plan to attend.

Class Rank: a student's standing as compared with that of the other members of the class according to his/her school GPA.

College Entrance Examination Board (CEEB): company that provides college entrance testing, such as SAT, TOEFL, PSAT. The ETS (Educational Testing Service) is the testing division.

Community College: a two-year college offering transfer programs: the first two years of a four-year program, preparatory to transfer to a four-year college; vocational programs: usually no more than two years in length, leading to employment in various specialties; certificate programs: of varying length, they involve detailed study in one particular field (such as real estate).

Credit, also Semester Hours, Unit Hours, Quarter Hours, Unit: a way of referring to the number of credits earned in a course. Approximately 64 total credits are needed for an AA degree, and 124 total credits for a B.A. or B.S. in schools on a semester calendar. If a class meets three hours per week, it is usually a 3-credit course. A full-time student at college generally takes five classes and earns 15 credits per semester.

Cumulative Record: the complete record of all courses completed and marks earned. A student's transcript is a copy of the cumulative record.

Degree: titles given to college graduates upon completion of a program. A four-year degree is generally a B.A. or B.S., a fifth- or sixth-year degree is often an M.A. or M.S., with a doctoral degree requiring approximately six additional years beyond the B.A.

E.O.P. (Educational Opportunity Program): a program designed to assist low-income, underrepresented minorities and first-generation college students with admissions, academic support services, and financial aid for most public and private universities. Eligibility criteria differ among all colleges. Contact the relevant college for further information.

Elective: a course needed for graduation credit, but not one of the specific courses required.

Fee Waiver: a form available to students of families with a low annual income. The fee waiver form is submitted instead of money when applying for college testing or admission. Requests for fee waivers are available in the College Office.

General Education Requirements (or Breadth Requirements): courses selected from several divisions required for a college degree. These are generally completed during the first two years of college. The second two years involve course work in major or minor areas.

GPA (Grade Point Average): a student's average grade, computed on a four-point scale: A = 4.0, B = 3.0, C = 2.0, D = 1.0, F = 0.

Impacted Program: a college degree program, such as engineering, communication, physical therapy, computer science, or business, that may be temporarily closed to new students due to heavy enrollment or may require supplementary screening of student records for selection of the strongest candidates.

Loans: money borrowed from a bank or a college for the purpose of attending college.

Lower Division: refers to courses usually completed in the first two years of college.

Major: the subject in which a student concentrates to earn a degree. For example, biology majors will have a degree in biology. Note: there are no set majors for prelaw, dental, medicine, and veterinary degrees—graduate work is necessary for each of these disciplines.

Master's Degree: A degree earned after a bachelor's degree. This degree usually takes about two years.

Minor: a secondary area of concentration; may or may not be required by an institution.

National Merit Scholarship Qualifying Test (NMSQT): based on the score a student earns on the PSAT in the junior year, he or she may be eligible to compete for the National Merit Scholarship.

Need Analysis: a technique used to estimate a student's need for financial assistance to help meet educational expenses. It consists of two major components: 1) estimating the family's ability to contribute to educational expenses; 2) estimating the student's educational expenses.

Prerequisites: courses, test scores, and/or grade level that must be completed before taking a specific course.

Private Colleges and Universities: those institutions that are not supported by state taxes. All funds for these colleges come from tuition, which is higher than at state colleges.

Professional/ Graduate School: a program in which a student can continue his or her education after a bachelor's degree. Professional schools train students in the fields of law, medicine, dentistry, business, pharmacy, etc. Graduate schools offer study in the fields of engineering, physics, education, math, etc.

Public Colleges and Universities: those institutions supported by state and local taxes.

Quarter System: the calendar used by most campuses. Each quarter is ten weeks long. There are three quarters in a school year with the option of a summer session as a fourth quarter.

ROTC: many colleges have units of the Reserve Officers' Training Corps that offer two- and four-year programs of military training culminating in an officer's commission. In some colleges, credits for the courses can be applied toward a degree. ROTC scholarships are available that pay full educational costs in both public and private colleges. A military obligation is required of ROTC scholarship recipients.

Technical/Vocational Schools: usually private institutions that charge fees for education in specific skills and trades (secretarial, welding etc.). Community colleges also offer vocational training.

TOEFL (Test of English as a Foreign Language): an English exam for foreign students. Register by mail. The test is held at various testing sites.

Transcript: a copy of a student's cumulative record, requested by all colleges and universities for admission purposes.

Tuition: a fee that is paid for instruction in a school, college, or university.

Undergraduate: a college student who has not yet received a bachelor's degree.

Upper Division Courses: courses designated for the junior and senior years of college.

Weighted Courses/Grades: a policy that rewards accelerated and/or extended academic performance by giving a "bonus" grade point for each designated course. Students completing courses so designated have traditionally been given extra consideration during the college admissions process.

Work-Study: a federally funded program that makes part-time jobs available to students with financial need. It is generally part of a financial aid package.